HEA

Higher Education Authority
An tÚdarás um Ard-Oideachas

R7U

The Higher Education Authority

An tÚdarás um Ard-Oideachas

Marine House, Clanwilliam Court, Dublin 2

College Entry in Focus: A Fourth National Survey of Access to Higher Education

Patrick Clancy

ISBN 0 - 904556 - 78 - 6

Dublin

Published by The Higher Education Authority

To be purchased from the
Government Publications Sales Office,
Molesworth Street, Dublin 2.

or through any Bookseller

Price € 25
September 2001

OPUS
MGA

contents

3

4

contents | List of Tables

contents | List of Figures

acknowledgements

I wish to acknowledge the co-operation and assistance of the many people who made possible this research. My first debt is to the students who completed a short questionnaire to supplement the data, which were available from existing records. I am grateful to the Presidents, Directors, Principals, Registrars, Admissions Officers and Records Staff of the colleges who facilitated access to anonymised student records. I owe a special debt to Dr. Martin Newell, Secretary of the Central Applications Office who in addition to providing access to anonymised student records also consented to the use of his office for the administration of the postal questionnaire. I thank Mr. Ivor Gleeson from the Central Applications Office for abstracting the required computerised data from the CAO records. I am also indebted to Professor Damian Hannan and Dr. Selina McCoy from the Economic and Social Research Institute for providing special tabulations from the School Leavers Surveys. I acknowledge the assistance of Deirdre Harte and Francis McCann from the Central Statistics Office who supplied me with some unpublished demographic statistics.

This research was funded by the Higher Education Authority. I thank the members of the Authority and the Chairman, Dr. Don Thornhill, who took a personal interest in the study. I am especially grateful to Mr. John Hayden, Secretary/Chief Executive of the HEA for his support and active interest in this and in each of the three earlier national surveys. I also acknowledge the assistance of Mr. Gerry O'Sullivan, Ms Maura O'Shea and Ms Sarah Barnett for making all arrangements for this publication.

Ms Joy Wall worked as Research Assistant for most of the duration of this research and made a very significant contribution to the project. I am pleased to acknowledge her commitment and professionalism. I also acknowledge the vital contribution made by Ms Philomena Butler and Ms Deirdre Fitzgerald who were responsible for most of the coding of the data on social background and also assisted in the collection and verification of the data. I was fortunate in being able to call on the assistance of Dr. Teresa Brannick for expert advise in respect of problems in data analysis. Ms. Aine O'Donovan provided assistance in the preparation and verification of some of the larger tables while Ms Sharon Bryan helped in the preparation of the maps and figures. My largest debt is too my wife Aine who in addition to her love and support also made helpful comments on an earlier draft of the report and saved the reader from some of the most infelicitous expressions.

Patrick Clancy
Sociology Department and Social Science Research Centre
University College Dublin

September 2001.

chapter one | Introduction

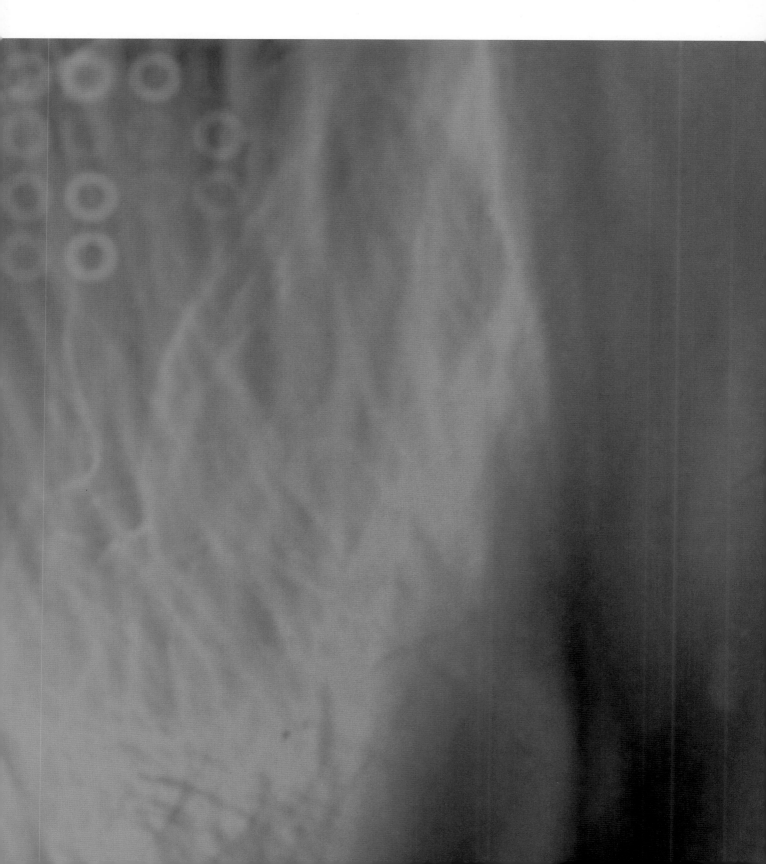

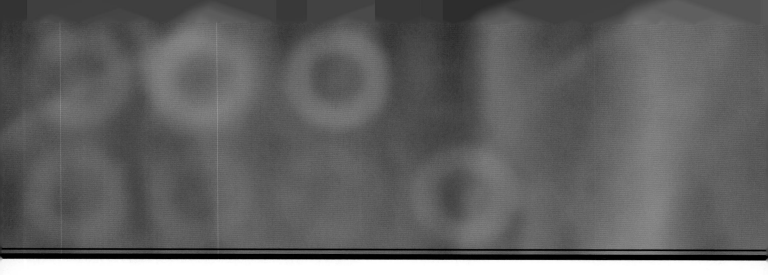

This study examines the pattern of participation in higher education in the Republic of Ireland. The report is based on a national survey of all those who enrolled as new entrants to full-time higher education in Autumn 1998. The study is the fourth national survey carried out by the author and in general, employs the same methodology and examines the same range of variables, which were analysed in the earlier reports (Clancy, 1982; 1988; 1995). Since this is part of a series of research studies, spanning a period of almost two decades, there is a particular focus on monitoring changes in the pattern of participation over time.

The report is divided into six chapters. This first chapter describes the scope of the study and the research methods used. In addition, to help place the study in context, it presents a brief description of the expansion and diversification of higher education in Ireland and internationally. The second chapter describes the distribution of higher education entrants by gender and age and examines their destination by college, sector and field of study. The third chapter examines the social background of entrants and assesses the degree of socio-economic group inequality in access to higher education. This part of the research has already been published separately (Clancy & Wall, 2000), thus, chapter three is primarily an edited version of the earlier publication and is included here for ease of reference and to correspond with the format of the earlier reports. The educational background of entrants forms the subject of the fourth chapter. The fifth chapter assesses national and county participation rates. It also examines variations in participation rates by postal district in the Dublin area. Chapter six examines a number of correlates of differential participation rates in an attempt to explain differences in admission rates by county. The final chapter of the report summarises the main findings of the research and explores some of the implications of the findings.

Our concern with the patterns of participation in higher education is linked to the increasing centrality of post-compulsory education in contemporary society. An important dimension of social change in recent decades has been the growth in educational enrolments among those who have passed the age of compulsory school attendance. This development has been reflected in higher retention rates at second level and, especially, in a massive expansion in higher education. A recent OECD report argues that:

A historic shift is occurring in the second half of the 20th century: tertiary education is replacing secondary education as the focal point of access, selection, and entry to rewarding careers for the majority of young people (OECD, 1999a: 20)

In Ireland this expansion has been explicitly linked to the achievement of key national objectives of employment creation and economic development. Several recent analyses of the economic achievements of the past decade have identified the changes in education as a crucial facilitator of the economic and social transformation (NESC, 1999; Nolan et al, 2000). Although in Ireland the widespread acknowledgement of the dividend accruing from educational expansion is of recent date, it should be noted that the reorientation of education policy towards human capital objectives has a longer lineage, having first found expression in the influential *Investment in Education* report published in 1965.

It is also significant that the current concern for social justice and combating disadvantage, the second, although perhaps more subsidiary, focus of contemporary education policy also finds its first expression in the *Investment in Education* report. The focus on education as a crucial mechanism of social exclusion is linked to the role which education plays in the status attainment process and reward structure of our society. This development is in turn related to the changes in the occupational structure, with a rapid growth in employment opportunities for those with technical and professional qualification and the contraction in employment opportunities for those who lack advanced education and training. As a consequence, educational qualifications have become the currency for employment. The higher the level of education attained the less likely is the prospect of unemployment. Census data from 1996 show that the unemployment rate among those with degree qualifications was just four per cent, by comparison with twenty-six per cent for those with only Primary level education. The unemployment rate for those with other levels of education was twenty, twelve and seven per cent, respectively, for those with Lower Secondary, Upper Secondary and Non-degree Third Level qualifications. Furthermore, for those who gain employment the rate of return on education credentials, as reflected in levels of remuneration, is impressive (Callan and Harmon, 1997; Barret et al, 1999).

The scale of expansion of higher education in Ireland is broadly similar to the experience in other European countries as illustrated in Table 1 which shows, for selected countries of the European Union, the percentage increase in enrolments each decade over the period 1950-1997. In 1997 there were more than twelve million students in tertiary education in the fifteen countries of the European Union (Eurostat, 2000). Over the period of a half century[1] there has been an eleven-fold increase in the enrolments in ten countries shown in this table (excluding Germany). The rate of increase for Ireland over the period was somewhat above the average, exceeded only by the Mediterranean countries of Portugal, Spain and Greece. The Irish pattern is also characterised by a relatively steady rate of increase by comparison with a more uneven pattern of growth in many countries. It is evident that for most countries the rate of increase was highest in the 1960s. However, the 1990s have also been characterised by very rapid increases in most countries. This compares with relatively modest growth rates in the 1980s. Germany achieved its fastest growth rate in the 1970s while Portugal had the fastest growth in the 1990s. One of the features of this expansion has been the remarkable growth in female enrolments. By 1991 the female rate of admission to higher education exceeds that of males in the majority of OECD countries – this

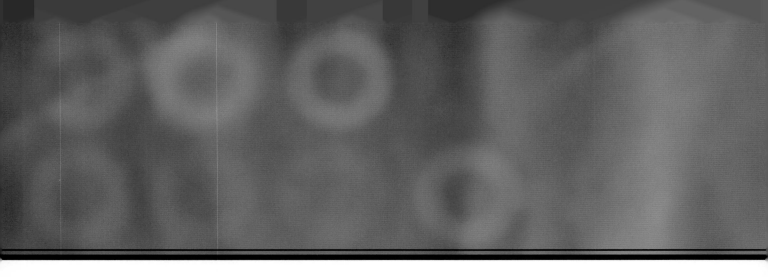

differential is especially marked in those countries, which have achieved highest overall enrolment rates (Clancy, 1994). In 1997, females accounted for fifty-two per cent of all higher education enrolments in the European Union. The female majority was evident in eleven of the fifteen countries, the exceptions being Germany, Greece, The Netherlands and Austria where females accounted for between forty-six and forty-nine per cent of total enrolments (Eurostat, 2000).

TABLE 1 PERCENTAGE INCREASE IN HIGHER EDUCATION ENROLMENTS EACH DECADE FROM 1950 TO 1997 AND RATIO OF 1997 TO 1950 ENROLMENTS IN SELECTED E.U. COUNTRIES

COUNTRY	1950–60 %	1960–70 %	1970–80 %	1980–90 %	1990–97★	1990/1950 Ratio
Belgium	68	140	57	27	56	12
Denmark	57	169	40	35	47	9
France	54	195	34	44	43	12
Germany	98	90	143	47	34	NA
Greece	57	192	41	61	124	20
Ireland	56	129	92	64	84	16
Italy	18	258	63	29	54	8
Netherlands	72	118	56	32	10	9
Portugal	58	107	84	106	240	22
Spain	38	157	210	75	63	20
United Kingdom	68	256	38	52	86	11

★ *To facilitate comparison over the entire period the figures for the period 1990-97 have been adjusted upwards to represent estimates for the full decade 1990-2000, based on the trends for the first seven years.*

Source: Figures for the period 1950-90 are taken from Clancy (1994), figures for 1990-97 are calculated from Eurostat Yearbook 2000: A Statistical Eye on Europe, (Eurostat, 2000).

The dramatic expansion of enrolment has been accompanied by a diversification of higher education systems resulting in more institutional diversity (Jallade, 1992; OECD, 1999a). In most countries the institutional diversity that is observed occurred outside the previously dominant university model. This 'external diversification' led to the development of two quite separate sectors resulting in the creation of *binary* systems, although frequently more than two sectors are evident and it may be more appropriate to talk of a diversified model (Teichler, 1988). Although less common, in some countries the diversification can be said to be 'internal' because it occurred within the university leading to the development of an integrated university model – Sweden and Spain are examples (see Clancy, 1994). More recently, some countries, such as Australia and Great Britain, which previously operated 'binary' systems have moved towards 'unified' systems. A recent analysis has suggested that while diversity may be the most characteristic feature of modern higher education systems it is not linked to any particular institutional structure (OECD, 1999a). It argues that, as a strategy, diversity 'may be pursued within unitary, binary or multi-sectoral systems' (p.41) and is not to be confused with particular macro-structural arrangements.

It is clear that the pattern of development of higher education in Ireland conforms to the dominant model. The main feature of the diversification was the development of a network of Regional Technical Colleges and the expansion of the existing Technological Colleges in Dublin and Limerick. The Dublin colleges have since been integrated to form the Dublin Institute of Technology while the Limerick college was designated as a Regional Technical College. More recently all RTCs have been redesignated as Institutes of Technology. The system was further diversified by the establishment of two National Institutes of Higher Education which have since become universities to form the University of Limerick and Dublin City University. The most recent addition to the higher education system has been a network of new private colleges which offer courses mainly in the business studies area.

The result of the sustained expansion and diversification is illustrated in Table 2, which shows the distribution of full-time enrolments by sector in 1968/69 and 1998/99 and the percentage change over the thirty-year period. While there was a five-fold increase in total enrolments the most striking feature of the growth pattern is the massive increase in the Institute of Technology sector. In 1968/69 this sector accounted for only six per cent of enrolments; this had increased to thirty-seven per cent by 1998/99. In contrast, while university enrolments increased by a factor of three and a half over the period, universities now account for a smaller proportion of total enrolments. While the Colleges of Education sector registered a modest increase of some forty per cent over the period it now accounts for only a small percentage (1.8%) of the total system. Over this period Carysfort College ceased to function as a college of education while Thomond College, the main centre for the training of specialist teachers, has now been incorporated into the University of Limerick. While the 'Other Colleges' sector has also increased over the period, the rate of increase (258%) is less than that of the total system. The composition of this sector has changed over the thirty-year period. In the late 1960s non state-aided religious colleges accounted for the majority of students in this sector; by the late 1990s private business colleges enrolled the majority of students in this sector.

TABLE 2	ENROLMENT OF FULL-TIME STUDENTS IN HIGHER EDUCATION BY SECTOR IN 1968-69 AND 1998-99, AND PERCENTAGE CHANGE 1968-1998

Sector*	1968-69		1998-1999		Percentage Change 1968-1998
	N	%	N	%	
Universities	18,056	78.0	63,328	54.3	+251
Institutes of Technology	1,449	6.3	43,476	37.3	+2900
Colleges of Education	1,498	6.5	2,092	1.8	+40
Other	2,140	9.2	7,652	6.6	+258
TOTAL	23,143	100.0	116,548	100.0	+404

★ *The total for the university sector in 1998/99 includes students from NCAD and BA students in St. Patrick's College and Mary Immaculate College*

SCOPE OF THE SURVEY

The study is confined to those who enrolled for the first time as undergraduates in the first year of study as full-time students in higher education in the Republic of Ireland. The delineation of what constitutes 'higher education' requires some elaboration. In a period of unprecedented growth of education and training opportunities for those who have completed compulsory schooling there is increasingly a blurring of boundaries between higher education and other forms of further education and training. While, as in the case of the earlier surveys, higher education is defined as consisting of courses of study which normally[2] demand as a minimum entry requirement a Leaving Certificate with at least grade D in five subjects, it is necessary to further specify that only courses which are offered in recognised higher education institutions are included. Thus, all Post Leaving Certificate courses (PLCs) are excluded from this definition. However, this study is the first to include all nursing education courses which have now become part of the higher education sector[3].

New entrants to a total of forty-three colleges are included in the survey[4]. Eight of these colleges are classified as belonging to the university sector. These include the four constituent universities of The National University of Ireland, University College Dublin, University College Cork, National University of Ireland, Galway and National University of Ireland, Maynooth[5]; The University of Dublin (Trinity College Dublin); Dublin City University; University of Limerick; and the Royal College of Surgeons in Ireland. A total of thirteen colleges make up the Institute of Technology sector. These include the Dublin Institute of Technology; the eleven former Regional Technical Colleges now designated as Institutes of Technology in Athlone, Carlow, Cork, Dundalk, Galway-Mayo, Letterkenny, Limerick, Sligo, Tallaght, Tralee, and Waterford; and Dunlaoghaire Institute of Art, Design and Technology, which incorporates the former Dunlaoghaire College of Art and Design. Ten colleges of education are included in the study. These include seven state aided colleges and three private colleges, the Mater Dei Institute of Education, Montessori College AMI and St. Nicholas, Montessori College. The state-aided colleges include two colleges of Home Economics, St. Catherine's, Blackrock, and St. Angela's Sligo and five colleges of education for primary teachers; St. Patrick's, Drumcondra; Mary Immaculate College, Limerick; Froebel College, Blackrock; St. Mary's College, Marino and Church of Ireland College, Rathmines. A total of twelve other colleges are included in the survey. These include The National College of Art and Design, The National College of Ireland, Shannon College of Hotel Management, the Milltown Institute of Theology and Philosophy, the American College Dublin and seven other private colleges whose main course offerings are in the areas of business studies and accountancy. Four of these colleges are based in Dublin, Dublin Business School, Griffith College, LSB College and Portobello College, two in Limerick, H S I College and Mid-West Business Institute and one in Cork, Skerry's College.

As was the case in the three previous national surveys this study does not attempt to examine systematically the pattern of participation in theological colleges or seminaries as it is felt that the pattern of recruitment to these colleges is not a matter for public policy and thus falls outside the scope of this research. In addition, the pattern of recruitment to these colleges is monitored annually by the Council for Research and Development of the Roman Catholic Church. However on this occasion it was decided to include some information on new entrants to the Pontifical University, St. Patrick's College, Maynooth and the Milltown Institute of Theology and Philosophy since both of these colleges enrol a significant number of lay students. Students at the Pontifical University are combined with students from NUI, Maynooth in Tables A1 and A21 and are classified as part of the university sector in aggregate tables on sector, field of study and county of origin while new entrants to the Milltown Institute are shown separately.

It is possible to estimate the number of new entrants to higher education in seminaries and other religious colleges who are excluded from this study. Apart from those who entered the colleges at Maynooth, Belfast and European Colleges it

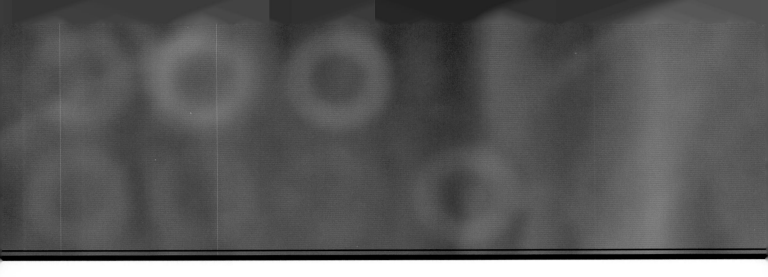

is known that some thirty-six students entered seminaries for the diocesan priesthood or for the Clerical Religious Orders. However in respect of both groups of entrants about half had previous third level education. Thus it is estimated that not more than twenty new entrants to higher education are excluded by virtue of the non-inclusion of the other theological colleges and seminaries.[6]

As in the case of the earlier surveys the focus of this study is on 'new entrants' in the first year of an undergraduate programme. Repeat students or students who were previously enrolled in higher education on another programme in the same college or in another college were not included in the study. Thus the number of new entrants to higher education is not the same as the number of first year students. This is an important distinction which is frequently ignored in the statistical data on many systems (OECD, 1993: 125) and has significant implications for the calculation of participation ratios. Where this distinction is not made double counting is involved and rates of admission to higher education are over estimates.

The tendency to conflate first year enrolments and first time entrants is understandable from the perspective of the institutions. This is especially the case where the students involved are first time entrants to the college even though they may have previously been enrolled in another college. In the present study it emerged that almost two and a half thousand of the full-time students registered in the first year of an undergraduate course were not new entrants to higher education. This represents seven per cent of first year enrolments. This is slightly less than that found in the 1992 and 1986 surveys where the rate was closer to eight per cent (8.3% in 1986 and 7.7% in 1992). It is unclear as to whether this represents a long-term trend or whether it merely reflects differences in willingness to disclose this information[7]. The proportion of first year enrolments which was made up of students who had some previous third level education varied by sector. It was lowest in the Colleges of Education (3.9%), and the Universities (5.2%). It was highest in the 'Other Colleges' sector (10.4%) followed by the Institute of Technology sector (8.5%). Although all of these percentages are lower than that reported in 1992 the differentials between sectors mirror those from the previous study.

DATA COLLECTION

The study is based primarily on an analysis of personal demographic and educational data, which were abstracted from individual student record forms. Access to this information was granted following contact with the principal, director or registrar of each college. Assurances of the strictest confidentiality were given: the names of students were not recorded, thus, it is impossible for the researcher to link any information with the identity of any individual student.

For the thirty-five colleges, which at the time of the survey, processed their applications through the Central Application Office (CAO), a standard application form was completed by all applicants. These data together with Leaving Certificate and other examination results when they become available are entered on computer file for processing. For the present study permission was granted by the Board of the CAO and by the principals or registrars of the affiliated colleges to obtain access to these data. Each of the colleges provided a computer listing of the CAO number and some additional information[8] on each student who registered on the first year of a full-time undergraduate course in Autumn 1992. By matching these ID numbers with the CAO master file it was possible to abstract most of the required data. However, since many colleges admit a small number of students directly without going through the CAO it was necessary to approach the colleges directly for these data.

While access to computerised records both from the colleges and from the CAO greatly facilitated the research it was necessary to supplement these sources by a direct approach to the new entrants to obtain data on their socio-economic background. This aspect of the research was accomplished with the assistance of the Director of the CAO who kindly agreed to send to all students, who accepted a place through the CAO system, a special form which was designed by the researcher to collect data on the socio-economic status of parents (see below for further details on this part of the research).

Eight of the colleges included in the survey were not at the time affiliated to the CAO system and, thus, operated their own independent admissions procedure. Two different research strategies were adopted with these colleges. In some cases it was possible to abstract all the data required from the student application and/or enrolment forms. In other cases where less comprehensive student data were available permission was sought to have all first year students complete a short questionnaire prepared by the researcher. The collection of data commenced in mid-November by which time it was felt that all colleges would have completed their enrolments for the year, thus avoiding the problem of duplication which could arise if a student enrolled initially in one college and subsequently transferred to another.

Irrespective of the data gathering strategy used the first task was the accurate identification of the first time entrants and the elimination from the survey of those who had previously been enrolled on a third level course. Students who apply thought the CAO system students are requested to provide details of previous third level education. In this way it was possible to identify most of those who were not new entrants. This information was supplemented by college records. In the case of those students who were admitted directly to the colleges we examined the application/enrolment forms to identify those with previous third-level education. All students who were known to have had some previous third level education were excluded from the main study. Having identified the target population, the research effort concentrated on achieving as complete a record as possible in respect of each student. Since the study aimed at complete coverage, considerable effort was expended in the pursuit of missing data and in the verification of these data. This effort was successful only because of the willing cooperation and forbearance of the admissions and student records' staff of the colleges.

The personal, demographic, social and educational data collected as described above constitute the main source of data for the study. Data provided by the Central Statistics Office and by the Department of Education and Science are also used to provide a context within which the survey findings can be interpreted. Demographic data on age, sex, social class and socio-economic status of the population, by area, from the 1996 Census of Population and from the 1997 Labour Force Survey are used as a basis for calculating rates of participation in higher education. The study also draws upon data published by the Department of Education in its annual Tuarascáil Staitistiúil and on unpublished data kindly provided on enrolment figures by school type and on retention data by county for the final year of the post-primary cycle in 1997/98. Students from this cohort formed the main target group from which the new higher education entrants are drawn.

Like the three previous studies this is a policy-oriented descriptive study of the pattern of participation in higher education in Ireland. Although the research is policy-oriented this report does not attempt to formulate any comprehensive recommendations for the future developments of higher education. The question of policy options has being considered separately in a range of recent reports. These include the report of the Steering Committee on the Future Developments of Higher Education (1995), the Report of the Review Committee on Post Secondary Education and Training Places (1999), the report, Access & Equity in Higher Education by Skilbeck and Connell (2000) and more recently the report by the Report of the Action Group on Access to Third Level Education (2001). The main aim of this report is to contribute to the information base which is available to decision makers. Thus, for example, our findings, in respect of the social background of higher education entrants, have been considered by the Action Group on Access when making its recommendations. Finally, since the report is written with a broad readership in mind the style of the report, like that of its predecessors, is, for the most part, non-technical and non-academic. Since the empirical analysis reported here does not exhaust the full potential of the data it is envisaged that the results of further analysis will be published in separate articles.

FOOTNOTES

1. The figures for the last decade (1990-2000) are estimates based on trends for the first seven years of this decade.

2. Almost all colleges admit some mature students who may not have the required educational credentials.

3. Only a small number of nursing education courses were included in the earlier studies. However, while this study includes all such students only a limited range of data were available in respect of these students. For example, data on educational attainment and social background are not included.

4. Data were also collected from Burren College of Art. However all of the students enrolled in this college had some previous third level education thus, they were not within the scope of this research.

5. The figures shown for NUI, Maynooth includes students from the Pontifical University. Since only limited data were collected in respect of students enrolled at the Pontifical University these students were not the subject of separate analysis.

6. The author is grateful to Ms Ann Hanley from the Council for Research and Development of Roman Catholic Church, who supplied the statistical information, which made possible this estimate.

7. Our information is necessarily based on that which students disclose in their application forms. We have not attempted a formal tracking of previous applications through the CAO or other systems.

8. The colleges also provided information in respect of each student on: course of study; county of origin; source of financial aid, if any; and registration status as of 13 November.

Females have had higher retention rates to Leaving Certificate for many years, yet until now, this did not translate into higher rates of admission to third-level. In 1998 the representation of females among higher education entrants fully reflects their proportionate representation among Leaving Certificate students[2].

The gender distribution of new entrants is related to the structure of the higher education system. Females constitute a significant majority (58%) of entrants to the university sector and a preponderance (90%) of entrants into the colleges of education. In contrast they form a smaller percentage (45%) of entrants into the Institute of Technology sector. In general the gender balance does not vary significantly by college within each sector. Females constitute the majority in seven of the eight colleges in the university sector, the exception being the University of Limerick where they are marginally in the minority, accounting for forty-nine per cent of admissions (Table A1). Males constitute the majority in twelve of the Institutes of Technology, although in several instances this gender differential is no more than one per cent. Cork Institute of Technology has the largest gender imbalance where males account for sixty-four per cent of the intake. Sligo Institute of Technology is the only college to have a majority (55%) of female admissions. While females constitute an overall majority of the intake into the 'Other Colleges' sector, the pattern does vary by college. The largest female majorities are evident in two of the smaller private business colleges, Skerry's College, Cork (90%) and HSI, Limerick (81%), and in the National College of Art and Design (80%). In contrast, males constitute the majority in two of the private colleges, Dublin Business School (68%) and Portobello College (64%).

Field of Study

In examining the distribution of new entrants by field of study the three previous surveys utilised sets of categories which have been widely used within the separate administrative structures of the HEA sector and non-HEA sector colleges. In the interests of comparability the same set of categories will be used in this report. For the HEA sector colleges (the universities and the NCAD[3]) the set of categories developed for the Higher Education Authority's *Annual Report and Student Statistics* will be used while for the other colleges the field of study categories used are those defined by the Boards of Study of the National Council for Educational Awards. However, before examining the detailed breakdown of new entrants within these separate fields of study categories it is appropriate to start with a summary composite table which shows the field of study of all new entrants.

Table 4 reveals that Technology is the field of study which enrolled the largest percentage (26%) of new entrants. Twenty-one per cent of students were enrolled in Commerce, seventeen per cent in the Humanities with a further twelve per cent in Science. The remaining twenty-four per cent of entrants were distributed among eight other fields of study[4].

Field of Study	1998 New Entrants				Representation of Females
	Male	Female	Total		
	%	%	N	%	%
Humanities	11.2	21.6	5,434	16.6	68.3
Art and Design	2.4	3.6	987	3.0	62.3
Science	10.8	13.2	3,938	12.0	57.7
Agriculture	1.9	1.5	547	1.7	47.0
Technology	43.0	10.7	8,497	26.0	21.7
Medical Sciences	2.2	7.2	1,579	4.8	78.3
Education	1.1	4.9	1,015	3.1	83.3
Law	1.3	2.0	544	1.7	63.5
Social Science	1.6	4.2	967	3.0	74.6
Commerce	20.4	22.5	7,028	21.5	55.0
Hotel, Catering & Tourism	2.0	4.7	1,164	3.6	72.6
Combined Studies	2.2	4.0	1,024	3.1	67.4
TOTAL	100.0	100.0	32,724★	100.0	52.7

★ *Total includes 82 students for whom data on gender was missing.*

The pattern of admission by field of study is strongly differentiated by gender. This differentiation is elaborated in Table 4 which in addition to showing the *distribution* of men and women by field of study also shows the *representation* of women within each field. In the former case the universities in question is all male students and all female students, the focus being on how they distribute themselves among the different fields of study. In the latter case when the representation of females is presented the unit of analysis is all students within a particular field of study, the focus being on the percentage of places taken by females. While, as already noted, females constituted slightly more than half (53%) of all entrants they formed a particularly large majority of entrants into Education (83%), Medical Sciences (78%), Social Science (75%) and Hotel, Catering and Tourism (73%). They were also in the majority in six other fields of study: Humanities (68%), Combined Studies (67%), Law (64%), Art and Design (62%), Science (58%) and Commerce (55%). In contrast, females constituted only twenty-two per cent of entrants to Technology, which, after Education, shares with Medicine the distinction of being the second most sex-typed field of study. Females were also slightly under-represented (47%) in Agriculture.

It is of interest to monitor changes in the pattern of enrolment by field of study over an eighteen-year period. In reporting on the 1986 and 1992 surveys it was noted that there was relatively little change in the disciplinary balance over the period 1980-92 (Clancy, 1988: 16). This generalisation also holds true for the period 1992-98 (Table 5). With the exception of Education in the period 1980-92, all fields of study participated in the enrolment growth. Between 1980 and 1986 Hotel, Catering and Tourism, and Social Science experienced the largest percentage increase in admissions although in each case they still formed a low percentage of overall enrolments. In the period 1986-92 Law (88%) and the Humanities (71%) showed the largest percentage increase, while Commerce, Agriculture, Science and Hotel, Catering and Tourism all had rates of increase which were in excess of the average. In the more recent period 1992-98, Combined Studies, a category first utilised in 1992, showed the largest percentage increase. Medical Sciences[5], Education and Hotel, Catering and Tourism also showed rates of enrolment growth greatly in excess of the average.

TABLE 5	PERCENTAGE CHANGE IN ENROLMENT BY FIELD OF STUDY BETWEEN 1980 AND 1986, 1986 AND 1992, AND 1992 AND 1998

	1980	1986	1992	1998	% Change 1980-86	% Change 1986-92	% Change 1992-98
Field of Study	N	N	N	N	%	%	%
Humanities	1,955	2,720	4,638	5,302	+39.1	+70.5	+17.2
Art and Design	506	683	847	987	+35.0	+24.0	+16.5
Science	1,898	2,531	3,817	3,938	+33.4	+50.8	+3.2
Agriculture	230	265	417	547	+15.2	+57.4	+31.2
Technology	3,364	4,240	5,856	8,497	+26.0	+38.1	+45.1
Medical Sciences	620	626	780	1,579	+1.0	+24.6	+102.4
Education	1,175	916	541	1,015	-22.0	-40.9	+87.6
Law	266	273	512	544	+2.6	+87.5	+6.3
Social Science	371	639	728	967	+72.2	+13.9	+32.8
Commerce	2,736	3,817	6,090	7,028	+39.5	+59.5	+15.4
Hotel, Catering & Tourism	239	449	667	1,164	+87.9	+48.6	+74.5
Combined Studies	-	-	241	1,024	-	-	+324.9
TOTAL %	-	-	-	-	+28.4	+46.5	+30.2
TOTAL N	13,360	17,159	25,134	32,724			

The data reported in Table 4 and the 1998 data from Table 5 are based on an amalgamation of data contained in the following two tables which describe, separately, the distribution of students by field of study for the HEA sector and non-HEA sector colleges. However before examining these more detailed distributions it is appropriate to take account of some variability between colleges in the way different subject areas are classified. For example, Mathematics can be classified as a Science subject or as one of the Humanities: Computer Studies can be classified as part of Science, Engineering or Business Studies in different colleges. Thus, in examining the distribution of students by field of study in the different colleges it is necessary to be aware of these different classifications (see Clancy, 1995: 221-2 for detailed information on the classification used).

The distribution of new entrants by field of study and gender in the HEA sector colleges is shown in Table 6. (This distribution is shown separately for each individual college in the Appendix, Table A2). Almost a third of entrants were admitted to Arts. Other fields of study which enrolled a large percentage of entrants were Science (17%), Commerce (14%) and Engineering (12%). Ten per cent were admitted to Medicine while the remaining students were distributed among the other fields of study shown in Table 6. This pattern of distribution does not differ significantly from that reported in the earlier studies.

As was evident from our examination of the composite table the distribution of students by field of study in HEA sector colleges is highly differentiated by gender. Social Science, Communication and Information Studies, Art and Design, Medicine, and Food Science and Technology all attracted a disproportionate number of female students. In contrast, Engineering and Agricultural Science and Forestry attracted a disproportionate number of males students. Economic and Social Studies, Dentistry, Commerce and Science reflect greater gender balance in recruitment with females forming a slight majority in all of these fields of study. These gender differentials are broadly similar to those found in previous surveys. While there is some evidence of an increase in female representation in what have been traditionally male dominated disciplines, this is by no means a universal trend. For example, while female representation in Engineering has increased marginally from almost nineteen per cent in 1992 to twenty-four per cent in 1998, their representation in Agricultural Science and Forestry in 1998 (28%) shows a decline from the thirty-nine per cent achieved in 1992. There has been a significant change in the gender balance in recruitment into Veterinary Medicine where females now constitute a majority. In 1986 females accounted for thirty-four per cent of entrants to Veterinary Medicine; this had increased to forty-four per cent in 1992 and sixty-three per cent in 1998. The findings reported in Table 6 substantiate the conclusion reached in the report of the previous survey that 'male admission rates to traditionally female dominated fields of study may prove more resistant to change' (Clancy, 1995: 36). Between 1992 and 1998 there has been no increase in the representation of males in Social Science which remains at about 12%. During this period their representation has declined in Art and Design (from 29% to 20%) while there have been smaller declines in their representation in Arts (from 38% to 32%) and in Communication and Information Studies (from 19% to 17%)

TABLE 6 DISTRIBUTION OF ENTRANTS TO HEA DESIGNATED COLLEGES BY FIELD OF STUDY AND GENDER, AND REPRESENTATION OF FEMALES IN EACH FIELD OF STUDY

Field of Study	Male	Female	Total		Representation of Females
	%	%	%	N	%
Arts	24.9	36.8	31.9	4,738	67.7
Education	1.3	0.7	0.9	141	42.6
Art and Design	0.5	1.3	1.0	143	80.3
Social Science	0.6	3.1	2.0	304	88.5
Economics and Social Studies	1.8	1.3	1.5	220	50.5
European Studies	0.8	1.4	1.1	170	71.2
Communication and Information Studies	0.1	0.5	0.4	54	83.3
Commerce	15.6	12.3	13.6	2,025	52.8
Law	2.2	2.5	2.4	351	61.5
Science	18.5	15.5	16.8	2,492	54.3
Engineering	21.1	4.6	11.5	1,702	23.6
Architecture	0.3	0.4	0.3	516	0.8
Medicine	5.0	13.2	9.8	1,456	79.0
Dentistry	0.6	0.4	0.5	71	52.1
Veterinary Medicine	0.4	0.5	0.5	72	62.5
Agricultural Science and Forestry	2.7	0.7	1.5	230	27.8
Food Science and Technology	0.5	1.1	0.8	123	75.6
Equestrian	0.3	0.5	0.4	62	69.4
Combined Studies	2.8	3.2	3.0	452	61.3
TOTAL	100.0	100.0	100.0	14,857	58.6

The distribution of new entrants by field of study and gender for the non-HEA sector institutions is shown in Table 7. (This distribution is shown separately for each individual college in the Appendix, Table A3). The largest percentage of students, thirty-one per cent, were enrolled in Business, Administrative and Secretarial Studies. Engineering was the field of study with the next largest enrolment, with nineteen per cent in General Engineering and a further six per cent in Construction Studies. Twelve per cent enrolled in Computer Studies with a further nine per cent in Science. Art and Design, Education, General Studies, and Hotel, Catering and Tourism each enrolled between five and six per cent of new entrants. As in the case of the HEA sector colleges, the pattern of enrolment by field of study in these colleges is broadly similar to that which prevailed in the 1992 survey. The main change has been an increase in the percentage of students who enrolled in Computer Studies (from 6% to 12%) with a corresponding decline in the percentages enrolled in Science (from 15% to 9%). The decline of three per cent in the percentage enrolled in General Engineering has been compensated for by increases in Education and Hotel, Catering and Tourism.

TABLE 7   DISTRIBUTION OF ENTRANTS TO NON-HEA DESIGNATED COLLEGES BY FIELD OF STUDY AND GENDER, AND REPRESENTATION OF FEMALES IN EACH FIELD OF STUDY

Field of Study	Male %	Female %	Total %	Total N	Representation of Females %
Construction Studies	9.7	2.0	6.0	1,074	15.6
General Engineering	32.5	5.0	19.3	3,456	12.4
Science	6.6	11.5	8.9	1,5906	1.6
Art and Design	3.7	5.9	4.7	844	59.2
Computer Studies	14.7	9.6	12.2	2182	37.4
Business, Administrative and Secretarial Studies	25.2	37.5	31.0	5,537	57.6
Hotel, Catering and Tourism	3.3	9.5	6.5	1164	72.6
Education	0.9	9.2	4.9	874	89.9
General Studies	3.4	9.7	6.4	1,146	72.3
TOTAL	**100**	**100**	**100**	**17,867**	**47.7**

Table 7 reveals a high level of gender differentiation in the distribution of students by field of study. This is most pronounced in respect of recruitment to Education and General Engineering. Less than thirteen per cent of entrants to

Engineering are female while the situation is reversed in respect of Education where males constitute only ten per cent of entrants. These patterns reveal little movement over a period of six years. Between 1992 and 1998 there has been no change in the gender balance of the intake into Education while in respect of Engineering the representation of females has increased by three per cent. Other fields of study which manifest a high level of gender differentiation are Hotel, Catering and Tourism and General Studies where the female representation is seventy-three and seventy-two per cent, respectively and Construction Studies where males account for eighty-four per cent of enrolments. There is least gender differentiation in Business, Administrative and Secretarial Studies, the field of study which attracts the largest percentage of enrolments in this sector. Science and Computer Studies reveal moderate and complementary levels of gender differentiation; females constitute the majority (62%) of entrants into the former while males form the majority (63%) of entrants into the latter field of study. It is of interest to note that the distribution within these two fields of study reveals growing gender differentiation over recent years. By comparison with the situation which prevailed in 1992, by 1998, the female majority in Science has increased by seven per cent while the male majority is six per cent greater in Computer Science.

Level of Study

An important feature of the diversification, which accompanied the enrolment growth in the 1970s, was the expansion of short-cycle programmes (Clancy, 1993). The main third level provision in the newly established Regional Technical Colleges was at certificate and diploma level. The sustained growth in the non-university sector has led to a situation whereby, from a comparative perspective, Ireland is characterized by having a high percentage of third level entrants enrolled on sub-degree level programmes (OECD, 1997). This is reflected in Table 8, which shows the distribution of entrants by level of study and sector.

TABLE 8   DISTRIBUTION OF NEW ENTRANTS BY LEVEL OF STUDY AND BY COLLEGE TYPE

COLLEGE TYPE	Degree	Sub-Degree	TOTAL	
	%	%	%	N
Universitites	94.9	5.1	100	14,623
ITs	14.9	85.1	100	15,683
Colleges of Education	89.3	10.7	100	1,052
Other	63.3	36.7	100	1,366
TOTAL	**55.1**	**44.9**	**100**	**32,724**

While the majority (55%) of entrants to higher education in 1998 were admitted to degree level courses forty-five per cent were admitted to certificate or diploma programmes. This differentiation is closely linked to the type of college attended. The vast majority of entrants to the university sector were enrolled on degree level courses, the main exception being those admitted into Nursing Studies programmes. Similarly, with the exception of those who entered the Montessori Colleges, the great majority of entrants to the colleges of education were enrolled on degree level programmes. In contrast the great majority (85%) of entrants into the Institute of Technology sector were enrolled on sub-degree programmes. The distribution of entrants, by level of study, to the 'Other Colleges' sector corresponds more closely to the average for all colleges; sixty-three per cent were enrolled on degree level programmes. It is, of course, necessary to point out that these data refer only to the level of programme on which the students embark. Because of the cumulative nature of the NCEA award structure very many students who earn a National Certificate progress to Diploma level and with the introduction of add-on degree programmes an increasing number of diploma recipients go on to study for a degree within the Institute of Technology sector. In addition, smaller numbers of certificate and diploma holders go on to study for a degree in Irish or UK universities. Thus, the designation of 'degree level' in Table 8 refers only to *ab initio* degrees.

The distribution of entrants by level of study in individual colleges is shown in Table A4. Within the Institute of Technology sector the Dublin Institute of Technology (DIT) had the largest percentage (38%) of students on degree courses. Waterford also had a relatively high level of admission to degree level courses (35%). Other colleges in this sector which had a significant percentage of entrants on degree level courses were Cork (16%), Limerick (14%) and Galway/Mayo (9%). Within the 'Other Colleges' sector there is considerable variability between colleges in the distribution of students between degree and sub-degree courses. All of the new entrants to the NCAD were on degree level courses while more than three-quarters of entrants to the American College Dublin and to two of the larger private business colleges, Griffith College and the Dublin Business School were at degree level. All of the entrants to Shannon College of Hotel Management and to three of the smaller private business colleges, HIS and Mid-West from Limerick and Skerry's College Cork, were enrolled on sub-degree programmes.

The differentiation between degree and sub-degree programmes is related to the field of study in which students enrol (Table 9). Students of the Humanities, Education, Agriculture and Law were disproportionately admitted to degree level courses. In contrast, sub-degree courses were more common for students of Art and Design, Hotel, Catering and Tourism, and Technology. Commerce students were more evenly divided between degree and sub-degree programmes although the majority (56%) had embarked on sub-degree level courses.

TABLE 9 FIELD OF STUDY OF ALL NEW ENTRANTS TO HIGHER EDUCATION IN 1998 BY LEVEL OF STUDY

Field of Study	Degree %	Sub-Degree %	TOTAL %	N
Humanities	96.6	3.4	5,434	100
Art and Design	21.3	78.7	987	100
Science	68.2	31.8	3,953	100
Agriculture	83.0	17.0	547	100
Technology	32.7	67.3	8,560	100
Medical Sciences	42.8	57.2	1,501	100
Education	93.4	6.6	1,015	100
Law	80.3	19.7	544	100
Social Science	68.0	32.0	967	100
Commerce	43.7	56.3	7,028	100
Hotel, Catering & Tourism	17.7	82.3	1,164	100
Combined Studies	62.9	37.1	1,024	100
TOTAL %	**55.1**	**44.9**	**32,724**	**100**

Age of New Entrants

In examining the age of new entrants it was decided to focus on age on October 1st 1998, this being the approximate median date of commencement of the academic year. Table 10 shows the age distribution by college type and, for comparative purposes, the comparable distribution for each of the three earlier national surveys. We note that just over half of the new entrants were aged eighteen at entry. Nineteen per cent were less than eighteen while twenty-one per cent were aged nineteen at the time of entry. The remaining ten per cent were aged twenty or over. Less than five per cent of entrants could be classified as 'mature students', being aged twenty-three or over at the time of entry. While the age distribution is broadly similar to that recorded in 1992 there is some evidence that new entrants are getting somewhat older. The reduction (from 31% in 1992 to 19% in 1998) in the number of entrants aged seventeen or under is quite significant and represents a continuing trend since 1980 when forty-four per cent of entrants were in this age group.

However, there is much less change at the other end of the age range. Between 1992 and 1998 there has been only a small increase in the percentage of 'mature students' (from 2.5% to 4.5%). Similarly, over the same six year period, there has been only a three per cent increase in the percentage of entrants aged twenty or over (from 6.9% to 9.9%).

TABLE 10   **AGE ON OCTOBER 1, 1998 OF NEW ENTRANTS TO HIGHER EDUCATION BY COLLEGE TYPE IN 1998 WITH COMPARATIVE DATA FOR ALL NEW ENTRANTS IN 1992, 1986 AND 1980**

| AGE | 1998 New Entrants | | | | | 1992 New Entrants | 1986 New Entrant | 1980 New Entrants |
| | Universities | Institutes of Technology | Colleges of Education | Other Colleges | TOTAL | TOTAL | TOTAL | TOTAL |
	%	%	%	%	%	%	%	%
Under 17	0.1	0.1	0.1	0.1	0.1	0.3	0.1	2.1
17	18.6	20.0	19.6	12.0	19.1	30.3	34.0	42.0
18	52.0	49.2	47.9	42.2	50.1	47.0	46.3	38.5
19	20.1	21.2	19.9	24.9	20.8	15.4	13.5	9.6
20	3.2	4.0	2.7	8.3	3.8	2.9	2.3	2.8
21	0.7	1.3	0.9	3.6	1.1	1.0	0.8	1.4
22	0.5	0.6	0.2	1.3	0.5	0.5	1.2}	2.3}
23-25	1.6	1.7	3.1	2.9	1.8	1.0		
26-30	1.3	0.9	1.8	2.2	1.2	0.6	0.4	0.7
31-40	1.1	0.7	2.0	1.3	0.9	0.6	0.3	0.5
Over 40	0.7	0.4	1.8	1.3	0.6	0.3	0.1	0.1
TOTAL %	100	100	100	100	100	100	100	100
TOTAL N	14,543	15,596	1,045	1,346	32,530	25,084	17,152	13,360

In general, the analysis of age distribution by college type in 1998 does not reveal any marked differences. The modal age at entry was eighteen for all college types. However, the colleges of education had the highest percentage (9%) of 'mature' entrants while the 'Other Colleges' sector had the highest percentage (21%) of entrants aged twenty or over. In contrast, both the university and Institute of Technology sectors have a younger age profile, with about seventy per cent of entrants aged seventeen or eighteen and less than ten per cent aged twenty or over. The age distribution of new entrants was very similar for males and females (Appendix, Table A5). In both instances the percentage of 'matures' is less than five per cent although females were somewhat more likely to be less than eighteen years at entry (20% versus 18%).

A more detailed analysis of the age of new entrants in individual colleges is provided in the Appendix (Table A6). Within the university sector, the modal age of entrants was eighteen in all colleges except the Royal College of Surgeons, where the largest percentage (27%) of entrants were aged nineteen at the time of entry and where almost half were aged twenty or over. Entrants to NUI, Galway were somewhat younger with twenty-four per cent under the age of eighteen and less than six per cent were aged twenty or over. NUI, Maynooth had the largest percentage (7.6%) of entrants over the age of twenty-five. In contrast, only one per cent of UCD entrants and two per cent of UL entrants were in this age category.

There was relatively little variability in the age of entry to the Institutes of Technology, where eighteen was the modal age for all thirteen colleges. Dun Laoghaire Institute of Art, Design and Technology had the most distinctive profile on this variable. Less than five per cent of its entrants were under the age of eighteen, by comparison with twenty per cent which was the average for this sector. In addition, the percentage of entrants to Dun Laoghaire who were over the age of twenty-five (11%) was more than five times the average for the sector. Within the Colleges of Education sector the Mater Dei Institute had the highest percentage (30%) of students under the age of eighteen while Montessori AMI College had the highest percentage of older students, with more than eighteen per cent over the age of twenty-one.

The modal age of entry was eighteen for all of the colleges within the 'Other Colleges' category. The Dublin Business School, NCAD, and American College Dublin had the lowest percentage of entrants under the age of eighteen. In contrast, the colleges with the highest percentage of entrants over the age of twenty-one were the Milltown Institute (27%), American College Dublin (21%) and Griffith College (17%).

The age distribution of new entrants by field of study is also presented in separate tables in the Appendix. In respect of HEA sector colleges (Table A7), the modal age of entrants was eighteen for all fields of study. Engineering and Science were the faculties which enrolled the largest percentage (23%) of students under the age of eighteen. In contrast, Veterinary Medicine, and Art and Design had less than three per cent of entrants in this age range. Looking at the distribution of older students we note that the highest percentages of entrants over the age of twenty-one were to be found in Medicine (21%), Social Science (14%) and Veterinary Medicine (11%).

In respect of non-HEA sector colleges (Table A8), the modal age of entrants was also eighteen for all fields of study. Art and Design had the smallest percentage (10%) of entrants under the age of eighteen and was amongst those with a significant percentage of entrants (9%) over the age of twenty-one. Almost eleven per cent of entrants into General Studies and more than eight per cent of entrants into Computer Studies were aged more than twenty-one at the time of entry.

Footnotes

1. If Arts students enrolled in St. Patrick's and Nursing students at St. Angela's are excluded the increase in enrolment in the Colleges of Education sector is 102%.

2. Females accounted for 52.5% of Leaving Certificate candidates in 1998 and 52.7% of higher education entrants. In contrast, in 1992 when females also constituted 52% of Leaving Certificate candidates they accounted for only 49% of higher education entrants. The removal of this gender anomaly reflects a change in classification, i.e. the recent inclusion of Nursing Studies as part of the higher education system, rather than any differential increase in the relative admission rates of females and male students

3. While the two largest Colleges of Education, St. Patrick's and Mary Immaculate, were recently included as part of the HEA sector, they are not included in this sector in this report as these changes occurred subsequent to the time of the survey.

4. See Clancy (1995: 221-2) for detailed information on the classification used.

5. This is explained by the recent incorporation of undergraduate Nursing Studies as part of the higher education system.

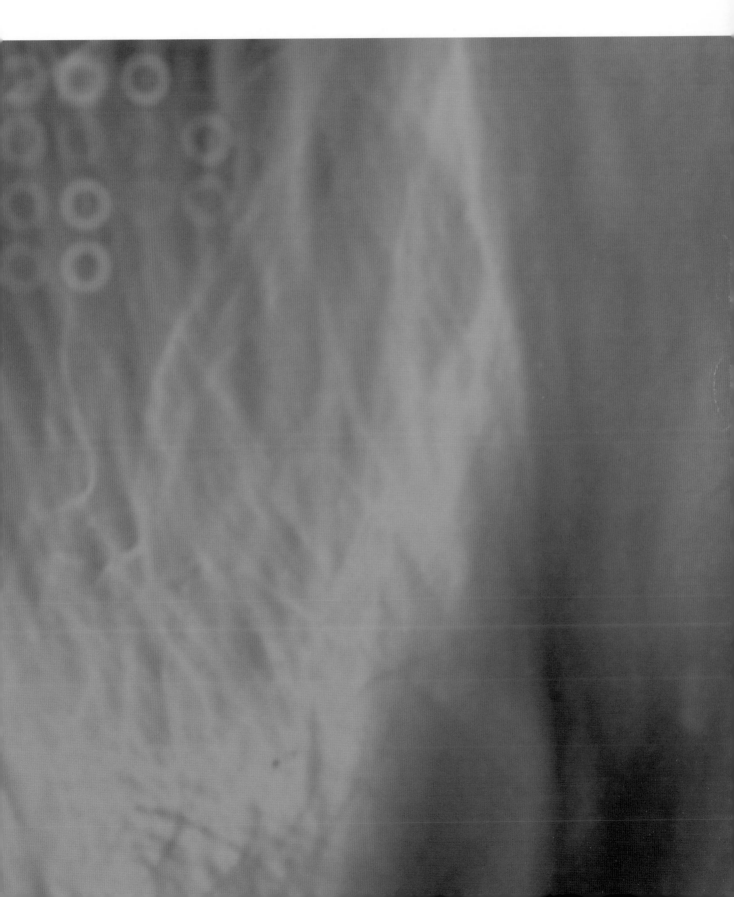

chapter three | Social Background of Entrants

An important aim of this study was to examine the social background of new entrants to higher education. Since this issue was first examined in the *Investment in Education* (1965) report it has remained an important one in educational research in Ireland. It has been a central concern in each of the earlier surveys. At the request of the Higher Education Authority and in view of current policy concerns in this area, the findings from this part of the 1998 survey have already been reported (Clancy and Wall, 2000). As mentioned in our introduction, this chapter is primarily an edited version of the earlier publication. The chapter is divided into four main sections. In the first section we describe the data sources that are used and some of the measurement problems, which we encountered. The second section presents the main findings of our study in respect of the three social background indicators that are used: parents' principal economic status; parents' socio-economic group; and parents' social class. In respect of the latter two indicators we use the new socio-economic group and social class categories, which were first used in the 1996 Census of Population. In the third section we monitor changes in the social background of entrants, comparing the findings from the present study with those from earlier studies. In the final section we present some findings from the School Leavers' Surveys on second level transitions, which bear directly on access to third level.

Data Sources and Measurement Problems

While the main study attempts complete coverage of the total higher education system, including private colleges, this report is confined to those colleges, whose students are admitted through the Central Application Office (CAO) system and to whom some form of state support applies, either in the form of free fees and/or where students are eligible to apply for a means tested maintenance grant. Thus, the colleges encompassed in this aspect of the study include all of the Universities (including the Royal College of Surgeons in Ireland and the Pontifical University, St. Patrick's College Maynooth); the Institutes of Technology; the Colleges of Education (state-aided); and three other colleges, The National College of Art & Design, The National College of Ireland, and the Milltown Institute of Theology and Philosophy. The study population for this aspect of the study is further confined to students from the Republic of Ireland.

The main source of data was a special postal survey, which sought information directly from students on their parents' social background. This practice of seeking data on parents' social background directly from the students was also followed in 1992, since by this time the CAO no longer collected data on parents' occupation from all applicants. Following discussions, the Secretary of the CAO kindly agreed to facilitate the research by arranging to send to all students who accepted a place through the CAO system a special questionnaire, designed by the researcher, to elicit the required data. Data was sought on parents' principal economic status, parents' occupation and employment status. In respect of principal economic status the questionnaire sought to differentiate between those who were employed, unemployed, on home duties, retired, deceased and 'other'. In requesting data on the occupation of parents, respondents were asked to give precise job title, and for those not in paid employment to record last occupation held. The questionnaire also sought data on employment status, differentiating between those who were self-employed with paid employees, self-employed without paid employees and those who were employees. Finally those, whose parents or guardians were farmers were asked to indicate size of farm. Overall the questionnaire was designed to collect data, which as far as possible matched that collected in the Census of Population. A copy of the form used is reproduced in Appendix B.

Questionnaires were sent to all CAO applicants, from the Republic of Ireland, who accepted a CAO offer in September 1998. Students were asked to return the completed form directly to the CAO office. While guarantees of confidentiality were provided, it was clear to students that compliance was voluntary and did not in any way affect the allocation or confirmation of a higher education place. A total of 22,914 questionnaires were returned. This represents a response rate of sixty-seven per cent since some 34,334 students from the Republic of Ireland accepted a third level place offered through the CAO. While a higher response rate would, of course, be welcome, this level of response to a postal questionnaire is high by contemporary standards. While it is lower than the almost seventy-five per cent response rate achieved in 1992, there is one significant difference in the procedures adopted. In 1992, the questionnaire was sent with the CAO offer letter and students were asked to return the completed questionnaire with their letter of acceptance. In contrast, because the latter procedure was not considered feasible, the 1998 questionnaire was sent after the students had accepted their offer. Students were asked to return the form in a special prepaid envelope in a special mailing. It is perhaps not surprising that the 1992 procedures, which might be perceived as more integral to the acceptance process, secured a higher level of compliance.

Not all of the questionnaire data returned has been used in this report. As described above, all students who had withdrawn or who had been identified as having previously been enrolled on a third level course were excluded from the study. An additional limitation applies to part of the analysis. Although only those students who accepted a place through the CAO system were sent a questionnaire, in about two thousand cases the ID on the student's questionnaire could not be matched with the ID supplied by the colleges. Thus, while these unmatched cases are included in the main aggregate tables on social background, they could not be used in that part of the analysis, which requires a link with individualised data[1].

As already mentioned in the introduction we use three different indicators of students' social background: (1) parents' principal economic status, (2) parents' socio-economic group and (3) parents' social class. While the measurement of the first of these does not present particular difficulties, socio-economic status and social class, which are determined on the basis of parents' occupation, do present a range of problems. Some of these measurement problems have been discussed in the reports on the earlier surveys (see Clancy, 1988: 22-23 and footnote[2]). Notwithstanding these problems, the attraction of using each of these categories is that it allows us to compare the social background of third level entrants with the relevant section of the national population. The use of socio-economic status is especially appropriate since this was first used in the *Investment in Education* report and in each of the three previous national surveys. The utilisation of the same set of categories allows us to monitor changes over time in the socio-economic profile of higher education entrants. However, in the light of the very rapid social and economic changes of recent years and because of the consequential changes in the occupational structure, whereby many new types of occupations were not reflected in the previous classification, the Central Statistics Office introduced a revised system of classification for the 1996 Census. The new classification is based on the *UK Standard Occupational Classification* and is described by the CSO as differing significantly from those used in previous censuses (CSO, 1998, p101). Apart from the need to cover new types of occupations, the CSO points out that the change in the classification system is necessary to facilitate computer automated coding and to meet the requirement to adhere to the international occupational classification, ISCO Com (88). In a third section of this chapter, where we seek to monitor change over time, we detail how we have chosen to deal with the difficulties, which this change in classification systems presents.

In view of the high incidence of missing data on parents' social background, it is appropriate, before presenting the main findings of this part of the survey, to address the question of the representativeness of the data which we have available. In all, four separate tests were carried out comparing those for whom data on social background were available with those for whom they were missing. These comparisons relate to type of post-primary school attended, financial aid status, higher education sector and for those at university, the percentages enrolled in professional faculties. It has been documented in previous research that each of these variables is linked to students' social background. Thus, if the pattern of missing data is class biased, it should be reflected in the distribution of these variables. The results are reported in the Appendix A (Table A9).

In respect of post-primary school attended there is a very close correspondence between the two distributions. The most critical categories in this comparison are Fee-paying Secondary Schools and Vocational Schools, for it is well established that the higher socio-economic groups are 'over-represented' in the Fee-paying Secondary schools while lower socio-economic groups are 'over-represented' in Vocational Schools (Hannan, et al, 1996). While students for whom data on social background are available are marginally more highly represented in Fee-paying Secondary Schools, they are also very slightly more represented in Vocational Schools. This test would suggest that there is no substantial bias in the incidence of missing data.

The second test relates to financial aid status. Here again the broad similarities between the two distributions do not suggest any consistent bias. While there are some differences between the type of means-tested financial aid being received and while there is a slightly higher percentage of those in the 'missing data' category with no financial aid, the differences do not appear highly significant. The third comparison relates to the type of college in which students enrolled. The differences here are more significant. Those for whom data are available are more highly represented in the university sector, while those for whom data on social background are unavailable are more highly represented in the Institute of Technology sector. Since, as we will see below, the lower socio-economic groups have their highest representation in the IT sector, this might suggest that the participation of the lower socio-economic groups may be understated in the data on social background.

The final comparison which is confined to those within the university sector, also lends some credence to this suggestion. It is well established that the most socially selective fields of study are the professional faculties of Law, Medicine, Dentistry and Architecture. We note from Table A9 that students from these faculties make up six per cent of those for whom we have data on socio-economic background by comparison with just two per cent of those for whom these data are missing. The latter two tests might suggest that our data on socio-economic background underestimate the representation of the lower socio-economic groups; but if this is so it is surprising that these differences are not reflected in the pattern of attendance at Fee-paying Secondary and Vocational schools and in the percentages of those in receipt of means tested maintenance support. On balance, we believe that since the data on type of second level school and financial aid constitute a more robust test, we can proceed with confidence that our respondents are broadly representative of the total cohort with respect to parents' social background. Accepting that there is some margin of error, the more likely direction of such error is that the study may exaggerate the level of 'under-representation' of the lower socio-economic groups.

Social Background of Higher Education Entrants

Principal Economic Status

The main interest in principal economic status of parents of higher education entrants centres on the incidence of employment and unemployment. The response categories included in the questionnaire also included 'home duties', 'retired', 'deceased' and a final 'other' category. Before examining the main distributions it is appropriate to note the main response categories which emerged from an analysis of those who ticked the 'other' category. The largest category was accounted for by the two per cent of respondents who provided insufficient information on parents for coding. A further two per cent of respondents reported that their father was absent while a half of one per cent reported that their mother was absent. A small number of respondents reported that their mother (0.4%) or father (0.1%) were students. All of these categories are excluded from Table 11. In addition, those whose fathers (3.8%) and mothers (1.5%) were deceased are also excluded from Table 11. Three further categories were identified. Those who were described as being on FÁS/CES schemes (1.3% of fathers and 0.5% of mothers) were included with the unemployed/ unable to work category, as were the small number of fathers (1.1%) and mothers (0.4%) who were described as 'disabled'. Finally eighteen respondents (1 father and 17 mothers) described their parents as 'carers of invalids'; these were included in the 'home duties' category.

For the majority (83.1%) of entrants to higher education, their fathers' principal economic status was classified as being in employment. Some nine per cent were classified as unemployed or unable to work, almost seven per cent as retired, and over one per cent as on 'home duties'. In contrast with the situation for fathers, the majority (53.8%) of the mothers of new entrants were classified as on 'home duties'. Forty per cent were classified as employed, with less than five per cent unemployed or unable to work and just over one per cent were described as retired.

Table 11 compares the distribution of higher education entrants, by parents' principal economic status, with the *ever married*, aged 45-54, from the 1996 Census of Population, which appears to be the most appropriate national distribution. The most emphatic finding relates to the situation of fathers who are unemployed or unable to work. While eighteen per cent of the national distribution of ever-married males aged 45-54 were classified as unemployed [3], less than nine per cent of higher education entrants have fathers who were unemployed. A higher percentage of fathers of higher education entrants were retired than was the case for the comparative national distribution. However, this latter finding may suggest that a wider age span of the national distribution might make a more appropriate comparison. For example, data from the *96 Census of Population* reveal that for the age group 45-64 (ever-married males) over eight per cent were retired. In this case, however, nineteen per cent of the national population were classified as unemployed, thus substantiating the main finding, that students with unemployed fathers are 'under-represented' [4].

probability of the young person going on to third level. Just over two per cent of entrants [whose]
father was unemployed or unable to work and where the mother was in employment. In c[or...]
couples nationally fall within this category. Similarly for those whose fathers are in employ[ment...]
mother does not appear to increase the rate of admission to higher education. However, in w[...]
with these findings, entrants from the modal family configuration, (father in employment a[nd...]
seem to be somewhat less numerous than might be expected on the basis of the national repr[...]

Fathers' Socio-Economic Group

As already mentioned, most analysis of the social background of students in Ireland is based o[...]
classified into one of the eleven socio-economic groups used in the Census of Population. Th[...]
of a new set of categories by which to classify the socio-economic status of the population pr[...]
for the present study. An appropriate comparison with the present national population requi[...]
categories. Furthermore, since the new categories are likely to continue in use for some years i[...]
is an even greater imperative. However, since this is the fourth in a series of studies, a major o[...]
to monitor change over time. For this purpose continuity with earlier studies was an import[...]
decided that the most realistic option was to code the data on socio-economic status and social [...]
of the data was done in accordance with the older set of socio-economic and social class categ[...]
completed the data was recoded in accordance with the new categories designed for the 199[...]

Conscious of the implications of such a necessary but radical change in socio-economic group[...]
have provided some data which allows us to quantify the magnitude of the change. The occupa[...]
have been reclassified to the new SEG classification. Thus both distributions can be compare[...]
author was given a copy of an unpublished crosstabulation between the old and the new SE[...]
Census population. The changes are, indeed quite significant. While eight of the eleven categor[...]
classifications the allocation of a significant number of occupations has changed. More signific[...]
the old classification system (Salaried Employees, Intermediate Non-Manual and Other Non[...]
single Non-Manual category is included in the new system to complement the Employe[...]
Professional and Lower Professional groups, which remain from the earlier classification. T[...]
the introduction of a new Own Account Workers category. An examination of the cr[...]
two classifications reveals that only fifty-eight per cent of the 1991 population belong [...]
both classifications.

TABLE 11	DISTRIBUTION OF HIGHER EDUCATION ENTRANTS BY PARENTS' PRINCIPAL ECONOMIC STATUS COMPARED WITH DISTRIBUTION OF EVER MARRIED MALES AND FEMALES (AGED 45-54) FROM 1996 CENSUS

Principal Economic Status	Fathers		Mothers	
	Higher Education Entrants %	Census 1996 Ever Married Males 45-54 %	Higher Education Entrants %	Census 1996 Ever Married Females 45-54 %
Employed	83.1	79.5	40.3	33.9
Unemployed/ Unable to Work	8.9	18.3	4.5	4.8
Home Duties	1.3	0.4	53.8	60.8
Retired	6.8	1.0	1.3	0.6
TOTAL %★	**100**	**100**	**100**	**100**
TOTAL N	**19,216**	**173,310**	**20,039**	**182,742**

*In respect of all distributions, those for whom data were unavailable are excluded from the table. In addition, the table excludes data in respect of 3.7% of entrants whose fathers were deceased and 1.4% of entrants whose mothers were deceased.

The comparison between the distribution of mothers of entrants and the relevant national distribution of *ever married* females aged 45-54, reveals a very close correspondence in respect of the incidence of unemployment. However, higher education entrants were somewhat more likely to have mothers in employment (40.3% versus 33.9%), while they were correspondingly less likely to have mothers classified as on 'home duties' (53.8% versus 60.8% of the comparions group).

By linking the data on fathers' and mothers' principal economic status we get the overall pattern in respect of both parents of higher education entrants. This cross-classification (Table 12) reveals that the modal family pattern was that the father was in employment while the mother was on home duties. This was the situation in respect of forty-three per cent of entrants. The next largest category, accounting for thirty-four per cent of entrants, contains those where both parents were employed. More than six per cent of entrants came from families where both parents were unemployed (1.7%) or where one was unemployed and the other was described as being on home duties (4.4%). An interesting feature of this table is the patterning of employment and unemployment between spouses. Mothers' employment was higher where fathers were also in employment. Where fathers were unemployed twenty-eight per cent (2.4/8.5) of mothers were employed while where fathers were employed, forty-three per cent (34.0/80.0) of the mothers of entrants were also in employment.

TABLE 12	PARENTS' PRINCIPAL ECONOMIC STATUS: FATH (TOTAL PERCENTAGE)

Fathers' Principal Economic Status	Mothers' Principal Economic			
	At Work	Unemployed /Unable to Work	Home Duties	Re
	%	%	%	
At Work	34.0	2.2	42.7	0
Unemployed/ Unable to Work	2.4	1.7	4.4	0
Home Duties	0.4	0.0	0.7	0
Retired	1.6	0.2	3.9	0
Deceased	1.3	0.2	1.7	0
TOTAL %	39.7	4.2	53.4	1
TOTAL N 19,774				

Having examined together the principal economic status of both parents it was felt desi with the appropriate national distribution. The most comparable national data base ava Force Survey (LFS) [5]. At our request the CSO supplied a special tabulation of 'couples', by principal economic status. While this distribution is not identical to a classification of measure and should enable us to judge the representativeness of higher education e principal economic status of their parents. Table A10 shows the classification of entrants of their parents and the 1997 LFS estimates of the national distribution of couples. To two distributions those students who had one or both parents deceased were not includ

It is clear from Table A10 that, with respect to the principal economic status of both par higher education entrants is broadly similar to the national distribution of couples. Th classification of higher education entrants by the joint principal economic status o significantly differentiate them from the national population. We have already noted, that unemployed are 'under-represented' in higher education, the employment of the mothe

Table 13 shows the distribution of respondents' fathers by socio-economic group together with the national distribution of the population under fifteen years from the 1996 Census. In addition, a participation ratio is calculated showing the relative distribution of higher education places between the different social groups. The participation ratio serves as a measure of the degree to which each social group is proportionately represented, 'over-represented' or 'under-represented' among third level entrants. The greater the deviation from 1.0, the greater the degree of unrepresentativeness. This analysis reveals very large disparities by socio-economic group.

Entrants from the Higher Professional group constituted 10.1% of total intake, although this group represented little more than five per cent of the national population. This gives a participation ratio of 1.94. In sharp contrast, entrants from the Unskilled socio-economic group accounted for little more than three per cent of the total, although this group contained more than eight per cent of the comparison population group, giving a participation ratio of 0.36. In all, four of the ten socio-economic groups are 'over-represented'. In descending order these are: Higher Professional, Farmers, Employers and Managers, and Lower Professional. Perhaps the most striking finding is the level of representation of the Farmers group. This group accounts for almost seventeen per cent of higher education entrants, although it represents little more than nine per cent of the comparison population group. In contrast the degree of 'under-representation' of the Agricultural Workers group (participation ratio = 0.35) is even greater than for the Unskilled. It is of interest to note that the representation of those classified in the new Own Account Workers group corresponds most closely to the proportionate size of this group in the national population. This group accounts for just over seven per cent of entrants and represents less than eight per cent of the comparison population group. Of the other three groups which are 'under-represented' it is of interest to note that the participation ratio of the Manual Skilled (0.71) and Semi-Skilled (0.70) are almost identical and that these rates are higher than that of the Non-Manual group (0.63). To our knowledge this is the first research study to have used this new SEG classification. Consequently, the usefulness and discriminatory power of the new socio-economic group classification have not yet been assessed.

TABLE 13 FATHERS' SOCIO-ECONOMIC STATUS OF 1998 ENTRANTS TO HIGHER EDUCATION & NATIONAL POPULATION UNDER 15 YEARS IN 1996 AND PARTICIPATION RATIO FOR 1998

Socio-Economic Groups	Higher Education Entrants in 1998	National Population Under 15 years in 1996	Participation Ratio 1998
	%	%	
Employers and Managers	21.6	14.8	1.46
Higher Professional	10.1	5.2	1.94
Lower Professional	10.1	7.7	1.31
Non-Manual	9.4	15.0	0.63
Manual Skilled	13.6	19.1	0.71
Semi-Skilled	7.4	10.6	0.70
Unskilled	3.1	8.5	0.36
Own Account Workers	7.2	7.8	0.92
Farmers	16.6	9.4	1.77
Agricultural Workers	0.7	2.0	0.35
TOTAL %	**100**	**100**	–
TOTAL N	**19,087**	**766,057**	–

Socio-Economic Group	% Distribution		Participation Ratio	
	Male	Female	Male	Female
Employers and Managers	21.6	21.6	1.46	1.46
Higher Professional	10.3	9.9	1.98	1.90
Lower Professional	10.6	9.7	1.38	1.26
Non-Manual	10.1	8.7	0.67	0.58
Manual Skilled	13.5	13.7	0.71	0.72
Semi-Skilled	7.2	7.6	0.68	0.72
Unskilled	2.8	3.3	0.33	0.39
Own Account Workers	7.0	7.5	0.90	0.96
Farmers	16.0	17.3	1.70	1.84
Agricultural Workers	0.8	0.7	0.40	0.35
TOTAL %	100	100	-	-
TOTAL N	8229	9290	-	-

TABLE 14 PERCENTAGE DISTRIBUTION AND PARTICIPATION RATIO OF NEW ENTRANTS TO HIGHER EDUCATION BY SOCIO-ECONOMIC STATUS AND GENDER

Thus far in our discussion of the socio-economic status of new entrants we have not differentiated by gender. It is clear from Table 14 that the participation ratios for males and females are strikingly similar. The two ratios are identical for the Employers and Managers group and almost identical for the Manual Skilled group. The male ratio exceeds the female ratio in respect of Higher Professional, Lower Professional, Non-Manual and Agricultural Workers' groups. In contrast, the female ratio exceeds the male ratio in the case of the Farmers, Own Account Workers, Semi-Skilled and Unskilled Manual groups. It has been assumed that the gender difference in favour of females for the Farmers' group, which has been a consistent finding in successive studies, is related to the pattern of inheritance whereby inheriting sons are less dependent on advanced education to secure their future status. However, the extent of this difference has greatly reduced.

Mothers' Socio-economic group

Usable data on mothers' socio-economic group are only available for 12,157 entrants. This is mainly accounted for by the fact that, as noted above, only forty per cent of respondents' mothers were in employment. While respondents whose mothers were not currently employed were asked to indicate last occupation held, this information was seldom supplied. It is assumed that respondents whose mothers had not been in the labour force for many years did not consider it relevant to record last occupation held. For those for whom data are available, the largest percentage of entrants (39.5%) had mothers who were categorised as Non-Manual while almost a third (31.8%) were from the Lower Professional group (Table 15). This distribution differs significantly from that of fathers, where fewer than twenty per cent were drawn from these two socio-economic groups. Just under eight per cent of entrants had mothers who were classified as Employers and Managers, while a similar percentage came from the Semi-Skilled group.

TABLE 15   MOTHERS' SOCIO-ECONOMIC GROUP

Socio-Economic Groups	%
Employers and Managers	7.9
Higher Professionals	3.6
Lower professionals	31.8
Non Manual	39.5
Manual Skilled	0.9
Semi Skilled	8.0
Unskilled	2.7
Own Account Workers	2.7
Farmers	2.5
Agricultural Workers	0.3
TOTAL %	**100**
TOTAL N	**12,157**

Parents' Social Class

The third measure of social background used is that of social class. This measure was first used in the 1992 study, having been developed in the mid 1980s to classify the national population in the 1986 Census of Population. The social class scale was devised by a Working Party in conjunction with the Central Statistics Office (see O'Hare *et al.*, 1991). An important rationale for the development of a census based social class scale arose from dissatisfaction with the socio-economic group classification, especially with the fact that it lacks a ranking procedure. An illustration of this is the grouping of all farmers in one category irrespective of farm size and income accruing from the farm. The social class scale is designed to classify the population according to an ordinal class structure. For example, farmers are allocated into one of five classes depending on the size of the farm, with those with farms of two hundred acres or more being assigned to class one and those with less than thirty acres assigned to class five.

Although this scale is not long in use, the adoption of a new occupational classification system has necessitated changes to the social class scale, which the CSO (1998, p.102) describes as 'similar though not identical to that used in 1986 and 1991'. In addition they have suggested that users should treat comparisons with figures from the 1986 Census with caution. Although less radical, this change in the social class scale has presented the same dilemma for this study as was the case with the socio-economic group classification. In response, we have followed the same strategy as that adopted in respect of the SEG classification. The data has been coded twice, firstly, in accordance with the old (1986) scale and then in accordance with the new social class categories. We will first present the results for the new scale.

Table 16 shows the distribution of entrants by parents' social class (1996 scale) with the comparable national distribution of children under 15 years. Applying the same procedures which we used in the case of socio-economic status, we calculated a participation ratio for each social class. We note that, with one exception, the higher the social class the higher the participation ratio. The Professional Workers' class had a participation ratio of 1.64 while the Managerial and Technical class had a participation ratio of 1.22. The main deviation from the comparable ranking of the two distributions is in respect of the Skilled Manual and Non-Manual classes. The participation ratio of the Skilled Manual class, at 1.00, is higher than that of the Non-Manual class, which stands at 0.79. The latter is amongst the 'under-represented' social classes, while the former is represented among higher education entrants, in exact proportion to its relative size in the national population. The other two 'under-represented' classes are the Semi-Skilled, at 0.82, and the Unskilled class, which is seriously 'under-represented', having only forty-six per cent of the places, which its proportionate size in the population would warrant. While the main finding relates to the low representation of the Unskilled, the ranking of the Non-Manual class, which is below that of both the Skilled and the Unskilled, is also highly significant.

TABLE 16   DISTRIBUTION OF HIGHER EDUCATION ENTRANTS BY PARENTS' SOCIAL CLASS AND NATIONAL POPULATION UNDER 15 IN 1996

Social Class	Fathers' Social Class	National Population Under 15 Years in 1996	Participation Ratio 1998	Mothers' Social Class
	%	%		%
Professional Workers	11.5	7.0	1.64	3.9
Managerial and Technical	34.5	28.2	1.22	40.6
Non Manual	16.2	20.5	0.79	35.2
Skilled Manual	24.0	23.9	1.00	6.4
Semi Skilled	10.2	12.4	0.82	10.9
Unskilled	3.6	7.9	0.46	3.0
TOTAL %	**100**	**100**	**-**	**100**
TOTAL	**18,999**	**767,984**	**-**	**12,149**

Data on the distributions of respondents by mother's social class are also reported in Table 16. However, as in the case of the socio-economic categories, since these data were only available for just over forty per cent of respondents, it was not considered appropriate to calculate participation ratios in respect of this distribution. What is clear is that the mothers of higher education entrants are heavily concentrated in two class categories, the Managerial and Technical and the Non-Manual; almost forty-one per cent belong to the Managerial and Technical class and thirty-five per cent to the Non-Manual class. Almost eleven per cent belong to the Semi-Skilled class while six per cent were classified as Skilled.

Having examined separately the social class of fathers and mothers of entrants, it is of interest to consider together the respective social classes of fathers and mothers, where both sets of data are available. This analysis is confined to those entrants whose fathers and mothers were in employment. The cross-classification of the social class of both parents for this sub-group is shown in Table A11, which also shows the 1997 Labour Force Survey estimate of the distribution of couples, with one or both parent aged 40-54 and both working, by social class. Having already demonstrated that the rate of admission to higher education is strongly influenced by fathers' social class, the purpose of the comparison is to ascertain whether the related class position of the mother has any influence on the rate of admission. In spite of the well documented trend towards 'homogamy' whereby 'like marry like', the difference in the occupational profile of males and females in our society leads to a situation whereby sixty-eight per cent of entrants have parents who are in different class groups. The LFS estimate suggest that, for the country as a whole, this was the situation of seventy-two per cent of couples where both parents are working.

Of much greater interest is the situation where there is a difference in the class position of fathers and mothers. In the case of forty-three per cent of entrants the mother had a lower class position than the father; this was the situation for forty per cent of couples nationally, as demonstrated in Table A11. More interestingly, the percentage of entrants where the mothers' class position is higher than the fathers (25%) is less than the corresponding percentage from the national distribution of couples (31%). This finding, which is counter intuitive, replicates that found in the 1992 survey. It should be considered in conjunction with the above finding in respect of the joint principal economic status of fathers and mothers. Both findings suggest that neither the employment of mothers nor, where employed, their relative class position, affects the rate of admission of their children to higher education.

Socio-Economic Group By Sector

It has been observed from the earlier national surveys that the social selectivity of higher education as a whole is complemented by further selectivity by sector and by field of study. The present study replicates these earlier findings (Table 17). We note that the Higher Professional and Employers and Managers groups are especially strongly represented in the university sector. While the Lower Professional group is also well represented in the university sector, it has its highest proportionate representation in the Other Colleges and Colleges of Education. The three manual (Skilled, Semi-Skilled and Unskilled) groups, the Other Agricultural and Own Account Workers groups have their highest proportionate representation in the Institute of Technology sector. The Farmers group is strongly represented in the Colleges of Education, while the Non-Manual group is most strongly represented in the Other Colleges sector.

More detailed information on the distribution of new entrants by socio-economic group for each college is given in the Appendix (Table A12). Looking first at the pattern of admission to the universities, we note that the Employers and Managers group is particularly strongly represented in the Royal College of Surgeons, Dublin City University, Trinity College Dublin and University College Dublin; this group forms between a quarter and a third of entrants to these colleges. Perhaps the most striking feature of the distribution is the strong representation of the Higher Professional group

TABLE 17   SOCIO-ECONOMIC STATUS OF NEW ENTRANTS TO HIGHER EDUCATION BY COLLEGE TYPE, IN 1998.

Socio-Economic Groups	Universities 1998 %	Institutes of Technology 1998 %	Colleges of Education 1998 %	Other Colleges* 1998 %	Total 1998 %
Employers and Managers	24.0	19.4	17.3	22.9	21.6
Higher Professional	14.9	5.5	5.9	12.7	10.1
Lower Professional	12.6	7.4	13.2	13.6	10.2
Non-Manual	9.5	9.3	9.1	13.1	9.4
Manual Skilled	9.6	17.7	13.5	14.8	13.6
Semi-Skilled	5.6	9.4	6.2	9.3	7.5
Unskilled	1.9	4.3	2.6	2.1	3.1
Own Account Workers	6.0	8.5	6.8	6.4	7.2
Farmers	15.3	17.7	24.9	5.11	6.6
Agricultural Workers	0.6	0.9	0.5	0.0	0.7
Total %	**100**	**100**	**100**	**100**	**100**
Total N	**8450**	**8303**	**646**	**236**	**17,635**

★ *Private Colleges are not included in this table.*

in the RCSI, where it constitutes forty-one per cent of entrants. The Higher Professional group is also stongly represented in TCD (24.4%) and UCD (20.4%). Taken together, the three Manual groups are more strongly represented at NUI, Maynooth (24.9%), UCC (21.2%), and DCU (19.3%). These groups have their lowest representation in RCSI (4.5%), TCD (10.2%) and UCD (13.3%). The Farmers social group is most strongly represented in the University of Limerick (25.3%) and NUI, Galway (18.7%).

Looking at the pattern of admission to the Institutes of Technology, it is noticeable that the three Dublin Colleges have a disproportionate number of students from the Employers and Managers and Higher Professional groups. This is most marked in the case of Dun Laoghaire Institute of Art, Design and Technology, where these two groups account for close to half (46.8%) of all entrants, but is also evident in case of the Dublin Institute of Technology (DIT) and Tallaght IT. Tallaght has a relatively high proportion of students from the Manual Skilled group. This is also the case for Dundalk, Athlone, Tralee and Carlow. In these colleges the representation of the Manual Skilled group exceeds the proportionate size of this group in the national population. The Semi-Skilled and Unskilled Manual groups are most strongly represented in Letterkenny (21.7%) and Dundalk (19%). Finally, within the ITs the Farmers group was most strongly represented in Tralee, Sligo, Athlone and Galway.

Turning to the Colleges of Education the most striking finding is the very high representation of the Farmers' group in St. Angela's (64.3%) and the Mater Dei Institute (43.1%). Indeed, the Farmers group is stongly represented in all colleges with the exception of Froebel College and St. Mary's, Marino. If the representation from the Employers and Managers and Higher Professional groups is considered together, we note that St. Mary's Marino, St. Patrick's Drumcondra and Mary Immaculate Limerick have the highest level of participation from these groups. Looking at the representation of the three Manual groups taken together, we note that they are most strongly represented in the Froebel College (40%), while they have their lowest representation in the Church of Ireland College (4.3%).

Looking at the 'Other Colleges' sector, we note the strong representation of the Employers and Managers group in the National College of Ireland, where it accounted for a third of all admissions. The NCAD has a high representation from the Lower Professional and Non-Manual groups, while the Milltown Institute of Theology and Philosophy also draws disproportionately from the Non-Manual group. The other feature of the pattern of admission to this sector is the strong representation of the Own Account Workers group in Milltown and the National College of Ireland.

The differential pattern of admission to the individual colleges is, of course, partly a reflection of the programmes of study available in these colleges. This relationship between students' socio-economic group and field of study is examined in the Appendix (Tables A13 and A14). In respect of HEA sector colleges, students from the Farmers socio-economic group are, not surprisingly, disproportionately represented in Veterinary Medicine, Equestrian Studies, Agricultural Science and Forestry, and Food Science and Technology. Education has also attracted a strong representation from the Farmers group, as well as from the Semi-Skilled group. The Employers and Managers group has a strong representation in Economic and Social Studies; in contrast, this group is poorly represented in Agricultural Science and Forestry. The Higher Professional group is especially strongly represented in Medicine and Law, while the Lower Professional group is 'over-represented' in Architecture and Art & Design. The Manual Skilled group has its highest proportionate representation in Social Science, Economic and Social Studies and Art & Design. The Semi-Skilled the Unskilled Manual and the Non-Manual groups are also well represented in Art & Design.

There are fewer socio-economic group differentials evident in the pattern of admission to the different fields of study in non-HEA sector colleges (Table A14). The largest differentials are evident in the strong representation of the Lower Professional and Farmers groups in Education, the Higher Professional group in Art & Design, and the Agricultural Workers group in Science and General Studies.

Financial Aid

Student support systems have long been a crucial feature of higher education policy. The main initiative in recent years has been the elimination of undergraduate fees for the vast majority of students. The main exception relates to those students who attend private colleges. Apart from state support for tuition fees, the main additional source of aid relates to maintenance grants. In Ireland, three separate schemes have evolved. Two of these schemes are now almost identical, although they were designed for students attending different sectors. The Higher Education Grant Scheme was first introduced for students attending the universities, while Vocational Education Committee Scholarships were introduced for students attending Institutes of Technology. In this analysis we will not differentiate between the two, simply designating them with the label 'Grant'. The third funding scheme is that provided by the European Social Fund Training Grant Scheme, which we will simply designate as 'ESF'. Since, with minor exceptions, all students qualify for fee remission, our interest in these three financial aid schemes is solely related to the payment of maintenance support. Eligibility criteria for maintenance support is identical, the value of the ESF training allowance is similar to that of the Higher Education Grant or VEC Scholarships and all three are subject to the same variability depending on the distance of a student's home from the college attended. In 1998 the maximum value of the maintenance grant was £826 for those whose normal family residence was within fifteen miles of the college, while for those who qualified for the non-adjacent rate the maximum value was £1,652. In addition to these publicly funded schemes, there are a small number of other forms of financial aid available. These include Entrance Scholarships or Exhibitions, Easter Week and Gaeltacht Scholarships. As noted in the introduction, all colleges supplied data on those students who were in receipt of a maintenance grant or other discretionary award. The distribution of entrants by type of financial aid is shown in Table 18, which presents the situation for all students from the Republic of Ireland, not just those for whom we have data in respect of parents' social background. It should be noted that, with the exception of those in the private colleges, the great majority of those who are categorised as having 'none' are exempt from the payment of tuition fees.

TABLE 18	DISTRIBUTION OF ALL NEW ENTRANTS, BY TYPE OF FINANCIAL AID AND BY COLLEGE TYPE

College Type	Grant	ESF	Other	None★	Total	
	%	%	%	%	%	N
Universities	27.4	0.0	2.3	70.7	100	13964
Institutes of Technology	4.8	40.5	0.1	54.6	100	15583
Colleges of Education	22.2	0.0	0.0	77.8	100	991
Other Colleges	11.4	4.8	0.0	83.8	100	438
TOTAL	**15.6**	**20.4**	**0.9**	**63.0**	**100**	**30976**

★This category includes students where no tuition fees were charged.

The pattern of student support varies by the type of college attended (Table 18). Overall, thirty-six per cent of entrants were in receipt of means-tested financial aid. The Institutes of Technology have the highest percentage (45.3%) of entrants in receipt of aid, while the Other Colleges sector has the lowest (16.2%). In the universities, twenty-seven per cent of entrants were in receipt of means tested financial aid, while in the colleges of education it was twenty-two per cent. It is of interest to note that the percentages of entrants in receipt of means tested aid are significantly lower than in 1992, when fifty-one per cent of entrants received such aid. However, it is necessary to exercise caution in making this comparison. In 1998, almost all students had their fees paid by the state while, in 1992, some of those in receipt of means tested aid qualified only for a level of grant which covered part or all of the fees. However, the comparison does point to the fact that by 1998, a smaller percentage of entrants satisfy the income criteria which qualify them for means tested support.

Returning to our focus on the social background on higher education entrants it is of interest to examine the relationship between the pattern of financial aid and the socio-economic background of entrants. Predictably, the pattern of financial aid differs significantly by socio-economic group (Table 19). The four Non-Manual groups have significantly lower percentages of students in receipt of financial aid. Eighty-seven per cent of entrants from the Higher Professional group receive no financial aid. The corresponding percentages for the Lower Professional, Employers and Managers, and Non-Manual groups are eighty-two, eighty-one and sixty-seven per cent, respectively. In contrast, the groups with the highest percentages of students in receipt of financial aid were the Unskilled (78.4%) and Agricultural Workers (75.6%) groups. For the remaining socio-economic groups the pecentages in receipt of aid range from fifty-nine per cent for the Semi-Skilled to fifty-five per cent for the Manual Skilled; the rate for Farmers is fifty-eight per cent, while fifty-seven per cent of Own Account Workers receive financial aid.

TABLE 19	DISTRIBUTION OF NEW ENTRANTS BY TYPE OF FINANCIAL AID AND SOCIO-ECONOMIC STATUS (FATHERS)

| Socio-Economic Group | Grant | ESF | Other | None* | TOTAL | |
	%	%	%	%	N	%
Employers and Managers	8.6	8.7	2.5	80.2	3802	100
Higher Professional	5.3	4.0	4.6	86.1	1789	100
Lower Professional	8.6	6.5	3.7	81.3	1795	100
Non-Manual	15.7	16.0	2.1	66.2	1664	100
Manual Skilled	22.5	32.5	1.2	43.8	2400	100
Semi-Skilled	26.0	32.0	1.4	40.1	1314	100
Unskilled	29.4	48.1	1.1	21.4	538	100
Own Account Workers	27.1	29.7	0.7	42.5	1275	100
Farmers	29.1	27.7	1.5	41.7	2931	100
Agricultural Workers	34.6	39.4	1.6	24.4	127	100
TOTAL %	17.7	19.8	2.2	60.4	-	100
TOTAL N	3119	3488	384	10,644	17,635	-

*This category includes students where no tuition fees were charged.

Farmers' Socio-Economic Group

A significant finding from this and earlier surveys is the high participation rate from the Farmers socio-economic group. It is possible to disaggregate this finding by farm size. In pursuing this analysis it is, of course, recognised that variations in the quality of land mean that acreage is not always the best measure of farm value. However, while this caveat would be important for individual cases it does not invalidate an aggregate analysis. Table 20 shows the distribution of higher education entrants from the Farmers socio-economic group and the national distribution from the 1991 Census[6] of *Ever Married* Farmers by farm size. We note that the modal farm size of parents of new entrants was between 50-99 acres (40%). Fewer than eight per cent had in excess of 200 acres, while less than nine per cent had under thirty acres. When we compare this with the national distribution we note that students from the larger farms were 'over-represented' while those from smaller farms were 'under-represented'. While students from farms of less than thirty acres accounted for fewer than eight per cent of entrants from farming families, this group represented more than thirteen per cent of the national distribution. In contrast, while almost eight per cent of entrants came from farms of more than 200 acres, this group accounted for just over five per cent of the national distribution. Thus, it is clear that the class differences in participation which are found in non-farm families are replicated within the farming sector.

TABLE 20	DISTRIBUTION OF 1998 NEW ENTRANTS FROM FARMERS' SOCIO- ECONOMIC GROUP BY FARM SIZE AND NATIONAL DISTRIBUTION OF EVER MARRIED FARMERS FROM 1991 CENSUS

Farm Size (Acres)	Higher Education Entrants	National Distribution of Farmers (Ever Married)
	%	%
200 acres or over	7.6	5.2
100 - 199 acres	30.6	21.8
50 - 99 acres	39.7	38.1
30 - 49 acres	14.6	21.4
Under 30 acres	7.6	13.5
TOTAL* %	100	100
TOTAL N	3076	65,893

*Information on farm size was not available for 101 (3.2%) entrants and 3,120 (4.5%) farmers for the 1991 Census.

To complement our analysis in Table 19, of the relationship between socio-economic group and the pattern of financial aid, it is of interest to examine how this relates to farm size. It is clear that the likelihood of receiving financial aid increases as farm size decreases (Table 21). Eighty-three per cent of students from farms of less than thirty acres were in receipt of means tested financial aid by comparison with twenty-two per cent of students from farms of more than 200 acres. However, the latter percentage is itself quite significant. For example, it is significantly greater than that for entrants from the Lower Professional group, fourteen per cent of whom were in receipt of means tested aid.

TABLE 21   DISTRIBUTION OF NEW ENTRANTS FROM THE FARMERS SOCIO-ECONOMIC GROUP BY FARM SIZE AND TYPE OF FINANCIAL AID

Farm Size	Type of Financial Aid				TOTAL	
	Grant	ESF	Other	None★		
(Acres)	%	%	%	%	%	N
200+	12.0	9.6	3.4	75.0	100	208
100–199	21.4	18.8	2.2	57.6	100	873
50 –99	34.1	29.6	1.0	35.3	100	1,131
30- 49	33.9	40.7	0.7	24.6	100	410
Under 30	39.1	44.0	–	16.9	100	207
Size not stated	33.7	36.8	2.1	27.4	100	95
TOTAL	**29.1**	**27.8**	**1.4**	**41.7**	**100**	**2,924**

★*This category includes students where no tuition fees were charged.*

Changes in Social Background of Entrants

Since this is the fourth national survey it is of great interest to assess trends in the social background of higher education entrants. Since admission rates to full-time higher education have more than doubled since the first national study was carried out in 1980, and since a key objective of public policy has been to reduce inequalities, it is timely to assess progress on this dimension. However, as discussed above, the changes in the socio-economic and social class classifications have complicated this assessment. In this section of the report we make three comparisons. We compare the findings from 1992 and 1998 in respect of the parents' principal economic status and social class. Data on these variables were first collected in 1992; thus comparisons cannot be made over a longer period. The most comprehensive assessment can be made in respect of parents' socio-economic status since these data have been collected for all four surveys. It was this imperative which caused us to code parents' occupational data twice.

Changes in Principal Economic Status

In reporting the findings of the 1998 survey, as summarised in Table 11 above, we compared the distribution of higher education entrants by principal economic status with the comparable distribution of *ever-married males and females* aged 45-54 from the 1996 Census of Population. Table 22 juxtaposes these findings with those from the 1992 study. The same categories are used, and to maximise comparability, the 1992 distribution is compared with that from the 1991 Census of Population for the ever-married males and females aged 45-54. The latter comparison differs from that used in the published report on the 1992 study (Clancy, 1995) where the national distributions from the 1992 Labour Force Survey were used.

It is clear from Table 22 that, in respect of fathers, both distributions are remarkably similar. In both surveys higher education entrants whose fathers are in employment are somewhat 'over-represented'. In both census years just under 80% of ever-married males, aged 45-54, were in employment, while just over 82% of entrants had fathers in employment. However, there is some evidence that the unemployed were less well represented in the 1998 survey. Less than nine per cent of entrants had fathers, who were unemployed, by comparison with just under 11% in 1992. The incidence of unemployment among the national distribution of ever-married males, aged 45-54, was almost identical for both years.

In contrast, higher education entrants, whose mothers were in employment, were 'over-represented' in the 1998 survey. While the 1992 entrants were broadly representative of the national population with respect to mothers' employment, in 1998 the percentage of entrants whose mothers were in employment was forty per cent by comparison with thirty-four per cent of the national population of 'ever-married females' aged 45-54. Correspondingly, higher education entrants, whose mothers were categorised as being on 'home duties', were 'under-represented'.

Principal Economic Status	Fathers				Mothers			
	Higher Education Entrants		Population Census Ever Married Males 45–54		Higher Education Entrants		Population Census Ever Married Females 45–54	
	%		%		%		%	
	1998	1992	1998	1992	1998	1992	1998	1992
Employed	83.1	82.4	79.9	79.6	40.3	25.5	33.9	22.2
Unemployed/Unable to Work	8.9	10.9	18.3	18.8	4.5	2.8	4.8	3.7
Home Duties	1.3	0.3	0.4	0.2	53.8	71.1	60.8	70.5
Retired	6.8	6.4	1.4	1.4	1.3	0.6	0.6	0.5
TOTAL %★	100	100	100	100	100	100	100	100
TOTAL N	19,216	18,040	175,310	145,935	20,039	19,020	182,742	151,767

★ In respect of all distributions, those for whom data were unavailable are excluded from the table. In addition, the table
   excludes data in respect of entrants whose fathers and/or mothers were deceased.

Changes in Fathers' Socio-Economic Group

The problems of assessing change over time in the socio-economic group background of higher education entrants are
not confined to the complications arising from changes in the classification system which necessitated a recoding of
parents' occupation in accordance with the older socio-economic group categories. A second problem, which has not
yet been discussed explicitly is that which arises from the choice of comparison population distributions. In each of the
four studies this research programme has used the national population under 15 years of age as the optimum basis for
calculating participation ratios. Socio-economic and social class census data for older age groups, for example for the 15-
19 aged group, are complicated by two factors. Firstly, part of this age cohort is already in the labour force and therefore
their socio-economic status is calculated on the basis of their own, rather than their parents' occupation. Secondly, by

age fifteen, migration has become a factor, with some of this age group residing away from home. This would include some in employment and some in full-time education. Since the Census of Population in Ireland is based on the *de facto* population resident in households on census night, not on those normally resident, those living away from home cannot be assigned to a socio-economic group by reference to the the social background of their parents.

The use of the under 15 age group for the purpose of calculating participation ratios suggests that the best comparative national distribution should be drawn from a year which predates the collection of the survey data. In this way we can be confident that the survey cohorts were part of that population distribution. However, because of the very rapid changes in the occupational distribution, it may be less acceptable to use a population distribution, which predates by a number of years the date of the survey. The changes in the occupational distribution, by socio-economic group, for the under 15 age group for the period 1971 to 1991, with an estimate for 1996 are shown in Table 19. The 1980 study used the population distribution of those under 15 years of age from 1971, although a revised distribution, based on an estimate of the situation in 1975, was used in subsequent comparisons of these findings (see Clancy, 1995; p.53). The participation ratios for the 1986 survey were calculated using the 1981 population distribution, while the 1992 study used the 1986 population distribution. In respect of the present study the options were circumscribed because of the changes in the CSO classification system. When the data, which used the 1996 SEG and social class categories were analysed (Tables 13 and 15), the 1996 Census of Population was used, even though the survey population falls just outside this population group. The great majority of those who entered higher education in 1998 would have been aged 15 or 16 at the time of the 1996 Census. However, the distribution of the under 15 age cohort by socio-economic and social class must be considered a very close proxy, being broadly representative of the socio-economic distribution of families from which the 1998 college entry cohort was drawn. To check the sensitivity of the socio-economic distributions to changes in the age range, we requested the CSO to make a special tabulation of the 13-14 age group from the 1996 Census to compare with that of the under fifteen age group (Table A15). While there are some small differences between the distributions, there is sufficient comparability to warrant the continued use of the larger age range, since this is available for all census years. Where the present survey data relate to the 'older' SEG and social class categories, the population distribution of those under 15 years from the 1991 Census would appear to be the most appropriate comparison group. However if this strategy were adopted we would then have participation ratios calculated on the basis of population distributions of those under 15 years which relate to Census findings of five, six or seven years prior to the survey year.

Because of the rapid changes in the occupational distribution, illustrated in Table 23, it was considered inappropriate to use population distributions, from a period of up to seven years prior to the time of entry to higher education. Because of these reservations we have recalculated participation ratios for each of the previous surveys using the Census distributions of those under 15 years old from the 1981, 1986, and 1991 censuses. All of these population distributions fall within a year of the relevant survey. To facilitate the analysis of change over time the participation rate for the present study was calculated using an estimated population distribution from the 1996 Census, since the older SEG categories were no longer in use for this Census. This estimation was made on the basis of the CSO crosstabulations from the 1991 Census, showing the relationship between the two classification systems. Using standardisation techniques it was possible to redistribute the 1996 SEG distribution among the old SEG categories on the basis of the proportionate correspondence which had been established by the crosstabulation of the two classification systems from the 1991 Census. The resulting distribution, as reproduced in Table 23 above, seems eminently plausible, since the allocation between the socio-economic groups is remarkably consistent with the overall trend for the twenty-five year period.

TABLE 23   PERCENTAGE DISTRIBUTION OF THE NATIONAL POPULATION UNDER 15 YEARS BY SOCIO-ECONOMIC STATUS IN 1971, 1981, 1986 AND 1991 AND ESTIMATED DISTRIBUTION FOR 1996

Socio-Economic Groups	1971	1981	1986	1991	1996
Farmers	20.3	14.3	12.4	11.4	9.8
Other Agricultural Occupations	4.3	2.9	3.0	2.7	2.1
Higher Professional	3.0	4.0	4.2	4.4	4.9
Lower Professional	3.1	4.3	4.9	6.1	7.6
Employers and Managers	7.1	9.2	8.8	8.8	9.9
Salaried Employees	2.7	2.7	2.7	3.0	2.6
Intermediate Non-Manual Workers	10.0	10.2	11.2	13.4	14.8
Other Non-Manual Workers	11.7	12.8	12.9	12.8	13.3
Skilled Manual Workers	21.4	25.4	25.9	23.7	21.8
Semi-Skilled Manual Workers	5.5	5.9	5.9	5.0	5.9
Unskilled Manual Workers	10.9	8.2	8.1	8.8	7.3
TOTAL %	100.0	100.0	100.0	100.0	100.0
TOTAL N *	842,12	1969,951	950,844	855,869	765,736

* Children whose social group was unknown are excluded from this table.

Table 24 presents this estimate of the 1996 population distribution of those under 15 years of age, together with the distribution of higher education entrants by fathers' socio-economic group, coded in accordance with the older classification system. The resultant participation ratios reveal large inequalities by socio-economic group. Consistent with the findings reported in Table 13 above, where the new socio-economic group classification is used, the Higher Professional group has the highest participation ratio at 2.18. The next highest group is the Employers and Managers with a participation ratio of 1.82. The other groups which are 'over-represented' are the Farmers, with a participation ratio of 1.63, the Salaried Employees group at 1.19 and the Lower Professional group who are marginally 'over-represented' with a participation ratio of 1.05. At the other end of the spectrum the Unskilled Manual group has the lowest representation with a participation rate of 0.48, followed by the Semi-Skilled Manual Workers group at 0.51. The Other Non-Manual

TABLE 24   DISTRIBUTION OF HIGHER EDUCATION ENTRANTS IN 1998 BY FATHER'S SOCIO-ECONOMIC STATUS (OLD CATEGORIES) & ESTIMATED NATIONAL POPULATION UNDER 15 YEARS IN 1996 WITH PARTICIPATION RATIOS BY SOCIO-ECONOMIC GROUP FOR 1998, 1992, 1986 AND 1980

Socio-Economic Groups	Higher Education Entrants in 1998 %	National Population Under 15 years in 1996 %	Participation Ratio 1998	Revised Participation Ratio 1992	Revised Participation Ratio 1986	Revised Participation Ratio 1980
Farmers	16.0	9.8	1.63	1.46	1.68	1.48
Other Agricultural Occupations	1.6	2.1	0.76	0.67	0.47	0.31
Higher Professional	10.7	4.9	2.18	2.36	2.86	2.95
Lower Professional	8.0	7.6	1.05	1.18	1.88	1.65
Employers and Managers	18.0	9.9	1.82	1.86	1.80	2.12
Salaried Employees	3.1	2.6	1.19	1.33	2.30	2.93
Intermediate Non-Manual Workers	10.7	14.8	0.72	0.76	1.10	1.09
Other Non-Manual Workers	9.2	13.3	0.69	0.73	0.44	0.45
Skilled Manual Workers	16.0	21.8	0.73	0.77	0.50	0.43
Semi-Skilled Manual Workers	3.0	5.9	0.51	0.52	0.42	0.46
Unskilled Manual Workers	3.5	7.3	0.48	0.34	0.16	0.15
TOTAL %	100.0	100	-	-	-	-
TOTAL N	19,229	765,736	-	-	-	-

Workers group has a participation ratio of 0.69 while the ratio for the Intermediate Non-Manual group is 0.72. The other 'under-represented' groups are Skilled Manual Workers (0.73) and Other Agricultural Occupations group with a participation ratio of 0.76.

For comparison purposes, Table 24 also includes the revised participation ratios calculated for each of the earlier studies. The main finding is one of continuity. Six groups (Higher Professional, Lower Professional, Employers and Managers, Salaried Employees, Farmers and Intermediate Non-Manual) were 'over-represented' in the 1980 and, with the exception of the Intermediate Non-Manual group, they remained 'over-represented' in each of the subsequent studies. Over this eighteen-year period the Higher Professional group has retained its position as the group with the highest proportionate representation in higher education, although the ratio has declined from 2.95 in 1980 to 2.18 in 1998. For the two most recent surveys the Employers and Managers group has the second highest participation ratio; its participation ratio for this group has remained very stable over the period. The group, whose ratios show the sharpest decline over the period, is that of Salaried Employees, although the decline in the most recent period is modest. The position of the Lower Professional group has oscillated over the period; its participation ratio increased between 1980 and 1986 and declined sharply since then. The consistent decline in the participation ratio of the Intermediate Non-Manual group has altered its relative position among the socio-economic groups. While in 1980 and 1986 it was slightly 'over-represented' it is now firmly located among the 'under-represented' groups, with a participation ratio very similar to that of the Skilled Manual and the Other Agricultural Occupations groups. A noteworthy feature of this survey, which replicates that from the 1992 study, is the high participation ratio of the Farmers group. Although the pattern of change has not been uniform over the period, it now has the third highest participation ratio, approaching that of the Employers and Managers group.

Turning to the 'under-represented' groups the general pattern is towards an increase in the participation ratios. Excluding the position of the Intermediate Non-Manual which we have discussed above, the 1998 participation ratio of all the 'under-represented' groups is significantly higher than the 1980 rate, although the pattern of change has been uneven over the period. For three of these groups (Other Non-Manual, Skilled Manual and Semi-Skilled Manual) the 1998 participation ratio is slightly lower than the 1992 ratio, although the differences are very small. In contrast, the two most 'under-represented' groups in 1980, Unskilled Manual Workers and Other Agricultural Workers, have shown a continuous increase over the eighteen-year period. Because of particular coding difficulties in the correct allocation of occupations between the Unskilled and Semi-Skilled Manual groups[7] it may be more appropriate to combine these two categories. When this is done the participation ratio of the combined Semi-Skilled/ Unskilled Manual group in 1998 is 0.49 rate; this compares with 0.41 in 1992, 0.27 in 1986 and 0.28 in 1980.

It should be noted that the main reason for using participation ratios is to examine the relative distribution of the higher education places between the social groups. They are not a measure of the participation rate. It is possible to enhance our understanding of the changing patterns of inequality by linking the foregoing analysis of changes in the participation ratios of the different socio-economic groups, to changes in the overall rates of admission to higher education. By multiplying the participation ratio for each social group by the overall rate of admission which prevailed in a particular year, we get an estimate of the proportion of the age cohort in each social group going on to higher education (Table 25). While it is important to treat these proportions as *estimates*, in the knowledge that they are subject to a margin of error [8], there is no reason to believe that there is any major bias in the data. Thus, with this caveat in mind, it is felt that this table presents a good overview of the changing patterns of admission to higher education by socio-economic group.

TABLE 25   ESTIMATED PROPORTION OF AGE COHORT ENTERING FULL-TIME HIGHER EDUCATION BY FATHERS' SOCIO-ECONOMIC GROUP IN 1980, 1986, 1992 AND 1998

Socio-Economic Groups	1998 (Revised)	1992	1986	1980
Farmers	.72	.53	.42	.30
Other Agricultural Occupations	.34	.24	.12	.06
Higher Professional	.97★	.85	.72	.59
Lower Professional	.47	.42	.47	.33
Employers and Managers	.81	.67	.45	.42
Salaried Employees	.53	.48	.58	.59
Intermediate Non-Manual Workers	.32	.27	.28	.22
Other Non-Manual Workers	.31	.26	.11	.09
Skilled Manual Workers	.32	.28	.13	.09
Semi-Skilled Manual Workers	.23	.19	.11	.09
Unskilled Manual Workers	.21	.12	.04	.03
TOTAL	**.44**	**.36**	**.25**	**.20**

★ This is an overestimate; see text and footnote no. 5 for details.

In view of the fact that the overall rate of admission to higher education in Ireland has risen from twenty per cent in 1980 to forty-four per cent (44.4%, see Chapter 5 below[9]) in 1998, it is no surprise that, with some exceptions (Salaried Employees, Lower Professionals, and Intermediate Non-Manual), most social groups experienced a progressive increase in the proportion going on to higher education. In addition, not unexpectedly, we note that the highest proportionate increase occurred for those lower socio-economic groups, which had very low participation rates in 1980. For the Unskilled Manual group the 1998 estimate is twenty-one per cent, compared with a mere three per cent in 1980. The proportionate increase for the Other Agricultural Occupations group is also impressive, rising from six per cent in 1980 to thirty-four per cent in 1998. The rates for the other three groups, which were 'under-represented' in 1980, have also increased significantly, if less dramatically. In 1980 each of these groups had a participation rate of nine per cent; the 1998 estimates are thirty-two per cent, thirty-one per cent and twenty-three per cent, respectively, for the Skilled Manual, Other Non-Manual and Semi-Skilled groups.

At the other end of the spectrum, the progressive increase in the estimated participation rate of those groups, which were already 'over-represented' in 1980, is striking. However, it is clear that the ninety-seven per cent estimate for the Higher Professional group is not credible, thus warranting the caution that these are *estimates* subject to a margin of error. In this context, it is of interest to note that if we apply similar procedures to the data in Table 13, which uses the new socio-economic group categories, the estimated participation rate for the Higher Professional group is eighty-six per cent. We should also take into account that the revised 1992 estimate for the Higher Professional group (using the old socio-economic groups) was eighty-five per cent. While the level of saturation for any social group is unclear, it may be little more than ninety per cent. It is our view that the Higher Professional group has reached this level and that the 'true' participation rate is about ninety per cent. While we accept that there is some error in the estimate of the absolute level of participation for the Higher Professional group, there is little doubt but that it continues to be the group which is most strongly represented in higher education. Furthermore it is unlikely that there is any scope for additional increases in the take-up rate for this group. The estimated 1998 participation rate for the Employers & Managers group is an impressive eighty-one per cent, having increased in each successive survey. The participation rate of the Farmers group is the third highest, having reached seventy-two per cent in 1998. Here also, the pattern is one of continuing improvement, with the increase between 1992 and 1998 (from 53% to 72%) being especially noteworthy.

By comparison with the former eight groups, the performance of three socio-economic groups (Lower Professional, Salaried Employees and Intermediate Non-Manual) reveals a pattern of very modest improvement. Indeed in the case of the Salaried Employees group, the 1998 estimated participation rate is still below the 1980 estimate, although there is evidence of improvement (from 48% to 53%) between 1992 and 1998. There is no obvious explanation as to why the Salaried Employees group should not have participated in the general increase in admission rates over the entire period covered by these studies. However, as noted in the report on the 1992 study, it is necessary to keep in mind, that even at present levels, this is still one of the groups 'over-represented' in higher education.

The pattern of change for the Lower Professional group is broadly similar to that of the Salaried Employees group. While it continues to be among the 'over-represented' groups, and while it has improved its participation rate between 1992 and 1998, the rate of increase over the longer period is modest. Finally, as already remarked, the Intermediate Non-Manual group, which joined the 'under-represented' in the 1992 study is also 'under-represented' in the present study. The 1998 estimate is that less than one-third of this social group entered higher education.

Changes in Fathers' Social Class

Our third indicator of changes over time in the social background of higher education entrants is that derived from the parents' social class, although this measure is only available for one of the previous surveys, that of 1992. However, as mentioned above, in spite of the recent availability of the measure, the changes introduced in the 1996 Census in the classification of occupations mean that a direct comparison is not possible. Since the data on parents' occupation from the present survey were re-coded in accordance with the old social class categories, the main difficulty arises from the unavailability of an appropriate population parameter for comparison. It was necessary to calculate an estimate of the 1996 population under fifteen years. This was done following the same procedures, which we used in respect of socio-economic groups. The CSO kindly provided access to the crosstabulation from the 1991 Census which showed the correspondence between the two classification systems. It was possible to redistribute the 1996 social class distribution among the 1991 categories on the basis of the proportionate correspondence established by the crosstabulation. The resulting distribution is reproduced in Table 26 as is the distribution of higher education entrants in accordance with the 'old' social class categories. The participation ratios, which are calculated from these two distributions, are juxtaposed with revised participation ratios from the 1992 study. The latter revisions were made using the 1991 Census distribution as a denominator, rather than the 1986 distribution which was used in the publication of the 1992 survey.

TABLE 26 FATHERS' SOCIAL CLASS (OLD CATEGORIES) OF 1998 ENTRANTS TO HIGHER EDUCATION AND ESTIMATED NATIONAL POPULATION UNDER 15 IN 1996 AND PARTICIPATION RATIOS FOR 1998 AND 1992

Social Class	Fathers' Social Class 1998	Estimated National Population Under 15 Years in 1996 %	Participation Ratio 1998	Revised Participation Ratio 1992
Higher Professional	26.6	14.5	1.83	2.09
Lower Professional	24.2	20.0	1.20	1.25
Other Non Manual	17.9	19.4	0.92	1.06
Skilled Manual	18.8	21.8	0.86	0.79
Semi Skilled Manual	8.1	15.0	0.54	0.62
Unskilled Manual	4.4	9.2	0.48	0.34
TOTAL★%	100	-	-	-
TOTAL	19,118	-	-	-

A comparison of the participation ratios gives us an indication of the change (if any) in the levels of inequality, by social class. The main finding is one of considerable consistency. The rank order of the social classes in terms of their participation ratios is common for the two studies. In both, the higher the social class, the higher the levels of participation in higher education. However, some changes are evident. For each of the social classes, which were 'over-represented' in 1992, the 1998 participation ratios have been reduced. The participation ratio of the Higher Professional class has declined from 2.09 to 1.83, while that of the Lower Professional Class has declined from 1.25 to 1.20. The ratio has also declined for the Other Non-Manual class, which at 0.92 (down from 1.06) is no longer among the 'over-represented' groups. In contrast, the relative position of two of the three social classes, which were 'under-represented' in 1992, has improved. The participation ratio of the Unskilled Manual class has increased from 0.34 to 0.48 while the ratio of the Skilled Manual group has increased from 0.79 to 0.86. The main exception to this trend is the Semi-Skilled Manual class whose relative share of the higher education places has declined; the participation ratio has fallen from 0.62 in 1992 to 0.54 in 1998. If the two lower social classes (Semi-Skilled and Unskilled Manual) are combined, the change in the participation ratios is a modest one, from 0.49 to 0.52.

Following the same procedure which we applied in respect of the socio-economic distributions, if we multiply the participation ratios for each social class by the overall rate of admission which prevailed in 1992 and 1996, we get an estimate of the proportion of the age cohort in each social class going on to higher education. These estimates are reported in Table 27. While these participation rates are 'estimates', which must be treated with the necessary caveats[10], they provide a clearer picture of the changing patterns of admission to higher education by social group. Since the overall rate of admission increased from thirty-six per cent in 1992 to forty-four per cent in 1998 it is of interest to note that all social classes participated in this increase. However, the rate of increase is not uniform. Two of the Manual groups have registered especially large increases. The Skilled Manual group shows the largest absolute increase, from twenty-eight to thirty-eight per cent, while the Unskilled Manual group registered the largest proportionate increase, rising from twelve per cent to twenty-one per cent. In contrast, the Semi-Skilled group registered only a small increase from twenty-two to twenty-five per cent. The other group to show a small rate of increase was the Other Non Manual group, which increased from thirty-eight to forty-one per cent. Both of the Professional groups showed significant increases of six and eight per cent, respectively for the Higher and Lower Professional groups.

TABLE 27	ESTIMATED PROPORTION OF AGE COHORT ENTERING FULL-TIME HIGHER EDUCATION BY FATHERS' SOCIAL CLASS 1992 AND 1998	
Socio-Economic Groups	**1998**	**1992**
Higher Professional	.81	.75
Lower Professional	.53	.45
Other Non-Manual	.41	.38
Skilled Manual	.38	.28
Semi Skilled Manual	.24	.22
Unskilled Manual	.21	.12
Total	**.46**	**.36**

Second Level Transitions

The focus of this, as well as of the three earlier studies, has been on the pattern of access to higher education. However, it is well established that the patterns of inequality, which are manifest at the point of entry to third level, are the result of a cumulative process of disadvantage which first manifest themselves much earlier in the educational cycle. The source of educational disadvantage is rooted in differential economic, social and cultural capital of families. It is reflected in unequal opportunities to access pre-school education, and in differential participation and performance at first level. However, differential participation and performance at second level serve as more proximate determinants of access to higher education. In research done by the Technical Working Group (1995) for the Steering Committee on the Future Development of Higher Education, the results of the School Leavers Survey were used to delineate the second level transitions which bear directly on access to third level (see also Clancy, 1999). This exercise was replicated for the purposes of the present study.

Each year a national sample of more than two thousand school leavers are interviewed almost a year after they have left second level education. The surveys are carried out annually by the ESRI for the Department of Enterprise, Trade and Employment (previously the Department of Labour). For the present analysis, samples for three years have been combined. The surveys were carried out in 1996, 1997 and 1998 and thus refer to school leavers from the school years 1994/95, 1995/96, and 1996/97. At our request the ESRI have prepared the following three tables which allow us to examine the inter-relationship between the principal socio-economic status of school leavers (based on fathers' occupation), educational level, attainment, and destination upon leaving school[11].

TABLE 28 PERCENTAGE DISTRIBUTION OF SCHOOL LEAVERS BY EDUCATIONAL LEVEL AND FATHERS' SOCIO-ECONOMIC GROUP 1996-1998 SURVEYS (N IN PARENTHESIS)

Fathers' Socio-Economic Group	No Qualification %	Junior Cert %	Leaving Cert %	Total N	%
Farmers	1.6 (18)	9.6 (109)	88.8 (1,009)	1,136	100
Other Agricultural	6.3 (10)	22.0 (35)	71.7 (114)	159	100
Higher Professional	0.3 (1)	7.7 (28)	92.0 (335)	364	100
Lower Professional	0.6 (2)	5.6 (19)	93.8 (320)	341	100
Employers & Managers	1.1 (9)	8.2 (65)	90.7 (721)	795	100
Salaried Employees	0.5 (1)	9.7 (18)	89.7 (166)	185	100
Intermediate Non-Manual	2.3 (13)	13.8 (77)	83.8 (466)	556	100
Other Non-Manual	3.7 (39)	19.6 (209)	76.7 (816)	1,064	100
Skilled Manual	3.1 (57)	17.0 (313)	79.8 (1,466)	1,836	100
Semi-Skilled Manual	3.2 (6)	21.6 (40)	75.1 (139)	185	100
Unskilled Manual	9.1 (79)	25.4 (220)	65.4 (566)	865	100
Unknown	10.5 (70)	21.8 (146)	67.7 (453)	669	100
TOTAL	**3.7**	**15.7**	**80.6**	**8,155**	**100**

The combined results of the three surveys reveal that the great majority of students (80.6%) attained Leaving Certificate level of education, while fewer than four per cent left without any qualification (Table 28). The remaining sixteen per cent attained Junior Certificate level of education before leaving school. Educational level is strongly related to fathers' socio-economic status. The percentage of students from the Unskilled Manual group, who left with no qualifications (9.1%), is two and half times greater than that of the average for all groups. In contrast, fewer than one per cent of those from the Higher Professional, Lower Professional and Salaried Employees groups left without any qualifications. Socio-economic differentials are also evident among those who left school having completed the Leaving Certificate. While just over sixty-five per cent of the Unskilled Manual group had achieved this level of education, the figures were over ninety per cent for the Employers and Managers, Higher Professional and Lower Professional groups.

Of those students who sat the Leaving Certificate, the modal category (32%) of attainment is 2-4 honours (i.e. Grade C or higher on Higher Level papers in two, three or four subjects); just under six per cent have less than 5 passes, while twenty-eight per cent have at least five honours[12]. This pattern of attainment is strongly influenced by fathers' socio-economic group (Table 29). A clear trend is evident whereby the higher the school leavers' socio-economic group, the higher the levels of attainment. For example, more than half the students from Higher Professional (55.9%) and Lower Professional (51.1%) groups have 'honours' in five or more subjects. This is true of just twelve and fourteen per cent, respectively, of those from Unskilled and Semi-Skilled Manual backgrounds. In contrast, these latter socio-economic groups are 'over-represented' among those with lower levels of attainment. For the Unskilled and Semi-Skilled Manual groups the incidence of those who failed to get at least five passes is twice the average for all groups. Similarly, these lower socio-economic groups have a significantly higher percentage of students who fail to attain honours in any subject.

TABLE 29 PERCENTAGE DISTRIBUTION OF SCHOOL LEAVERS WHO SAT THE LEAVING CERTIFICATE BY LEVEL OF ATTAINMENT AND FATHERS' SOCIO-ECONOMIC GROUP, 1996-1998 SURVEYS, (N IN PARENTHESIS)

Fathers' Socio-Economic Group	< 5 Ds	5 passes, no hons	1 Honour	2-4 Hons	5+ Hons	Total	
	%	%	%	%	%	N	%
Farmers	4.1 (33)	15.4 (125)	12.8 (104)	37.6 (305)	30.2 (245)	812	100
Other Agricultural	9.6 (9)	21.3 (20)	17.0 (16)	27.7 (26)	24.5 (23)	94	100
Higher Professional	1.0 (3)	8.6 (25)	3.4 (10)	31.0 (90)	55.9 (162)	290	100
Lower Professional	4.3 (12)	7.2 (20)	6.2 (17)	31.2 (86)	51.1 (141)	276	100
Employers & Managers	4.4 (26)	16.4 (97)	11.7 (69)	29.0 (171)	38.5 (227)	590	100
Salaried Employees	2.1 (3)	14.8 (21)	14.1 (20)	34.5 (49)	34.5 (49)	142	100
Intermediate Non-Manual	3.5 (13)	16.5 (61)	10.8 (40)	34.6 (128)	34.6 (128)	370	100
Other Non-Manual	8.9 (59)	27.5 (182)	16.6 (110)	27.1 (180)	19.9 (132)	663	100
Skilled Manual	5.2 (60)	23.7 (273)	15.7 (180)	34.1 (392)	21.3 (245)	1,150	100
Semi-Skilled Manual	10.1 (12)	30.3 (36	)12.6 (15)	32.8 (39)	14.3 (17)	119	100
Unskilled Manual	12.1 (52)	33.6 (144)	11.2 (48)	31.1 (133)	11.9 (51)	428	100
Unknown	8.1 (24)	33.0 (98)	14.1 (42)	25.6 (76)	19.2 (57)	297	100
TOTAL	**5.82**	**1.1**	**12.8**	**32.0**	**28.2**	**5,231**	**100**

TABLE 30 PERCENTAGE OF SCHOOL LEAVERS WITH LEAVING CERTIFICATE WHO ENROLLED IN HIGHER EDUCATION BY LEVEL OF ATTAINMENT AND FATHERS' SOCIO-ECONOMIC GROUP, 1996-1998 SURVEYS.

Fathers' Socio-Economic Group	5 passes, no hons %	1 Honour %	2-4 Hons %	5+ Hons %	Total %
Farmers	22.0	33.3	67.9	91.8	63.5
Other Agricultural	30.0	18.8	65.4	95.5	54.8
Higher Professional	32.0	30.0	70.5	90.7	77.2
Lower Professional	15.0	76.5	54.8	93.6	73.7
Employers & Managers	22.7	33.3	55.6	95.1	63.0
Salaried Employees	14.3	45.0	69.4	95.9	66.9
Intermediate Non-Manua	6.1 2	5.6	68.3	89.1	62.3
Other Non-Manual	14.4	22.4	65.4	93.8	48.6
Skilled Manual	9.4	29.8	62.6	88.1	49.7
Semi-Skilled Manual	11.8	20.0	46.2	93.8	38.1
Unskilled Manual	9.2	8.3	62.5	84.6	38.1
Unknown	13.8	29.3	55.4	86.0	43.4
TOTAL	**14.3**	**28.9**	**63.1**	**91.4**	**56.2**

The third table in this section (Table 30) examines the relationship between socio-economic group, level of attainment in the Leaving Certificate and levels of enrolment in higher education. This analysis is confined to those who attained at least five passes in the Leaving Certificate Examination. Overall, fifty-six per cent of those with at least five passes in the Leaving Certificate transferred into higher education. It is clear that this transition is strongly influenced by both level of attainment and socio-economic group membership. Not surprisingly, as educational attainment increases, so too does the likelihood of proceeding to higher education. On average, only fifteen per cent of those with just a pass Leaving Certificate (no honours) transferred to third level; this compares with over ninety-one per cent of those with five or more honours. It is also evident from Table 30 that the percentage going on to higher education is related to socio-economic status. For example, the percentage of the Higher Professional group entering higher education (77.2%) is twice that of the Unskilled and Semi-Skilled Manual groups. However, the most interesting feature of Table 30 is the way in which level of attainment and socio-economic group interact to determine level of enrolment in higher education.

While there are some exceptions, the general pattern is that where attainment levels are modest the percentages going on to higher education are lowest for the manual groups. In the Unskilled Manual group the percentage of those with just a pass Leaving Certificate and the percentage of those with just one honour are nine and eight per cent, respectively. This compares with more than thirty per cent for the Higher Professional group. However, for those with higher Leaving Certificates results the socio-economic differentials in the transition to higher education are almost non existent. While it is the case that for those with 2-4 honours the Higher Professional group has the highest transition rate (70.5%) and the Semi-Skilled Manual group the lowest (46.2%), it is also noticeable that the transition rate for the Unskilled Manual group exceeds that of the Employees and Managers and Salaried Employees groups. This absence of significant socio-economic group differentials is most marked for those with the highest level of attainment (5 or more honours). For those high achievers the effect of fathers' socio-economic group is small; for eight of the socio-economic groups the transition rate exceeds ninety per cent. And while the Unskilled Manual group has the lowest transfer rate, the Semi-Skilled, Other Agricultural and Other Non-Manual groups have transfer rates which exceed the average rate for all groups.

It is possible to summarise the foregoing findings from the School Leavers Survey in a single table where we focus on a series of educational transitions which highlight differential participation and achievement rates by fathers' socio-economic group (Table 31). Since our focus is on participation in higher education the first crucial transition is whether students continue in school to take the Leaving Certificate. As we have already observed in our discussion of Table 28, nineteen per cent of students leave school without reaching the Leaving Certificate stage. The retention rate to Leaving Certificate level varies by social group with only seven per cent of the two Professional groups failing to make this transition by comparison with thirty-five per cent of the Unskilled Manual group.

The second 'transition' relates to the level of achievement of those school leavers who stay to complete the Leaving Certificate. To progress to higher education it is not enough to sit the Leaving Certificate, it is also necessary to reach a satisfactory level of performance. In Table 31 we present, for each socio-economic group, the percentage of those who both survive to Leaving Certificate level and reach two separate threshold levels of achievement: those with at least five passes in the Leaving Certificate and those with with at least two Cs or better on Higher level papers. These levels of achievement might be considered the minimum necessary for different forms of higher education. In respect of the lower threshold, the differences by socio-economic status are not dramatic, although there is an eleven per cent difference between the Higher Professional group and the Unskilled Manual group. However, as was evident from Table 29, above, class differences are more marked at higher levels of attainment. Of those who remain to take the Leaving Certificate, only forty-three per cent of the Unskilled Manual group achieve at least two honours, by comparison with eighty seven per cent of the Higher Professional group.

The third transition, which we document in Table 31 concerns those who have both survived to Leaving Certificate level and achieved a minimum attainment threshold in this examination. We display, separately, for those with at least five passes and for those with at least two honours, the percentage who went on to higher education. On average fifty-six per cent of students who attain at least five passes in the Leaving Certificate are enrolled in higher education; this compares with seventy-six per cent of those with at least two grade Cs at honours level. For those with modest levels of attainment, the comparative class differences observed in these transition rates are highly significant. However, when the comparison is restricted to those with at least two honours in the Leaving Certificate, the socio-economic group differences are more modest.

In summary, the series of transitions, which these data allow us to examine, make it clear that parental socio-economic status is a powerful determinant of progress through the educational system. The effect of social background is especially evident in three transitions. First, retention rates to the end of the senior cycle are highly class specific. Second, for those who stay on to complete the Leaving Certificate, levels of achievement are also highly class specific; the percentage differences between the socio-economic groups are especially significant at this transition. Third, the likelihood of those with modest levels of performance going on to higher education is strongly related to class. However, for those who survive to Leaving Certificate and achieve a high level of attainment in this examination the socio-economic group differences in transition rates are not very significant.

TABLE 31 EDUCATIONAL TRANSITIONS: DIFFERENTIAL PARTICIPATION AND ACHIEVEMENT RATES BY FATHERS' SOCIO-ECONOMIC GROUP: SCHOOL LEAVERS SURVEYS 1996,1997,1998.

Fathers' Socio-Economic Group	Percentage Reaching Leaving Cert.	Of those Reaching Leaving Cert. Level:		Of those with at least 5 passes in Leaving Cert., % enrolled in Higher Education	Of those with least 2C's at Hon. Level, % enrolled in Higher Education
		% with at least 5 passes	% with at least 2Cs at at Hons. Level		
Farmers	88.8	95.9	67.8	63.5	78.5
Other Agricultural	71.7	90.4	52.2	54.8	79.6
Higher Professional	92.0	99.0	86.9	77.2	83.3
Lower Professional	93.8	95.7	82.3	73.7	78.9
Employers and Managers	90.7	95.6	67.5	63.0	78.1
Salaried Employees	89.7	97.9	69.0	66.9	82.7
Intermediate Non-Manual	83.8	96.5	69.2	62.3	78.5
Other Non-Manual	76.7	91.1	47.0	48.6	77.6
Skilled Manual	79.8	94.8	55.4	49.7	72.4
Semi-Skilled Manual	75.1	89.9	47.1	38.1	60.7
Unskilled Manual	65.4	87.9	43.0	38.1	68.5
TOTAL	**80.6**	**94.2**	**60.2**	**56.2**	**76.4**

Since a major concern of this report is to monitor changes over time it is instructive to compare the findings, which we have just reported, with those from the earlier analysis, relating the School Leavers Surveys of 1991/93 (see Technical Working Group, 1995 and Clancy, 1999). These surveys covered those who left school during the school years 1989/90, 1990/91 and 1991/92. The changes from the late eighties/early nineties to the mid/late nineties, with respect to the educational level of school leavers, are summarised in Table 32 where we show the percentage difference between the two distributions. The overall pattern of change in educational level of school leavers is shown in the final row of the table. There has been a small reduction (2.1%) in the percentage of school leavers with no qualifications, almost no change in the percentage of those with a Junior Certificate, and a corresponding increase (2.8%) in the percentage of those with Leaving

Fathers' Socio-Economic Group	No Qualification %	Junior Cert %	Leaving Cert %
Farmers	-1.1	-4.3	+5.5
Other Agricultural	-6.0	-2.7	+8.7
Higher Professional	+0.3	+4.8	-5.1
Lower Professional	+0.2	+2.2	-1.9
Employers & Managers	-0.7	+0.4	0.0
Salaried Employees	-1.1	+5.0	-3.5
Intermediate Non-Manual	-1.2	+1.9	-0.5
Other Non-Manual	-4.0	-2.1	+6.2
Skilled Manual	-2.8	-1.1	+3.9
Semi-Skilled Manual	-6.7	-6.8	+13.4
Unskilled Manual	-7.1	-5.8	+12.9
Unknown	-21.9	+2.9	+19.1
TOTAL	**-2.1**	**-0.6**	**+2.8**

TABLE 32   CHANGES BETWEEN 1991-93 AND 1996-98 IN THE PERCENTAGE DISTRIBUTION OF SCHOOL LEAVERS BY EDUCATIONAL LEVEL & FATHERS' SOCIO-ECONOMIC GROUP

Certificate level of education. However, the most interesting feature of the table is that the most emphatic trend concerns the lower socio-economic groups. While there is a general reduction in the percentage of those who left school with no qualification, this trend is especially noticeable among the lower socio-economic groups, and among those for whom data on socio-economic background are missing. This pattern of change is also reflected in the percentage of those with Leaving Certificate level of education. We note that there has been an increase of thirteen per cent in the percentages of the Semi-Skilled and Unskilled Manual groups with this level of education. The other socio-economic groups which show an increase in the percentages with Leaving Certificate level of education are Other Agricultural, Other Non-Manual and Farmers.

We have noted above that, from the perspective of access to higher education, continuing in school to the Leaving Certificate represents merely the first crucial transition. The second 'transition' relates to the level of achievement of those school leavers who stay to complete the Leaving Certificate. In Table A 16 (Appendix) we monitor the pattern of change over time in respect of this transition. Overall, there is some evidence of an increase in the level of attainment of those students who sat the Leaving Certificate; the numbers getting five or more honours increased by almost seven per cent, with a corresponding decline in the percentage with lower levels of attainment. The exception to this overall trend is the marginal increase (0.7%) in the percentage who failed to get at least five passes. There is no clear pattern in the changes in performance by socio-economic group. For those getting five or more honours the increase has been greatest for the Intermediate Non-Manual, Farmers, Lower Professional, Skilled Manual and the Employers and Managers groups. The Unskilled Manual and those whose socio-economic group is 'unknown' have shown the greatest increase in the percentages getting two to four honours. Interestingly, the group which registers least change in the level of attainment is the Higher Professional group; the small increase in the percentage with two or more honours is more than compensated for by an increase in the percentage who have no subject at honours level.

TABLE 33 CHANGES BETWEEN 1991/93 AND 1996/98 IN THE PERCENTAGE OF SCHOOL LEAVERS WITH LEAVING CERTIFICATE WHO ENROLLED IN HIGHER EDUCATION BY LEVEL OF ATTAINMENT AND FATHERS' SOCIO-ECONOMIC GROUP

Fathers' Socio-Economic Group	5 passes, no hons %	1 Honour %	2-4 Hons %	5+ Hons %	Total %
Farmers	+13.4	+0.5	+12.2	+3.7	**+17.0**
Other Agricultural	+24.1	+2.1	-3.0	+8.8	**+23.0**
Higher Professional	+26.4	-27.1	+3.5	-3.5	**+0.6**
Lower Professional	+5.5	+60.5	-10.1	+12.5	**+13.3**
Employers & Managers	+6.6	-6.4	-9.9	+5.5	**+2.5**
Salaried Employees	-2.8	+16.4	+8.7	+12.2	**+15.4**
Intermediate Non-Manual	-0.2	-1.2	+5.5	+3.6	**+13.4**
Other Non-Manual	+6.7	+5.5	+19.3	-6.2	**+17.7**
Skilled Manual	+1.3	+8.7	+6.9	+14.6	**+14.6**
Semi-Skilled Manual	+6.7	-15.7	+9.4	+12.0	**+12.0**
Unskilled Manual	+4.7	+3.5	+18.1	+17.6	**+17.6**
Unknown	+13.8	+29.3	+5.4	+12.6	**+12.6**
TOTAL	**+6.1**	**+2.4**	**+3.6**	**+12.1**	**+12.1**

The third transition, which we document in Table 33, is in respect of those who have both survived to Leaving Certificate level and achieved a minimum attainment threshold in the Leaving Certificate. Here we show the percentage difference in the level of transfer to higher education by socio-economic group and level of academic attainment. The overall comparison of the two cohorts reveals an increase of twelve per cent in the numbers going on to higher education. This increase is greatest for those with five or more honours, but is also significant (+ 6.1%) for those with no subject at honours level. There is also an increase in the transfer rate, although more modest, for those with intermediate levels of attainment. The groups which show the greatest increase in transfer rates are, Other Agricultural, Other Non-Manual, Unskilled Manual, Farmers and Salaried Employees. In contrast, there is only a minimal change in the transfer rate of those from the Higher Professional and Employers and Managers groups, perhaps because the rate of transfer for these groups was already close to saturation by the early 1990s. It should be noted that our interest in this comparison is limited to general trends, we do not propose to comment on the pattern of change in respect of individual cells in Table 33, since the small numbers in some cases suggest caution against 'over interpretation'.

This analysis of the findings of recent School Leavers Surveys serves to complement our survey findings in respect of access to higher education. It is clear that the social group differentials in participation, which we have documented in this report find their origins in differential patterns of participation and performance through the second level system. While our data on third level entrants relating to 1998 is not precisely matched by the data on the School Leavers Surveys, which relate to students who left school during the previous three years, the match is sufficiently close to warrant an examination of the complementary trends. Looking at the situation of the Semi-Skilled and Unskilled Manual groups, we observe from the School Leavers Survey that some eight per cent left school without any qualification, while a further twenty-five per cent left after the Junior Certificate. Of those who sat the Leaving Certificate and for whom data on attainment level were available, some twelve per cent got less than five passes in the examination.

Finally, for those with at least a pass Leaving Certificate, thirty-eight per cent went on to higher education. Thus, sixty-seven per cent of Semi-Skilled and Unskilled Manual groups sat the Leaving Certificate, of whom eighty-eight per cent got at least five passes, of whom thirty-eight per cent went on to higher education. This analysis suggests that the percentage of this combined group going on to higher education was twenty-two per cent (.67 x .88 x .38). Since the data from the School Leavers Survey includes a small number of students who were registered on part-time higher education courses, these should be subtracted from the overall figure to maximise comparability between the two sources. For the Semi-Skilled and Unskilled Manual groups, the participation rate in part-time higher education was two per cent, thus, the participation rate in full-time higher education was twenty per cent. This estimate, which is an average figure for the years 1995, 1996 and 1997, is entirely consistent with the findings from the 1992 and the present survey. In 1992, the estimated participation rate of the Semi-Skilled and Unskilled groups was just over fourteen per cent, while it was twenty-two per cent in 1998. Thus, our analysis of the School Leavers Survey, in addition to documenting the second level transitions, which account for socio-economic group inequalities in access to higher education, also serves to confirm the validity of our estimates of the participation rates in this and the previous survey.

Footnotes

1. A decision to use the 'unmatched cases' in the aggregate tables was taken following a examination of the correspondence between the two distributions. The two distributions were almost identical in respect of socio-economic group and social class.

2. For some occupations a correct designation to socio-economic group and social class requires details in respect of grade (e.g. civil servants) or industry (e.g. technician). Where these details were not available these occupations were initially assigned a separate code and were subsequently reallocated on the basis of their proportionate distribution in the national population. Thus, for occupations listed as civil servants, with no further details, one third were coded 'Employers and Managers' and two thirds were coded 'Intermediate Non-Manual' for the old SEG categories and Non-Manual for the new SEG categories. When using the old SEG and social class categories, for occupations described as technicians, with no further details, one quarter were allocated to the Lower Professional group and three-quarters were allocated to the Skilled Manual group. A further coding problem arose in respect of respondents who listed two occupations, e.g. Farmer and some other occupation. Respondents were classified on the basis of the occupation, which assigned them to the highest of the two SEG and social class categories.

3. The unemployment rate for males in this age cohort is significantly greater than that for all ever-married males aged 15 years or over (10.7%). However, the unemployment rate for females in this age cohort differs little from that of the total cohort of ever-married females.

4. We use the term 'under-represented' and 'over-represented' in this report to describe the situation where there are significant departures from proportionality in the distribution of higher education places between different social groups. It should be noted that the use of the term 'over-represented', with respect to a particular group, does not indicate that we believe it is necessary or appropriate to effect a reduction in the absolute level of representation of this group. The achievement of greater equity can be effected by an increase in the representation of the group or groups which are currently 'under-represented'.

5. These data were not available for 1998, when the Labour Force Survey was replaced by the Quarterly National Household Survey.

6.   This information has not been published in respect of the 1996 Census of Population.

7.   A particular difficulty arises in the case of 'factory workers' where the socio-economic group allocation, between Semi-Skilled and Unskilled, is contingent on the nature of the industry in which the person is employed. In these cases where insufficient information was available, respondents were initially allocated to a separate category and were subsequently reallocated on a proportionate basis between the Semi-Skilled and unskilled categories.

8.   Possible sources of error include: those which arise from possible unrepresentativeness in the response rate by social group; coding errors with the survey data and census data; the use of the national population under 15 years of age as the denominator in the calculation of participation rates; the remaining discrepancy between the survey years and the years of the Census, which provide the population parameters for the calculation of the participation rates; the change in the SEG categories which necessitated the calculation of an 'estimate' of the national population distribution by socio-economic group (old categories). All of these issues have been discussed in the report.

9.   This is a revised figure from that reported by Clancy and Wall. This will lead to consequential changes in Table 25 and Table 27. The original estimate of 46% did not take account of first year students who were not new entrants.

10.   See note 8 above.

11.   I am grateful to Dr. Selina McCoy for preparing these tables.

12.   The percentage with less than five passes differs significantly from the national figure of 9.5% (average for the years 1995,1996 and 1997) of those who sat the Leaving Certificate examination. Part of this difference may be due to missing information on education attainment, which seems to be disproportionately concentrated among the low achievers. In addition since these data on achievement are self-reported there may be some grade inflation.

Having examined the social background of entrants this chapter focuses on educational background. An analysis of the operation of the second level system is crucial to an understanding of the pattern of access to higher education. In this study the post-primary school attended and the educational attainment of entrants were examined and the educational profile of the entrants was compared with that of the total cohort from which they were drawn. The results of this analysis are reported in this chapter.

chapter four | Educational Background of Entrants

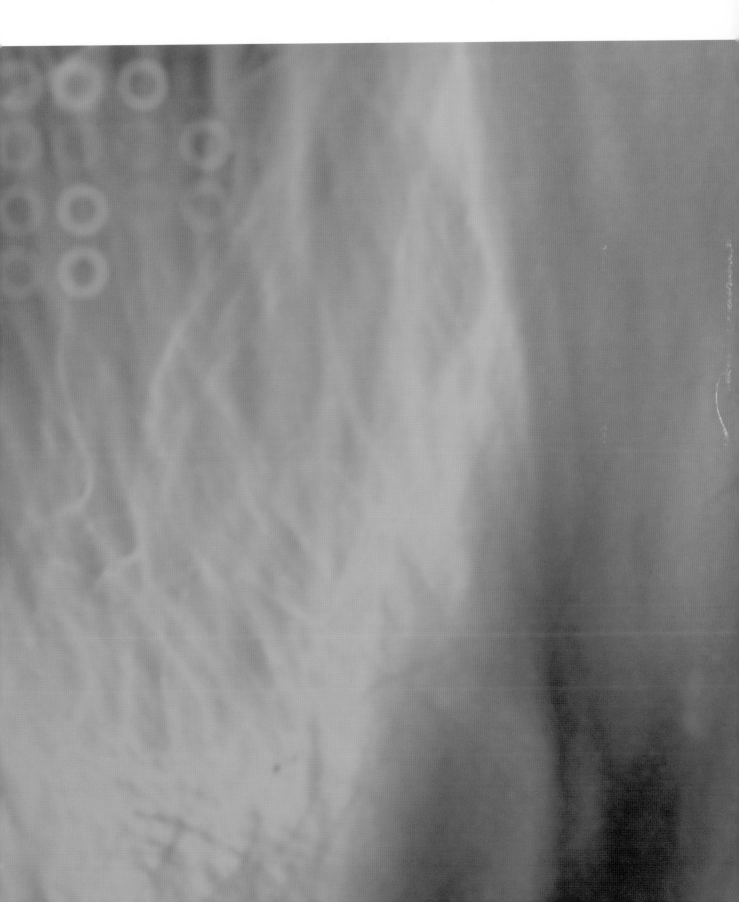

Post-Primary School Attended

Data on post-primary school attended were sought in respect of both last school attended and on principal school attended. Frequently it is desirable to make this distinction because of the pattern of repeating, whereby some students, having completed their Leaving Certificate in one school, their principal school, subsequently transfer to another school for the repeat year. However, in this analysis we rely mainly on data on principal school except in those cases where the only information available was that on last school attended. Students whose post-primary education was received outside the state (N=809) are not included in this analysis. In addition these data were not available for almost twelve per cent of entrants.

Seventy per cent of entrants attended secondary schools while a further fourteen per cent attended vocational schools. Eleven per cent attended community schools. The remainder were divided between comprehensive schools and 'other' schools, consisting mainly of private non-recognised schools. Table 34 examines the relationship between type of post-primary school attended and the type of third-level college in which the entrants enrolled. The destination of entrants coming from secondary and comprehensive schools was very similar with forty-seven per cent enrolled in a university and a further forty-eight to forty-nine per cent enrolled in the IOTs sector. In contrast entrants from vocational schools were disproportionately represented (67.5%) in the IOTs sector with less than thirty per cent enrolling in the universities. Third level entrants from community schools were also more strongly represented in the IOTs and somewhat under-represented in the universities. Finally, it is of interest to note that both the universities and the 'other colleges' attracted a disproportionate share of students from the private non-recognised schools.

TABLE 34 DISTRIBUTION OF NEW ENTRANTS BY TYPE OF HIGHER EDUCATION COLLEGE ENTERED AND BY TYPE OF POST-PRIMARY SCHOOL ATTENDED

College Type	Secondary %	Vocational %	Comprehensive %	Community %	Other Schools %	TOTAL %	TOTAL N
Universities	46.7	29.3	47.0	37.8	60.2	43.9	12,371
Institutes of Technology	48.1	67.5	48.8	57.5	34.2	51.3	14,460
Colleges of Education	3.1	2.2	2.6	3.1	1.1	2.9	818
Other Colleges	2.1	1.0	1.6	1.6	4.5	1.9	546
TOTAL %	100	100	100	100	100	100	-
TOTAL N	19,747	3,824	728	2,990	906	-	28,195

The information on post-primary school origin is more meaningful when considered in conjunction with post-primary school enrolment data. The most appropriate comparator is that provided by aggregate enrolment data in the final year of the post-primary cycle for each school type in 1998. This made it possible to calculate for each school type a transfer rate i.e. the percentage of the 1997/98 Leaving Certificate class which enrolled in third-level education in Autumn 1998. For the purpose of this analysis it is assumed that the number of students who were new entrants to higher education in 1998 and who were not part of the 1997/98 Leaving Certificate cohort, will be compensated for by the number of students from the 1997/98 Leaving Certificate cohort who will enter higher education subsequent to 1998.

Table 35 presents the distribution, by school type, of the Leaving Certificate cohort, excluding repeat students and those taking the Applied Leaving Certificate[1] and those in private non-recognised schools, and the 1998 higher education entrants. Sixty-five per cent of Leaving Certificate students attended secondary schools (7% in fee-paying and 58% in non-fee paying). A further twenty per cent attended vocational schools while the remaining fifteen per cent were distributed between Community (12%) and Comprehensive (2.5%) schools. However, when we compare this distribution with the distribution of new entrants we note that secondary schools have a higher proportionate representation among third level entrants. In particular, we note that while nine per cent of higher education entrants came from fee-paying secondary schools, these schools only accounted for seven per cent of Leaving Certificate enrolments. This differential pattern is summarised by the transfer rate, which has been calculated for each school type. In calculating the transfer rate the number of third level entrants shown in Table 35 is adjusted upwards by to take account of missing data[2]. Overall, the 1998 new entrants, represented over fifty-four per cent of the Leaving Certificate class of 1997/98. The overall transfer rate for secondary schools was sixty per cent; the rate for fee-paying secondary schools was seventy-one per cent compared with fifty-nine per cent for non-fee paying secondary schools, In contrast, the transfer rate for vocational schools was thirty-eight per cent. The transfer rate for comprehensive schools (57%) was broadly similar to that of non-fee paying secondary schools while the rate for community schools was fifty per cent.

TABLE 35 **DISTRIBUTION OF 1997/98 LEAVING CERTIFICATE STUDENTS AND 1998 NEW ENTRANTS TO HIGHER EDUCATION BY SCHOOL TYPE**

School Type	Leaving Certificate Students		*New Entrants to Higher Education		Transfer Rate **
	N	%	N	%	%
Fee-Paying Secondary	3,921	6.9	2,451	9.0	70.6
Non-Fee-Paying Secondary	33,132	58.4	17,296	63.4	59.0
Vocational	11,384	20.1	3,824	14.0	38.0
Comprehensive	1,445	2.5	728	2.7	57.0
Community	6,830	12.0	2,990	11.0	49.5
TOTAL	**56,712**	**100**	**27,289**	**100**	**54.4**

*   *Excludes Applied Leaving Certficate (N=1,957) students who are not eligible for direct entry into higher education*
* *   *Before calculating the transfer rate the number of new entrants recorded in colum four was multiplied by 1.13 to account for the missing data in respect of post-primary school attended.*

The differential transfer rates to higher education, from the different types of post-primary schools, represent only the final stage of a sequence of differential selectivity which is operative through the whole post-primary system. A key feature of this progressive selectivity is the differential retention rates for the different types of post-primary school. The majority of those who were new entrants to higher education in 1998 would have begun a five-year post-primary programme in 1993 or, for those completing a six-year cycle, in 1992. In the previous national surveys we have used aggregate enrolment data as published in the annual Statistical Report of the Department of Education and Science to estimate overall retention rates and retention rates by school type, over the five or six year post-primary cycle. It was known that this type of analysis of aggregate data was subject to some error, if only because of some mobility between schools and because of the complications arising from the fact that some students completed the post-primary programme in five years while others who included a transition year took six years. However, it provided a good snapshot of the operation second level system. For example in the 1992 study it was estimated that the Leaving Certificate enrolment in 1991/91 represented a retention rate of seventy-four per cent for those who commenced the second level cycle in 1987/88. It was estimated that this retention rate varied significantly by school type from sixty per cent for vocational schools to eighty-one per cent for secondary schools (Clancy, 1995: 81).

It is no longer necessary to rely on this kind of aggregate analysis for the calculation of overall retention rates since the Department of Education and Science has now introduced an individualized tracking system which allows for a more accurate calculation of retention. The author has been given access to the results of this analysis which reveals that overall school based retention is now seventy-eight per cent. That is of the 70,851 students who commenced their second level education in the year 1992/93, seventy-eight per cent complete the second level programme: forty-seven per cent complete the Leaving Certificate in 1997 and a further thirty-one per cent completed the Leaving Certificate in 1998.

Because of the different methodologies involved it is not possible to make strict comparisons between the retention rates calculated by the Department of Education and Science and the cruder aggregate analysis on which our estimates have been calculated in previous surveys. For example if we replicate, for the 1998 Leaving Certificate cohort, the methodology utilised in previous surveys, we estimate that the retention rate to Leaving Certificate was almost eighty-three per cent[3]. Notwithstanding the five per cent difference between the two estimates (78% versus 83%), it is clear that there has been a steady improvement in retention rates over the past two decades[4]. This generalization represents a long-term trend even if the buoyancy of the labour market in recent years has arrested this progress.

Educational Attainment of Entrants

As in the case of the earlier studies detailed information on the academic attainment of entrants was collected for the present study. This analysis was confined to those students who had sat the Leaving Certificate Examination. Students who presented GCE or other foreign examination results are not included in the analysis. In addition, no examination data were available in respect of four per cent of entrants. Some of this latter group would have been admitted as mature students where the normal academic prerequisites would not have applied. This left a total of 30,679 students for whom examination data were analysed.

Because of the competition for places in higher education many students seeking a place present more than one examination result. While in the past it was possible in some colleges to combine the results from more than one sitting to maximize the points score this is no longer possible. However, it is still possible to combine results from more than one year to satisfy basic matriculation requirements. For example, where Irish or a modern continental language is a basic requirement for entry into a programme, students who meet this requirement in their first sitting of the Leaving Certificate and who repeat the examination to achieve the necessary points for entry may opt not to take each subject in the repeat sitting. This strategic behaviour is directed at maximizing the points score since all colleges now calculate a points score based in the best results achieved in six subjects in any one sitting of the Leaving Certificate examination.

However since this is the fourth national survey and since a major objective of the study is to monitor change over time it was considered necessary, in the interest of comparability, to apply the same criteria in the measurement of the attainment levels of entrants. At the time of the 1980 and 1986 surveys and to a limited extent in 1992 it was possible to combine results from different years and from different examinations (the Leaving Certificate and University Matriculation examinations) to accumulate the highest points score. Thus in these surveys a student's level of academic attainment was assessed on the basis of a composite examination score, where for each subject a student was credited with the highest grade achieved over all examination sittings. To facilitate comparisons with previous studies a similar procedure was adopted in this analysis. This measure is described as the composite measure of attainment. In addition, a second scoring procedure was adopted where account was taken only of the best result achieved in a single examination sitting. This measure of attainment was based in the results achieved in the Leaving Certificate in the most recent year in which at least six subjects were taken[5]. This latter measure will be most useful for comparisons with future studies.

In seeking to examine the educational attainment of entrants we first examine the distribution of subjects presented by students in the Leaving Certificate examination and the highest level of achievement in these subjects (Table 36). The data presented in this table is based on the composite measure of attainment. The penultimate column of this table shows the number of students who had taken each subject and for whom information was available on the results achieved in these examinations. The first ten columns of Table 27 show the percentage distribution of students by level of achievement in each subject. The columns marked 'other' combine in single categories, for both higher and lower level papers, those who received grades of E, F and no grade. Furthermore, in the interest of economy of presentation this table does not show separately the distribution of students within each letter grade. Thus, for example those categorised under grade B combines those who were awarded B1, B2 and B3.

It is clear from Table 36 that the vast majority of entrants had taken English (98%), Mathematics (98%) and Irish (94%). Only two other subjects, French (67%) and Biology (51%) had a take-up rate of more than fifty per cent. Forty-four per cent of entrants had taken Geography while just over a third had taken Business Organisation (35%) and Home Economics (both programmes combined, 34%). Only four other subjects had a take-up rate of over twenty per cent: German and History were taken by twenty-three per cent while twenty-two per cent had Physics and twenty per cent had Accounting. Almost eighteen per cent had taken Chemistry while more than ten per cent had taken Art (13%), Technical Drawing (11%) and Economics (11%). In contrast many of the language subjects had take-up rates of less than one per cent. These included Latin, Spanish, Italian and a group consisting of Greek, Dutch, Danish and Portuguese, which are categorized as 'Other Languages'. Within the Mathematics and Science group, subjects which have low take-up rates include Applied Mathematics (4%) Agricultural Science (4%) and Physics & Chemistry (2.5%). Two of the subjects in the Technical group have relatively low take-up rates; these are Construction Studies (10%) and Engineering (6%). Finally the two subjects in Music and Musicianship were taken by a total of just over three per cent of entrants.

TABLE 36   EDUCATIONAL ATTAINMENT BY SUBJECT OF 1998 NEW HIGHER EDUCATION ENTRANTS

	Higher Level					Lower Level					Total	
	A	B	C	D	Other	A	B	C	D	Other		
	%	%	%	%	%	%	%	%	%	%	N	%*
Languages												
English	6.1	19.6	33.6	18.5	0.5	1.1	6.3	10.4	3.8	0.1	30,152	98.2
Irish	4.6	17.7	19.1	6.0	0.1	0.3	8.8	23.9	16.6	2.7	28,925	94.2
French	5.7	18.7	25.7	15.5	1.0	0.1	5.6	16.0	10.7	1.1	20,565	67.0
German	8.1	26.6	29.8	13.4	0.5	0.7	8.0	8.7	3.8	0.4	7,163	23.3
Latin	23.2	34.4	30.5	9.3	1.3	-	-	0.7	0.7	-	151	0.5
Spanish	12.42	3.6	24.3	15.5	1.2	0.9	8.1	10.4	2.9	0.8	869	2.8
Italian	14.3	27.3	23.4	16.9	1.3	-	9.1	3.9	3.9	-	77	0.3
ClassicalStudies	6.3	22.9	38.1	23.1	6.1	-	0.3	0.8	1.3	1.0	603	2.0
Other Languages	15.8	36.8	36.8	10.5	-	-	-	-	-	-	19	0.1
Mathematics & Sciences												
Maths	6.1	11.0	8.8	3.2	0.1	17.5	25.8	17.7	9.2	0.5	30,008	97.8
Biology	12.3	24.6	26.3	17.3	3.5	0.7	5.1	6.8	2.8	0.5	15,551	50.7
Chemistry	15.6	26.4	24.7	17.0	5.9	0.4	2.8	4.0	2.5	0.7	5,428	17.7
Physics	10.5	21.8	23.4	18.7	5.6	1.6	6.6	6.6	4.1	1.2	6,750	22.0
Physics & Chemistry	19.2	28.7	20.5	12.4	4.8	1.0	2.7	4.7	4.0	1.8	766	2.5
Applied Maths	27.5	35.2	19.3	8.5	2.7	1.9	1.5	1.5	1.1	0.8	1,236	4.0
Agricultural Science	7.2	34.9	36.7	15.6	0.9	-	0.9	2.1	1.5	0.3	1,149	3.7

*The figures in this column refer to the percentage of higher education entrants who took each subject in the Leaving Certificate.

TABLE 36 Cont.

TABLE 36 Cont. — EDUCATIONAL ATTAINMENT BY SUBJECT OF 1998 NEW HIGHER EDUCATION ENTRANTS

	Higher Level					Lower Level					Total	
	A	B	C	D	Other	A	B	C	D	Other		
	%	%	%	%	%	%	%	%	%	%	N	%
Business Studies												
Accounting	14.0	24.7	23.0	15.8	5.5	5.1	6.2	3.3	1.9	0.7	6,161	20.1
Business Organisation	10.3	30.2	30.3	15.3	2.1	1.9	5.0	3.6	1.3	0.1	10.663	34.7
Economics	12.1	35.0	27.2	14.3	2.1	2.2	3.8	2.2	1.0	0.1	3,381	11.0
Economic History	3.1	22.5	36.3	25.2	9.4	-	0.5	0.7	1.2	0.7	413	1.3
Agricultural Economics	11.2	26.0	33.2	26.5	2.6	-	-	-	0.5	-	196	0.6
Technical												
Technical Drawing	12.3	22.6	20.5	13.0	2.1	7.9	11.0	7.3	2.7	0.5	3,453	11.2
Construction Studies	9.9	48.5	32.1	4.2	0.2	0.1	1.7	2.7	0.7	0.1	3,034	9.9
Engineering	13.1	39.3	30.6	7.3	0.2	0.7	5.1	3.1	0.7	-	1,760	5.7
Social Studies												
Art & Music												
Home Econ.S&S & General	9.7	33.2	33.6	16.1	2.3	0.4	1.7	2.0	0.8	0.1	10,364	33.8
History	10.6	26.8	29.6	16.6	2.6	6.3	3.4	2.4	1.3	0.3	7,144	23.3
Geography	9.0	33.1	38.2	14.0	0.7	1.1	1.9	1.4	0.5	0.0	13,536	44.1
Art	8.3	31.6	37.6	16.0	0.9	0.6	1.9	2.0	1.0	0.1	3,906	12.7
Music & Musicianship A&B	10.4	41.0	38.2	8.6	0.1	-	1.0	0.8	0.1	-	993	3.2

The second element of the educational profile of entrants which is shown in Table 36 is the distribution of students by the highest level of attainment in each of these subjects. The pattern shown is one of considerable diversity. For seventeen of the twenty-nine subjects[6] the modal level of attainment was grade C on a higher level paper. In the case of two of the Languages (Latin and Italian) the modal level of attainment was grade B on a higher level paper while the level of attainment in Irish represents the most significant departure from the modal distribution. In this instance the modal level of attainment was grade C on a lower level paper. In the case of three of the subjects from the Mathematics and Science group (Applied Mathematics, Physics & Chemistry and Chemistry) the modal level of attainment was grade B on a higher level paper. The level of attainment in Mathematics represents a more significant departure from the norm in this group. Here the modal level of attainment was grade B on a lower level paper. For all three subjects in the Technical group and for two of the subjects (Economics and Accounting) in the Business Studies group the modal level of attainment was grade B on a higher level paper. An additional feature of these distributions is the disproportionate number of students having high grades in those subjects taken by very small numbers of students[7]. More than fifteen per cent of entrants had a grade A on a higher level paper in Applied Mathematics (27.5%), Latin (23%), Physics & Chemistry (19%) and Other Languages (16%). In contrast, the percentage of entrants with an A grade on higher level papers in the three subjects taken by almost all students (English, Mathematics and Irish) ranged from five to six per cent. Finally, for subjects with a moderate take-up rate the percentages achieving an A grade ranged from seven for Agricultural Science to nineteen for Chemistry.

The distribution of students by subjects taken in the Leaving Certificate Examination and by levels of attainment in these subjects is more meaningful when compared with a similar distribution for the total cohort from which the new entrants are drawn. Data are now available annually on the results of the Leaving Certificate Examination. A comparison between these two distributions enables us to assess the extent to which the higher education entrants are representative of the Leaving Certificate cohort[8].

When we compare the distribution of new entrants by subjects taken in the Leaving Certificate Examination (last complete sitting) with the total 1998 Leaving Certificate cohort we note that the pattern of differential take-up of subjects was broadly similar. The same five subjects, Mathematics, English, Irish, French and Biology had the highest percentage take-up in both populations. However, some differences are evident. In relation to the three subjects with the highest take-up rate (Mathematics, English and Irish) the percentage taking these subjects was slightly higher in the Leaving Certificate cohort than for new entrants. This may be explained by the fact that while, typically, these subjects are needed by all students for matriculation purposes they are not always taken in the last complete examination sitting which is used in the calculation of a points score.

In contrast with the situation for English and Irish, higher education entrants were more likely than the total Leaving Certificate cohort to have taken other language subjects in the Leaving Certificate. The take-up rate for French and German was about five per cent higher for the higher education entrants. The only exception to this general trend was in the case of Italian where the percentage of Leaving Certificate students taking this exam was slightly higher than that for higher education entrants. Looking at the Mathematics and Sciences group, higher education entrants were more likely to have taken Physics, Chemistry, Applied Mathematics and Physics & Chemistry. They were less likely to have taken Agricultural Science. In the case of the subjects classified in the Business Studies group higher education entrants were more likely to have taken Economics, Economic History, and Accounting and somewhat less likely to have taken Business Organisation. Each of the three Technical subjects had a lower take-up rate by the higher education entrants by comparison with the total Leaving Certificate cohort. Finally in relation to the less homogenous Social Studies, Art and Music category in Table A17, while higher education entrants had a higher take-up rate than the total cohort in Music and Musicianship (both programmes combined), they had a lower take-up rate in Home Economics (both programmes combined), Art, History and Geography.

Much larger differences between the two populations are evident when we examine the two distributions by level of attainment in each subject. Predictably, the higher education entrants had significantly higher levels of attainment in all subjects by comparison with the total Leaving Certificate cohort. These differences are evident if we look at the attainment levels in the three subjects with the highest take-up rates. While the modal level of attainment in Mathematics, English and Irish is the same for both distributions the percentage of higher education who had grades A or B on higher level papers is twice that for the entire Leaving Certificate cohort. This latter generalisation also holds for French, Biology, Geography, Business Organisation and Home Economcis although in the case of French the modal level of attainment does differ for the two distributions. The largest percentage of entrants who took French attained grade C on a higher level paper while in the case of the entire Leaving Certificate cohort the modal level of attainment was grade D on a lower level paper. For each of the three Technical subjects (Technical Drawing, Construction Studies and Engineering) there is a similar divergence between both distributions. In each case the modal level of attainment for higher education entrants was grade B on a higher level paper while in the case of the entire Leaving Certificate cohort grade C on a higher level paper was the mode.

Returning to our more exclusive focus on higher education entrants, the main objective in our analysis of the Leaving Certificate examination data was to identify the level of prior academic achievement of students. A secondary objective of this analysis was to monitor changes over time on this variable. Consequently, the measure of differential attainment used here corresponds to that used in the three earlier surveys. It is based on the number of subjects in which students achieved grade C or higher on a higher level paper. Furthermore, in the interest of comparability, for this computation the composite result is used, taking account of all examination sittings. The distribution of students, by type of higher education college attended, on this measure of attainment is presented in Table 37. A striking feature of the distribution is the wide range of student attainment. Six per cent of higher education entrants had no subject with a grade C or higher on a higher level paper (henceforth referred to as "honours") while a total of fifteen had less than two honours thus falling short of the minimum matriculation requirement for university entry. In contrast, sixty per cent of entrants had four or more honours while thirteen per cent had seven or more subjects with this level of achievement.

TABLE 37	DISTRIBUTION OF NEW ENTRANTS BY LEVEL OF PRIOR ACADEMIC ATTAINMENT AND BY TYPE OF COLLEGE					

Number of Honours*	Universities %	ITs	Colleges of Education %	Other Colleges %	TOTAL %	TOTAL N
0	0.4	10.8	1.3	10.5	6.0	1,742
1	0.2	17.5	1.4	11.7	9.4	2,711
2	1.0	21.1	1.6	22.0	11.9	3,440
3	3.4	20.5	1.4	21.8	12.6	3,648
4	11.1	15.2	1.7	18.1	13.1	3,795
5	22.6	8.8	13.1	9.4	14.9	4,310
6	34.7	4.6	49.6	5.0	18.9	5,481
7	23.1	1.3	28.1	1.4	11.5	3,337
8	3.3	0.1	1.8	0.1	1.5	444
9	0.3	0.0	-	-	0.1	36
10 +	0.0	-	-	-	0.0	2
TOTAL %	100	100	100	100	100	-
TOTAL N	12,436	14,524	901	1,085	-	28,946

* Honours = Grade C or higher on higher level paper.

Significant differences were evident in the level of attainment of entrants to the different types of third level college. The pattern of attainment is broadly similar for the universities and the Colleges of Education with the modal level of attainment being six honours. While the universities had a smaller percentage (1.6%) of entrants with less than three honours and a larger percentage of entrants with eight or more honours (3.6% versus 1.8%) the Colleges of Education had a significantly higher concentration of students with six or seven honours (78% versus 58%). Almost forty-two per cent of entrants to the Institutes of Technology had two or three honours while a further thirty-three per cent had either one of four subjects with this level of achievement. Eleven per cent of entrants to this sector had no subject at honours level. The distribution of entrants by level of attainment to the heterogeneous 'Other Colleges' sector is broadly similar to that in the IT sector. The majority (62%) of entrants have two, three or four subjects at honours level.

The variability in the prior academic attainment of higher education entrants by college type is complemented by a similar variability by field of study. The distribution of entrants by level of academic attainment and field of study in HEA sector colleges is shown in the Appendix (Table A18). It is clear that the highest levels of attainment are to be found in the professional faculties. For example, more than a half of entrants to Veterinary Medicine had seven honours, while a further third had eight or more subjects at this level of attainment. The comparable figures for Medicine were sixty-one per cent with seven honours and twenty-three with eight or more subjects at this level. The academic profile of entrants to Architecture and Dentistry are broadly similar. The fields of study which had the highest percentages of students with less than four honours were Art and Design[9] (45%) and Equestrian Studies (30%). Finally, it is of interest to note that if we look at the modal level of attainment for ten of the nineteen disciplines shown in Table A18 the mode was six honours while for five others fields of study the modal level was seven.

The level of prior academic attainment of entrants by field of study for non-HEA sector colleges is shown in Table A19. In this instance the highest achievers were disproportionately concentrated in Education where eighty-one per cent had six or more honours. For four of the nine fields of studies shown in this table (Construction Studies, Business, Administrative & Secretarial Studies, Hotel, Catering & Tourism and General Studies) the modal level of attainment was three honours while in the case of General Engineering, Science and Computer Studies the mode was two honours. General Engineering had the highest percentage (35%) of students with less than two honours, followed by Art & Design (30%) and Computer Studies (29%).

While the link between attainment levels and field of study as described above is well known the link between subject specialisation at second level and third level field of study has received less attention. This was explored in the report on the 1992 study following an earlier paper which has examined the situation in respect of entry to universities (Clancy and Brannick, 1990). Table 38 shows separately for males and females the relationship between the average number of subjects taken from each of five Leaving Certificate subject groupings and third level field of study. The modal pattern for the total entry cohort was to have three Language subjects, two subjects from the Mathematics and Science group, one from the Business group, none from the Technical group and one from the heterogeneous 'Other' subject group.

TABLE 38 AVERAGE NUMBER OF LANGUAGE, MATHEMATICS AND SCIENCE, BUSINESS, TECHNICAL AND "OTHER" SUBJECTS TAKEN AT LEAVING CERTIFICATE LEVEL BY GENDER AND THIRD LEVEL FIELD OF STUDY

Third-Level Field of Study	\multicolumn{10}{c}{LEAVING CERTIFICATE SUBJECT GROUPINGS}								
	Language Subjects		Mathematics and Science Subjects		Business Subjects		Technical Subjects		"Other" Subjects	
	M	F	M	F	M	F	M	F	M	F
Humanities	3.07	3.16	1.86	1.86	0.81	0.52	0.16	0.02	1.44	1.57
Education	2.91	3.07	2.09	2.02	0.55	0.53	0.69	0.02	1.08	1.46
Art & Design	2.54	2.93	1.61	1.58	0.42	0.37	0.82	0.05	1.53	2.00
Social Science	2.91	3.03	1.92	1.92	0.90	0.63	0.32	0.01	1.19	1.50
Law	3.09	3.15	2.25	2.06	0.81	0.60	0.16	0.01	1.17	1.35
Commerce	2.87	3.02	1.74	1.73	1.27	1.03	0.26	0.01	1.06	1.25
Science	2.90	3.01	2.69	2.60	0.51	0.39	0.31	0.02	0.85	1.08
Technology	2.70	2.97	2.08	2.12	0.55	0.59	0.88	0.11	0.88	1.27
Medical Science	2.99	3.15	3.56	3.05	0.40	0.40	0.09	0.01	0.69	0.82
Agriculture	2.91	3.01	2.46	2.56	0.56	0.54	0.49	0.01	0.91	1.11
Hotel, Catering and Tourism	2.84	2.99	1.74	1.78	0.76	0.62	0.36	0.02	1.43	1.58
Combined Studies	3.02	3.17	1.98	1.89	1.06	0.83	0.14	0.02	1.07	1.17
TOTAL	**2.85**	**3.08**	**2.12**	**2.06**	**0.80**	**0.69**	**0.59**	**0.05**	**1.05**	**1.42**

Within this overall pattern significant gender differentials were evident. Female students were more likely to have taken an extra Language subject; ten per cent of females had more than three languages by comparison with only four per cent of males (See Appendix Table A20). Females were also more likely to have taken more subjects from the 'Other' group. Twenty-eight per cent of males had no subject from this group by comparison with only thirteen per cent of females while the pattern was reversed for those who took two or more subjects from this subject group (25% for males versus 41% for females). In contrast, male entrants were somewhat more likely to have taken more subjects from the Mathematics and Science group and the Business Studies group. Twenty-four per cent of males had three or more subjects from the Mathematics and Science group by comparison with twenty-one per cent of females. Fifteen per cent of males compared with eight per cent of females had two or more subjects from the Business Studies group. The gender differentials were greatest in the take-up of Technical subjects. Although the overall take-up rate of these subjects was low, less than three per cent of females had any subject from this group by comparison with thirty-eight per cent of males.

Having reviewed the pattern in the take-up of Leaving Certificate subjects we now turn to examine how these are related to third level field of study destinations. Although the variance in the take-up of language subjects is limited, with the majority of females (86%) and males (77%) taking three languages, Table 38 reveals a relationship between number of language subjects taken and field of study. For both males and females, students with more than three languages were more likely to enrol to study Law, Humanities, and Combined Studies while females who entered Medicine were also more likely to have more than three languages. In contrast, those with fewer Language subjects at Leaving Certificate level were more likely to study Art and Design and Technology. The take-up of Science subjects was strongly linked to third level field of study destination for both male and female entrants. Students who entered Medical Sciences had an average of more than one extra Mathematics and Science subject. Entrants to Science and Agriculture also had more Mathematics and Science subjects while those who entered courses in Art and Design, Commerce and Hotel, Catering & Tourism and the Humanities had fewer Mathematics and Science subjects in the Leaving Certificate.

The pattern of take-up of Leaving Certificate Business subjects was also linked to field of study destinations. Predictably, this was most evident in respect of those who entered Commerce who tended to have significantly more Business subjects. Entrants to Combined Studies and Social Science also tended to have more Business subjects at Leaving Certificate level. In contrast, those who entered Medical Science, Art and Design and Science tended to have fewer Business subjects at Leaving Certificate. Although the overall level of take-up of subjects from the Technical subjects group was low, especially for females, there was a clear link between the taking of these subjects at the Leaving Certificate and third level field of study. Predictably, those who entered the field of Technology were more likely to have studied Technical subjects at second level. This was also the case for those who entered Art & Design and, for males, those who entered Education. This latter finding reflects the pattern of entry to courses at the University of Limerick for the training of specialist second level teachers. Entrants to Medical Science were least likely to have taken a Technical subjects at second level.

The final column in Table 38 shows the relationship between the pattern of take-up of subjects from the heterogeneous 'Other' subjects group and third level field of study destination. Students who entered programmes in Art and Design, Hotel, Catering and Tourism, and the Humanities had significantly higher take-up rates in these subjects while students in Medical Science, Science and Agriculture had significantly lower take-up rates in these subjects.

A consistent finding in much recent research including our studies of the 1986 and 1992 entry cohorts has been the superior academic performance of females in the Leaving Certificate Examination. The present study replicates this finding. Table 39 reveals that female entrants had a higher level of prior academic attainment. While eighteen per cent of male entrants had less than two honours this was the case for only thirteen ten per cent of females. In contrast while thirty-eight per cent of females had six or more honours subjects this was true of only twenty-six per cent of male entrants.

TABLE 39   DISTRIBUTION OF NEW ENTRANTS BY LEVEL OF PRIOR ACADEMIC ATTAINMENT AND BY GENDER

Number of Honours*	Male %	Female %	TOTAL %
0	6.4	5.6	6.0
1	11.5	7.4	9.4
2	15.0	9.0	11.9
3	14.4	11.0	12.6
4	13.4	12.9	13.1
5	13.4	16.3	14.9
6	14.5	23.1	18.9
7	9.6	13.3	11.5
8	1.7	1.4	1.5
9	0.1	0.1	0.1
10 +	0.0	–	0.0
TOTAL %	100	100	100
TOTAL N	13,943	15,002	28,945

* *Honours = Grade C or higher on higher level paper.*

It is of interest to compare the findings on the level of prior academic attainment of new entrants in the present study with that found in the three previous national surveys. In the report on the 1992 study we noted a continuing rise in the level of attainment of new entrants between 1980 and 1992. Table 40 reveals that this continuing rise in attainment has been halted. There is very little difference between the 1992 and 1998 distributions in terms of the level of academic attainment of new entrants. While the percentage of entrants with less than two honours has risen from four per cent in 1992 to six per cent in 1998 the percentages with six or more honours has increased over the period. In 1992 twenty-eight per cent of entrants had this level of attainment while this increased to thirty-two per cent by 1998.

TABLE 40   DISTRIBUTION OF NEW ENTRANTS BY LEVEL OF PRIOR ACADEMIC ATTAINMENT, 1980, 1986 AND 1992

Number of Honours*	1980 %	1986 %	1992 %	1998 %
0	12.2	7.8	3.9	6.0
1	11.5	10.7	9.1	9.4
2	14.6	12.4	14.0	11.9
3	15.3	13.7	14.9	12.6
4	15.2	14.1	15.4	13.1
5	12.6	13.5	14.9	14.9
6	10.3	13.7	14.3	18.9
7	6.8	11.5	11.5	11.5
8+	1.7	2.5	2.0	1.6
TOTAL %	100	100	100	100
TOTAL N	12,775	16,613	23,761	28,946

* *Honours = Grade C or higher on higher level paper.*

Table 41 permits us to examine more closely changes between 1986 and 1992 in the distribution of entrants by level of prior academic attainment. Here we show the percentage difference between the 1986 and 1992 distributions of entrants by college type and level of attainment. The overall pattern of change shown in the final column replicates that shown in the previous table with an increase of two per cent in the percentage with less than two honours and an increase in the percentage of entrants with six of more honours. It is clear from Table 41 that the slight increase in the percentage of entrants with less than two honours is accounted for by the pattern of recruitment to the Institutes of Technology where more than four per cent of entrants had no subject with grade C or higher on a higher level paper. By contrast in the other three sectors there has been a reduction in the percentage of entrants with less than two subjects at honours level. Both the Colleges of Education and the Universities continue to show a rise in the attainment of entrants. This is most notable in the case of the Colleges of Education where there has been an increase of twenty-eight per cent in the percentage of entants with six or more honours subjects. The heterogeneous 'Other Colleges' sector also reveals a rise in the academic attainment of entrants. However some caution is necessary in the interpretation of this finding since the composition of this sector has changed over time as has the comprehensiveness of data available.

TABLE 41   CHANGES BETWEEN 1992 & 1998 IN THE PERCENTAGE DISTRIBUTION OF NEW ENTRANTS TO HIGHER EDUCATION BY LEVEL OF PRIOR ACADEMIC ATTAINMENT, AND BY TYPE OF HIGHER EDUCATION COLLEGE

Number of Honours*	Universities	ITs	Colleges of Education	Other Colleges	TOTAL
0	-0.1	+4.1	+0.4	-3.2	**+2.1**
1	-0.1	+0.3	-1.0	-4.7	**+0.3**
2	-0.9	-4.3	-0.1	-1.7	**-2.1**
3	-2.8	-2.7	-4.0	+2.4	**-2.3**
4	-4.9	+0.4	-14.4	+4.4	**-2.3**
5	-0.5	+1.5	-8.6	+1.9	**0.0**
6	+9.4	+0.7	+16.5	+1.0	**+4.6**
7	+0.4	-0.1	+11.8	-0.2	**0.0**
8+	-0.5	0	-0.6	+0.1	**-0.4**

* Honours = Grade C or higher on higher level paper.

Number of Examination Years

Our final variable relating to the academic profile of entrants concerns the incidence of repeating the Leaving Certificate examination. For many years one of the consequences of intensified competition for places in higher education has been the increased incidence of students repeating the Leaving Certificate in order to improve their competitive position. In the present study information was sought on the number of years in which students sat the Leaving Certificate Examination. Eighty-five per cent of entrants had sat these examinations in only one year. The incidence of repeating the Leaving Certificate does not vary significantly (Table 42). It was lowest among those who entered the Colleges of Education at less than fourteen per cent while it was highest (18%) among those who entered the 'Other Colleges' sector. It is of interest to note that there has been a continuous reduction since 1986 in the incidence of repeating the Leaving Certificate. In 1986 almost a quarter of entrants (24%) had repeated. By 1992 this had reduced to twenty-two per cent. The reduction to fifteen per cent in 1998 represents a more emphatic change.

TABLE 42 DISTRIBUTION OF NEW ENTRANTS TO HIGHER EDUCATION BY NUMBER OF YEARS IN WHICH EXAMINATIONS WERE TAKEN AND BY TYPE OF HIGHER EDUCATION COLLEGE

College Type	One Year %	More than One Year %	TOTAL %	N
			Leaving Certificate Examinations	
Universities	84.3	15.7	100	12,330
ITs	85.3	14.7	100	14,437
Colleges of Education	86.2	13.8	100	820
Other Colleges	81.7	18.3	100	545
TOTAL	**84.8**	**15.2**	**100**	**28,13**

Footnotes

1. Normally, students with a Leaving Certificate Applied are not eligible for direct entry into higher education.

2. Since school data were unavailable for almost twelve per cent of the entry cohort from the Republic of Ireland the numbers shown in column 4 were adjusted upwards: these values were multiplied by 1.13.

3. This rate was lowest in Vocational Schools (73%) and higher in the Community/Comprehensive (88%) and Secondary (85%) sectors. The finding that the Community/Comprehensive sector has a higher retention rate than the Secondary sector is surprising and is probably accounted for the growth in this sector, mainly from school rationalization, during the course of the five/six year cycle leading up to 1997/98. Changes in the structure of the second level system lead to movement between schools and between sectors.

4. While it was not possible to take account of the incidence of repeat Leaving Certificates in 1980 and 1986 our estimates suggest that retention improved by more than twenty per cent over this period. Our estimates suggest a further improvement of about thirteen per cent between 1986 and 1992 (Clancy 1995:82) and a further increase of about eleven per cent between 1992 and 1998.

5. For the purpose of this analysis it is assumed that the best overall result is that which was achieved in the most recent year in which at least six subjects were taken.

6. In this table no differentiation is made between the two separate Home Economics programmes or the separate Music and Musicianship programmes. In addition, as noted in the text, the 'Other Languages' group combines those taking Greek, Dutch, Danish and Portuguese.

7. Economic History stands as an exception to this generalization.

8. While these distributions afford us the optimum comparison the distributions are not strict comparators. For the higher education entrants the total on which the percentages in each attainment category are calculated is based on the number for whom examination data were available for at least five subjects. The total on which the relevant percentages for the Leaving Certificate cohort are calculated is the number of Leaving Certificate candidates who presented in each subject. Since a small number of candidates present in only one or very few Leaving Certificate subjects and since these are included in the aggregate result for each subject this distribution is a slight overestimate of the take-up rate for each subject.

9. Admission to Colleges of Art and Design is determined by the quality of Portfolio presented by students, in addition to Leaving Certificate grades.

chapter five | Rates of Admission to Higher Education

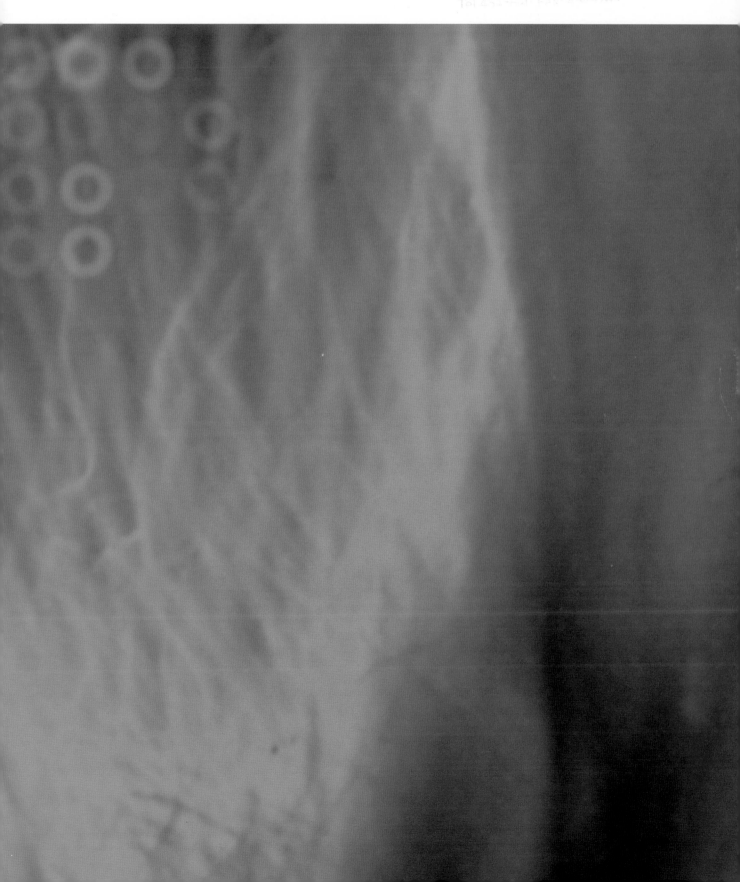

Admission to Colleges in the Republic of Ireland

An important objective of this study and of the three previous national surveys was to calculate precise participation rates at national and county level. It is felt that trends in participation are best measured by 'admission rates' rather than by 'enrolment rates', The latter are calculated by relating total enrolments to the population of the age group to which 70–80 per cent of students belong. However, these enrolment rates provide only a crude index of participation since the actual rates are as much influenced by the duration of courses and the age distribution of the student population as by the actual number of students enrolled. In contrast, admission rates provide a less ambiguous indicator since they are calculated solely on the basis of the flow of new entrants. A further refinement necessary in the calculation of precise admission rates is the exclusion of first year students who were previously enrolled on a third level course in an earlier year[1]. Following the practice first established by the OECD (1972) admission rates are calculated on the basis of the average of the populations of the single years of age from which more than seventy-five per cent of the new entrants come.

In the present study the permanent home address of each student was recorded. A total of 554 students were foreign students while a further 255 were from Northern Ireland. These students were excluded from this part of the analysis leaving 31,915 students from the Republic of Ireland.

On the basis of our analysis of the age of new entrants (see Chapter 2) we calculated their age at the time of the 1996 Census of Population. The great majority of them would have been aged 15 and 16 at this time. Thus, half of the number of persons in this two-year cohort represented the denominator on which rates of admission to higher education were calculated. Table 43 presents, for each county and for the country as a whole, the number of new entrants to higher education together with the size of the relevant age cohort on which admission rates were calculated. It also shows the resultant admission rates for 1998 and, for comparative purposes, the 1992, 1986 and 1980 admission rates.

TABLE 43 RATES OF ADMISSION TO HIGHER EDUCATION BY COUNTY IN 1998 WITH COMPARATIVE DATA FOR 1992, 1986 AND 1980

COUNTY	1998 NEW ENTRANTS	SIZE OF AGE COHORT	ADMISSION RATE 1998	ADMISSION RATE 1992	ADMISSION RATE 1986	ADMISSION RATE 1980
Carlow	387	872	.444	.392	.32	.29
Dublin	7,118	18,876	.377	.328	.20	.17
Kildare	1,189	2,891	.411	.349	.24	.16
Kilkenny	634	1,551	.409	.321	.27	.20
Laois	433	1,124	.385	.311	.23	.15
Longford	343	699	.491	.376	.30	.21
Louth	833	1,954	.426	.350	.25	.23
Meath	1,110	2,446	.454	.366	.25	.16
Offaly	518	1,370	.378	.317	.20	.15
Westmeath	675	1,379	.489	.379	.31	.20
Wexford	984	2,246	.438	.342	.22	.18
Wicklow	865	2,109	.410	.366	.23	.18
Clare	966	1,933	.500	.429	.30	.20
Cork	3,999	8174	.489	.372	.28	.22
Kerry	1,319	2,502	.527	.433	.35	.25
Limerick	1,665	3,308	.503	.374	.27	.20
Tipperary	1,360	2,801	.486	.362	.27	.19
Waterford	786	1,909	.412	.325	.28	.23
Galway	2,147	3,788	.567	.460	.33	.28
Leitrim	252	477	.528	.420	.34	.19
Mayo	1,275	2,288	.557	.422	.31	.23
Roscommon	542	1,080	.502	.409	.28	.20
Sligo	609	1,096	.556	.419	.35	.25
Cavan	487	1,076	.453	.334	.24	.16
Donegal	962	2,744	.351	.274	.19	.21
Monaghan	457	1,122	.407	.273	.24	.16
TOTAL	**31,915**	**71,808**	**.444**	**.359**	**.25**	**.20**

For the country as a whole the rate of admission to higher education was forty-four per cent. This rate represents a significant increase on the 1992 (36%), 1986 (25%) and 1980 (20%) rates. The rates varied significantly by county. Galway had the highest rate of admission at an impressive fifty-seven per cent. Seven other counties had admission rates of over fifty per cent. These were in descending order: Mayo (56%), Sligo (56%), Leitrim (53%), Kerry (53%), Limerick, Roscommon and Clare, each at fifty per cent. Donegal had the lowest rates of admission at thirty-five per cent. Three other counties had admission rates of less than forty per cent. In ascending order these were: Dublin (38%) Offaly (38%) and Laois (39%). Other counties with relatively low rates were, Monaghan, Kilkenny, Wicklow, Kildare and Waterford, all of which had admission rates of forty-one per cent. These differential county admission rates are illustrated on a map (Figure 1). A clear regional pattern is evident. The eight counties with admission rates in excess of fifty per cent are all from the West, the five Connaught counties, Kerry, Limerick and Clare. In contrast, the counties with the lowest rates are two of the three Ulster counties (Donegal and Monaghan), Dublin, the Midland counties of Laois and Offaly, two counties from the East (Wicklow, and Kildare) and two counties from the South-East (Kilkenny, and Waterford).

Figure 1.

Rates of Admission by County

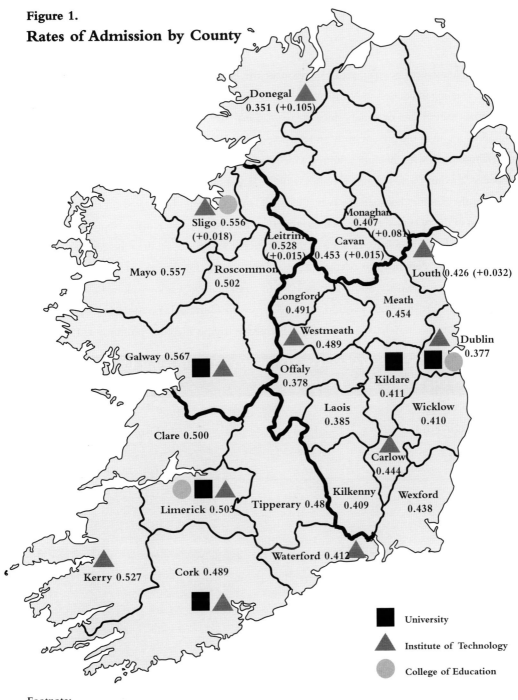

Donegal
0.351 (+0.105)

Sligo 0.556
(+0.018)

Leitrim
0.528
(+0.015)

Monaghan
0.407
(+0.081)

Cavan
0.453 (+0.015)

Mayo 0.557

Roscommon
0.502

Louth 0.426 (+0.032)

Longford
0.491

Meath
0.454

Galway 0.567

Westmeath
0.489

Dublin
0.377

Offaly
0.378

Kildare
0.411

Wicklow
0.410

Clare 0.500

Laois
0.385

Carlow
0.444

Limerick 0.503

Tipperary 0.48

Kilkenny
0.409

Wexford
0.438

Kerry 0.527

Cork 0.489

Waterford 0.412

■ University

▲ Institute of Technology

● College of Education

Footnote:

The admission rates shown are those calculated on the basis of admission to colleges in the Republic of Ireland. However, where the rate of admission is altered by more than one percentage point, by the inclusion of students admitted to colleges in Northern Ireland, the consequent increases are shown in parentheses.

While there are special circumstances governing the situation of the border counties because of the significant flow of students from the Republic going to colleges in Northern Ireland (which we will examine below) it is of interest to monitor the relative changes in participation rates by county since the last national survey. Figure 2 presents a crosstabulation between the county admission rates found in the present study and those found in 1992. For the purpose of the crosstabulation both variables have been trichotomised with the nine counties, which have the highest rates being designated as "high", the next eight counties classified as "medium" and the nine counties with the lowest rates classified as "low". If there were no changes in the relative ranking of the counties between the two studies, all counties would be located on the diagonal. This is the case in respect of eighteen of the twenty-six counties indicating that there is, indeed, a remarkable consistency between the findings of the two surveys as far as the relative ranking of the counties is concerned. Of the nine counties with the highest participation rates in 1992 seven continued to occupy this position in 1998. Of the two counties which changed their ranking Westmeath slipped by a single place from ninth in 1992 to tenth in 1998. Carlow's altered position in the ranking is more significant: in 1992 it was in eighth position, in 1998 it was in fourteenth position. In contrast, Limerick and Longford improved their relative position having both being classified as having 'medium' positions in 1992.

FIGURE 2   RELATIVE COUNTRY RATES OF ADMISSION TO HIGHER EDUCATION IN 1998 BY RATES OF ADMISSION IN 1992

Admission Rates to Higher Education		High	1998 Medium	Low
1992	High	Galway Mayo Sligo Leitrim Kerry Roscommon Clare	Westmeath Carlow	
	Medium	Limerick Longford	Cork Tipperary Meath Louth	Kildare Wicklow
	Low		Cavan Wexford	Waterford Kilkenny Monaghan Laois Offaly Dublin Donegal

There is also little evidence of change in relative ranking when we look at those counties with low rates of admission to higher education. Of the nine counties which had low admission rate to higher education in 1992, seven of them had a similar relative ranking in 1998. Two counties, Cavan and Wexford improved their relative postions over the period, having moved from having 'low' admission rates in 1992 to having 'medium' rates in 1998. Their relative improvement has been at the expense of Kildare and Wicklow, both of which were designated as having 'low' admission rates in 1998 in contrast to their designation as 'medium' in 1992.

Admission to Colleges in Northern Ireland

The foregoing description of the rates of admission to higher education relates only to those students who were admitted to colleges in the Republic of Ireland. However, an important feature of Irish higher education in recent years has been the significant flow of students going to Northern Ireland colleges. The increasing propensity to travel outside the state to avail of higher education is partly a consequence of the 1986 European Court ruling which defined the terms under which students could avail of higher education in other countries of the European Union. While the reintroduction of student tuition fees in the Great Britain and Northern Ireland and the elimination of tuition fees for undergraduate students in the Republic of Ireland has altered the opportunity structure in the different jurisdictions there continues to be a significant movement of students from the Republic of Ireland to the United Kingdom especially to Northern Ireland colleges. This latter flow was examined in the 1986 and 1992 studies and was also included as part of this study.

Aggregate data were provided by the Department of Education in Northern Ireland on the flow of students from the Republic of Ireland admitted on the first year of undergraduate courses to colleges in Northern Ireland. Following this each of the colleges, which was identified as having some students from the Republic, was contacted to identify the number of students from the Republic of Ireland among its first year undergraduate enrolment. The county of origin of these students was identified. In all the colleges identified a total of 649 students. Predictably the two universities, which are the main providers of higher education in Northern Ireland, enrolled the majority of these students. The University of Ulster was the main provider with almost half (326) the total. Queen's University, Belfast was the next largest provider (169) followed by the North West Institute (89). Both of the Colleges of Education had some students, St. Mary's (15) and Stranmillis (4). Finally four other Colleges of Further and Higher Education had some students from the Republic of Ireland: these were distributed as follows: Belfast Institute (27); Fermanagh College (11); Newry and Kilkeel Institute (7); and North Down & Ards Institute (1).

Table 44 shows the distribution, by county of origin, of new entrants on the first year of an undergraduate programme to colleges in Northern Ireland. This table also shows the impact that the inclusion of these students has on the rates of admission to higher education. However since the focus of this study is on first time entrants to higher education and since these figures are likely to include some who had previously been enrolled in a third level college (estimated to be about eight per cent), the figures for each county were adjusted downward by eight per cent. It is evident from Table 44 that while all counties, with the exception of Carlow, had some first year students in colleges in Northern Ireland there is a distinct regional pattern in the student flow. Almost half the students came from Donegal (315) with significant numbers also coming from two of the other boarder counties of Monaghan (98) and Louth (66). The changes in admission rates consequent on the inclusion of these students are particularly important in the case of Donegal (+10.5), Monaghan (+8.1), and Louth (+3.2). In addition the following counties show an increase in admission rate of at least one percentage point when students in Northern colleges are included in the calculations: Sligo (+1.8), Cavan (+1.5) and Leitrim (1.5).

TABLE 44 DISTRIBUTION OF HIGHER EDUCATION ENTRANTS FROM THE REPUBLIC OF IRELAND WHO ENROLLED IN NORTHERN IRELAND COLLEGES WITH CONSEQUENT CHANGES IN ADMISSION RATES BY COUNTY

COUNTY	Number of New Entrants	Admission Rate Excluding Students in Northern Colleges	Admission Rate Including Students in Northern Colleges **	Changes in Admission Rates
Carlow	0	.444	.444	0.0
Dublin	25	.377	.378	0.1
Kildare	8	.411	.414	0.3
Kilkenny	4	.409	.411	0.2
Laois	0	.385	.385	0.0
Longford	1	.491	.492	0.1
Louth	66	.426	.458	3.2
Meath	10	.454	.458	0.4
Offaly	1	.378	.379	0.1
Westmeath	4	.489	.492	0.3
Wexford	7	.438	.441	0.3
Wicklow	5	.410	.413	0.3
Clare	1	.500	.500	0.0
Cork	7	.489	.490	0.1
Kerry	2	.527	.528	0.1
Limerick	4	.503	.505	0.2
Tipperary	2	.486	.472	0.0
Waterford	1	.412	.412	0.0
Galway	15	.567	.571	0.4
Leitrim	8	.528	.543	1.5
Mayo	7	.557	.560	0.3
Roscommon	5	.502	.506	0.4
Sligo	22	.556	.574	1.8
Cavan	18	.453	.468	1.5
Donegal	315	.351	.456	10.5
Monaghan	98	.407	.488	8.1
TOTAL	**649 ★**	**.444**	**.453**	**0.9**

★ *The total includes 13 students who were known to come from the Republic of Ireland but for whom home address was unavailable*

** *Before calculating the revised admission rates the number of entrants to Northern Ireland has been adjusted downwards by eight per cent to take account of those with previous third level education.*

While the inclusion in our calculations of students going to Northern colleges in not particularly significant, nationally, with an increase of less than one percentage point in the overall admission rate, it is, as we have demonstrated, highly significant for some counties. This requires us to modify our findings in respect of the ranking of counties on overall admission rates. Donegal and Monaghan now join the other boarder counties of Louth and Cavan within 'medium' admission rates. In the case of Donegal it moves from the bottom to tenth place in the ranking of counties while in the case of Monaghan it moves from twenty-second to twelfth place in the ranking. The net effect of the inclusion of data from colleges in Northern Ireland is to sharpen the regional differentiation in admission rates. Dublin now has the lowest overall rate of admission to higher education and all of the counties in the lower third of the ranking now come from the East, Midlands and South East. These are in ascending order Dublin, Offaly, Laois, Kilkenny, Waterford, Wicklow, Kildare, Wexford and Carlow.

Admission Rates by Type of College

Returning to our main focus on rates of admission to colleges within the Republic of Ireland we now examine variability between counties in the rates of admission to the different college types. Table 45 displays the relative ranking of counties in the admission rates to the different forms of higher education. The range of variation by county for each college type is larger than the rate for higher education as a whole. The rate of admission to the universities is highest in Galway, Cork, Clare and Limerick. In each of these countries more than a quarter of the age cohort enrolled on university programmes. Kerry, Longford and Tipperary also had admission rates to university which were in excess of the average rate for the country as a whole. At the other end of the distribution Donegal, Louth, Monaghan, Offaly, Waterford and Laois had rates of admission to university that were well below the average for the state as a whole. However if the flow of students into Northern Ireland universities were taken into account the rates for Monaghan (19.1) and Donegal (17.3) would be closer to the overall national rate. In these circumstances the counties with the lowest rates of admission to university education would be Offaly, Waterford, Louth, Laois, Wexford, Carlow and Kilkenny.

Turning to the rate of admission to the Institute of Technology sector the counties with the highest rates of admission were Mayo, Sligo, and Leitrim each of which had more than thirty per cent of the age cohort admitted to this sector. Westmeath, Louth, Roscomnom, Galway and Kerry also had high rates of admission to this sector. It would appear that proximity to a college within the county or in an adjacent county is an important determinant (see discussion in next chapter). The counties with the lowest rates of admission to this sector were Dublin, Wicklow, Kildare, Laois and Kilkenny.

TABLE 45   RELATIVE RANKING OF COUNTIES ON RATES OF ADMISSION TO HIGHER EDUCATION BY TYPE OF COLLEGE

All Colleges		Universities		Institutes of Technology		Colleges of Education		Other Colleges	
Galway	.567	Galway	.263	Mayo	.326	Sligo	.038	Dublin	.034
Mayo	.557	Cork	.255	Sligo	.314	Mayo	.036	Wicklow	.032
Sligo	.556	Clare	.253	Leitrim	.304	Roscommon	.029	Kildare	.027
Leitrim	.528	Limerick	.251	Westmeath	.287	Monaghan	.026	Meath	.020
Kerry	.527	Kerry	.230	Louth	.282	Tipperary	.024	Limerick	.018
Limerick	.503	Longford	.210	Roscommon	.282	Kilkenny	.023	Leitrim	.017
Roscommon	.502	Tipperary	.210	Galway	.280	Kerry	.020	Sligo	.015
Clare	.500	Leitrim	.191	Kerry	.271	Cavan	.020	Louth	.013
Longford	.491	Mayo	.189	Longford	.261	Clare	.019	Tipperary	.013
Westmeath	.489	Sligo	.189	Cavan	.252	Carlow	.018	Kilkenny	.012
Cork	.489	Wicklow	.186	Carlow	.251	Wexford	.018	Westmeath	.012
Tipperary	.486	Dublin	.185	Wexford	.245	Galway	.018	Wexford	.012
Meath	.454	Westmeath	.183	Meath	.243	Leitrim	.017	Monaghan	.012
Cavan	.453	Roscommon	.183	Monaghan	.243	Meath	.015	Carlow	.011
Carlow	.444	Kildare	.180	Waterford	.242	Limerick	.015	Clare	.010
Wexford	.438	Meath	.176	Tipperary	.238	Longford	.014	Waterford	.010
Louth	.426	Cavan	.170	Donegal	.237	Donegal	.014	Cavan	.010
Waterford	.412	Kilkenny	.165	Offaly	.230	Laois	.013	Laois	.008
Kildare	.411	Carlow	.163	Limerick	.220	Wicklow	.011	Offaly	.007
Wicklow	.410	Wexford	.163	Clare	.217	Cork	.011	Cork	.007
Kilkenny	.409	Laois	.159	Cork	.217	Kildare	.010	Kerry	.007
Monaghan	.407	Waterford	.151	Kilkenny	.209	Dublin	.009	Mayo	.007
Laois	.385	Offaly	.132	Laois	.205	Louth	.009	Roscommon	.007
Offaly	.378	Monaghan	.126	Kildare	.194	Offaly	.009	Longford	.006
Dublin	.377	Louth	.122	Wicklow	.181	Westmeath	.009	Galway	.006
Donegal	.351	Donegal	.096	Dublin	.148	Waterford	.009	Donegal	.003
State	.444	State	.195	State	.217	State	.015	State	.018

In contrast with the situation in the other sectors the county rate of admission to colleges of education is not sensitive to location. While eight of the ten (including private) Colleges of Education are located in Dublin, it shares with Waterford, Westmeath, Offaly and Louth the lowest level of admission to this sector. In contrast, with the exception of Sligo, none of the counties with the highest rate of admission to this sector has a college located within the county.

With the exception of the Shannon College of Hotel Management and three small business colleges (two in Limerick and one in Cork) all of the colleges in the 'Other Colleges' sector are located in the Dublin area. Thus, it is no surprise that Dublin and the adjacent counties of Wicklow, Kildare and Meath have the highest admission rates to these colleges. However, given the relatively small size of this sector, in nine counties these colleges cater for less than one per cent of the age cohort.

More comprehensive data on the pattern of recruitment to all colleges is provided in the Appendix. Table A28 shows the distribution of students by county of permanent residence for each of the forty-five colleges. These data make possible a more detailed exploration of the relationship between county of origin and higher education college. A multivariate analysis of these data is presented in the next chapter.

The Dublin Region

In our analysis of regional variations in the rate of admission to higher education in this and the three previous national surveys the county has been the main unit of analysis. However it is acknowledged that counties are not homogenous regions and that aggregate county rates mask large differences between areas. This is especially the case in a densely populated county such as Dublin, which is especially heterogeneous in terms of its economic and social conditions. An earlier study examined differential participation rates in higher education from different parts of Dublin city and county (Clancy and Benson, 1979). In addition the 1980 national survey included some analysis of intra-county variability in admission to higher education through an examination of variations by Rural and Urban districts in three counties, Wexford, Tipperary and Mayo (Clancy, 1988). More recently, the report on the 1992 survey (Clancy, 1995) contained a detailed analysis of participation by postal district in the Dublin area. This was complemented by research for the Technical Working Group on the Future Development of Higher Education where Professor Sexton, using CAO/CAS data for 1993, examined variations in the pattern of applications, offers, acceptances and admissions to higher education by area of Dublin city and county (Technical Working Group, 1995). This section of the chapter seeks to contribute to this body of data on intra-county variability in admission to higher education.

The present analysis is based on an examination of the address records of all those students whose county of permanent residence was Dublin. Those from Dublin city are disaggregated by Postal Districts, while those from Dublin county are treated as a separate category. Because of coding difficulties we have not attempted to provide a definitive disaggregation of the county enrolment into the three new county council areas of Dun Laoghaire/Rathdown, South Dublin and Fingal although tentative estimates are provided. Having successfully classified all higher education entrants from Dublin2 into the appropriate area code we faced a particular difficulty in the identification of the size of the relevant age cohort in each area. Since the postal districts do not coincide with the District Electoral Districts or Wards it was necessary to estimate population data for each Postal District3. As was the case in the analysis of county and national admission rates the denominator in the calculation of admission rates by Postal District was half the number of persons aged 15 and 16 at the time of the 1991 Census.

Table 46 presents the distribution of higher education entrants by postal district. The districts north and south of the city are shown separately as well as that for County Dublin. Five of the districts in the south of the city have admission rates in excess of fifty per cent. The district with highest admission rates was Dublin 18 with an impressive seventy-seven per cent. This was followed by Dublin 6 (70%), Dublin 14 (68%), Dublin 4 (59%) and Dublin 16 (56%). 4%). Dublin County also had an admission rate of fifty per cent. Our tentative estimates suggest that the rate is especially high in South Dublin (74%) while Fingal and Dun Laoghaire-Rathdown have rates of less than fifty per cent. Only one district in the North city (Dublin 3) had an admission rate of more than fifty per cent (54%) although in Dublin 15 and Dublin 9 the rates exceeded forty per cent. In contrast, to these areas with high participation rates districts with the lowest participation rates were Dublin 10 (7%), Dublin 17 (8%) and the North Inner City (9%). Other districts with admission rates which were less than half the average for Dublin City and County were Dublin 22 (13%), Dublin 11 (14%), and Dublin 20 (17%). These differential admission rates are illustrated on Figure 3. What is clear from the graphical representation is that the pattern of admission to higher education reflects the socio-economic patterning of the population, which has been mapped from Census of Population data in a number of studies, most recently by McManus and Brady (1994).

TABLE 46 RATES OF ADMISSION TO HIGHER EDUCATION IN DUBLIN BY POSTAL DISTRICTS

Postal Districts	Higher Education Entrants	Size of Age Cohort	Rate of Admission ★
1 North Inner City	17	205	.089
3 (Clontarf – Marino)	190	376	.544
5 (Raheny – Harmonstown)	268	752	.383
7 (Cabra – Arran Quay)	110	597	.198
9 (Whitehall – Beaumont)	261	701	.401
11 (Finglas – Ballymun)	161	1222	.142
13 (Howth – Sutton)	337	911	.398
15 (Castleknock – Blanchardstown)	472	1253	.405
17 (Priorswood – Darndale)	35	448	.084
2 South Inner City	21	116	.195
4 (Ballsbridge – Donnybrook)	156	283	.593
6 (Rathmines – Terenure)	481	735	.704
8 (Kilmainham – Inchicore)	72	366	.212
10 (Ballyfermot – Chapelizod)	25	377	.071
12 (Crumlin – Kimmage)	170	917	.199
14 (Rathfarnham – Clonskeagh)	351	552	.684
16 (Ballyboden – Ballinteer)	590	1144	.555
18 (Foxrock – Glencullen)	336	469	.771
20 (Palmerstown)	73	455	.173
22 (Clondalkin – Neilstown)	142	1204	.127
24 (Tallaght – Firhouse)	426	1755	.261
Dublin County ★★★	1883	4046	.501
Dublin City and County	7,118★	18,876★★	.377

★ *The total number of entrants includes 541 students whose precise address was unknown. In calculating admission rates these have been redistributed between the districts on a pro rata basis.*

★★ *The totals add up to 18,884 because of rounding errors.*

★★★ *Although this may be subject to some margin of error a separate analysis of the three counties, Dublin Fingal, Dublin South and Dun Laoghaire-Rathdown, suggests that the admission rates were: Dublin South - 74% : Dublin Fingal - 49%: and Dun Laoghaire-Rathdown - 47%.*

Figure 3.
Rates of Admission to Higher Education in Dublin by Postal Direct.

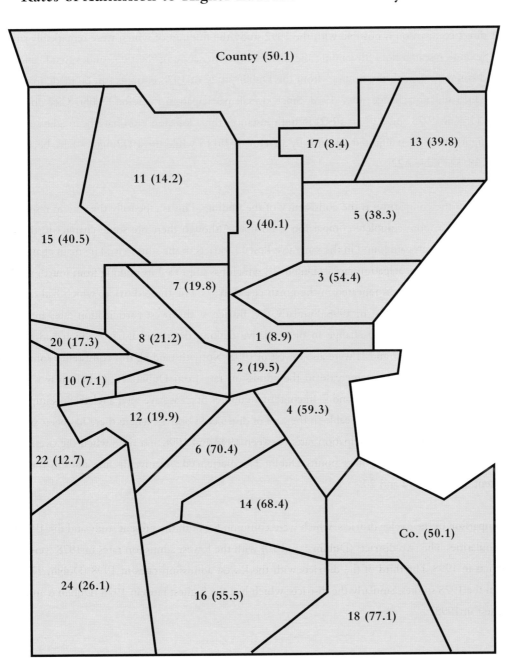

It is of interest to compare these findings on the geographical origin of third-level entrants from Dublin with the findings of previous studies. A direct comparison is possible with the 1992 study, the findings of which were remarkably similar to those from Professor Sexton's research notwithstanding the slightly different scope of the two studies (see Clancy, 1995: 117). A more restricted comparison with the findings from the Dublin study of 1978 entrants can be made in respect of those postal districts which did not change since 1978. Since overall participation rates for Dublin City and County differed for each study (15% in 1978 and 32% in 1992) in both instances the admission rates have been adjusted to 1998 equivalents. The 1978 figures have been adjusted upwards by a factor of 38/15 while the 1992 figures have been adjusted upwards by a factor of 38/32 (Table A22).

The most striking feature of the comparison is the consistency of the findings. This is especially the case in respect of the 1992 and 1993 studies where a more complete comparison is possible. Although there are some changes in the relative ranking the highest participation rates are found in the same five Postal Districts in the south city. The main change within these districts is the increase in the participation rate in Dublin 18 which has improved its ranking from fourth in 1992 to first in 1998. This pattern of consistency is repeated in the north city districts. The three districts, which had the highest participation rates in 1992, were also highest in 1998. Similarly, the districts with lowest participation rates are common for both studies. While there has been some change in their relative ranking the three districts which had the lowest participation rates in 1998 (Dublin 10, 17 and 1) were also lowest in 1992. Notwithstanding this consistency some changes are evident. We have already noted the large increase in the admission rate from Dublin 18. Other areas which have improved their rates are postal districts 2, 13, 5, 6, and 7. In contrast a number of areas have seen a relative dissimprovement in their participation rates. This is especially noticeable in the case of districts 11 and 22 where there has been an absolute decline of three percentage points4 in the participation rates between 1992 and 1998 at a time when the overall rate for Dublin city and county increased by six percentage points. Dublin 24 experienced a relative decline and this was also true though to a lesser extent in districts 12 and 20.

The more limited comparison of the twelve districts, which were common for both the present study and the 1978 survey, also reveals striking similarities. The two districts (Dublin 1 and 10) with the lowest admission rates in 1978 were amongst the three lowest districts in 1998. The third of the districts with the lowest admission rates in 1998 (Dublin 17) was not identified seperately in the 1978 studies. Similarly the districts, which had the highest rates in 1978 (Dublin 6 and 4), were still amongst the highest in 1998.

The final aspect of our analysis of the pattern of admission to higher education in Dublin examines the intra-county variability in the type of higher education on which students enrol. We have already noted that low level of admission to higher education is Dublin is characterized by a particular deficit in access to courses in the Institute of Technology sector. While the rate of admission to courses in the university sector is only marginally below the national average, the rate of admission to the IT sector is about a third below the national average (see Table 45 above). This is not a recent phenomenon having been noted in the reports on the earlier surveys and also noted in the Report of the Technical Working Group on the Future Development of Higher Education. The latter report in addition to documenting the low admission rates to Certificate and Diploma programmes also noted how access to different forms of higher education

TABLE 47	RATES OF ADMISSION TO HIGHER EDUCATION IN DUBLIN BY POSTAL DISRICTS AND LEVEL OF STUDY		
Postal Districts	Degree Admission Rate	Non-Degree Admission Rate	Ratio of Degree/ Non Degree
1 North Inner City	.032	.058	0.6
3 (Clontarf – Marino)	.388	.161	2.4
5 (Raheny – Harmonstown)	.233	.151	1.5
7 (Cabra – Arran Quay)	.099	.099	1.0
9 (Whitehall – Beaumont)	.256	.142	1.8
11 (Finglas – Ballymun)	.065	.073	0.9
13 (Howth – Sutton)	.262	.138	1.9
15 (Castleknock – Blanchardstown)	.276	.128	2.2
17 (Priorswood – Darndale)	.031	.053	0.6
2 South Inner City	.168	.028	6.0
4 (Ballsbridge – Donnybrook)	.473	.122	3.9
6 (Rathmines – Terenure)	.526	.178	3.0
8 (Kilmainham – Inchicore)	.103	.109	0.9
10 (Ballyfermot – Chapelizod)	.037	.034	1.1
12 (Crumlin – Kimmage)	.100	.100	1.0
14 (Rathfarnham – Clonskeagh)	.487	.200	2.4
16 (Ballyboden – Ballinteer)	.355	.200	1.8
18 (Foxrock – Glencullen)	.601	.173	3.5
20 (Palmerstown)	.090	.083	1.1
22 (Clondalkin – Neilstown)	.053	.074	0.7
24 (Tallaght – Firhouse)	.102	.159	0.6
Dublin County	.337	.164	2.1
Dublin City and County	**.234**	**.142**	**1.6**

varied by district within Dublin city and county. This report also pointed to the greater variability in admission rates on to degree level courses. This intra-county variability by level of course is examined in Table 47.

It is evident from Table 47 that the ratio of degree to non-degree students is significantly higher in Dublin (1.6) than for the country as a whole (1.2, see Table 8 in Chapter 2 above). This confirms the finding reported by the Technical Working Group and is also consistent with the findings from the two previous national surveys which pointed to a shortage of sub-degree places in Dublin. Table 47 also demonstrates that the variability in admission rates by postal district is significantly greater for degree programmes than for non-degree programmes. In respect of degree admission rates the range is from three to sixty per cent of the age cohort. In contrast, the range in admission rates for non-degree programmes is from three to twenty per cent. However, perhaps the most interesting feature of Table 47 is the way in which the ratio of degree to non-degree entrants varies by the socio-economic patterning of the population. This ratio is highest (6.0) in Dublin 2 and is 3.0 or over in the more affluent areas of Dublin 4, Dublin 18 and Dublin 6. In contrast, this ratio is less than 1.0 in Dublin 1, 17, 24, 22, 11 and 8. This aggregate analysis appears to confirm the findings from the individualised data. Areas with a high concentration of lower socio-economic groups tend to have low overall admission rates to higher education and for those who are admitted to higher education they are significantly more likely to enrol in the non-university sector.

Footnotes

1. It will be recalled from our discussion in Chapter 1 that the focus on 'new entrants' excludes repeat students and those who were previously enrolled in higher education on another programme. It was established that the number of new entrants was about seven per cent less than the number of first year students. Thus, as is frequently the case in both national and cross country comparisons, estimates of admission rates to higher education made on the basis of first year enrolments will be some percentage points higher than those based on 'new entrants' to higher education.

2. For 541 students it was not possible to identify the precise address. In the calculation of admission rates these have been redistributed between the districts on a pro rata basis.

3. The author is indebted to Professor Jerry Sexton who kindly supplied data, which assisted in the preparation of these estimates for each Postal District. The estimates were made with the help of maps provided by the Central Statistics Office. Since there are 322 DEDs or Wards and only 22 Postal Districts most DEDs fell wholly within Postal Districts. The need for estimation only arose where the Postal District boundaries cut across DEDs; in these cases the maps, which included housing details, provided the basis for a proportionate allocation of the population of the DEDs to the different postal districts.

4. In 1992 the participation rates for Dublin 11 and 22 were 17.5 and 15.6, respectively (Clancy, 1995:115).

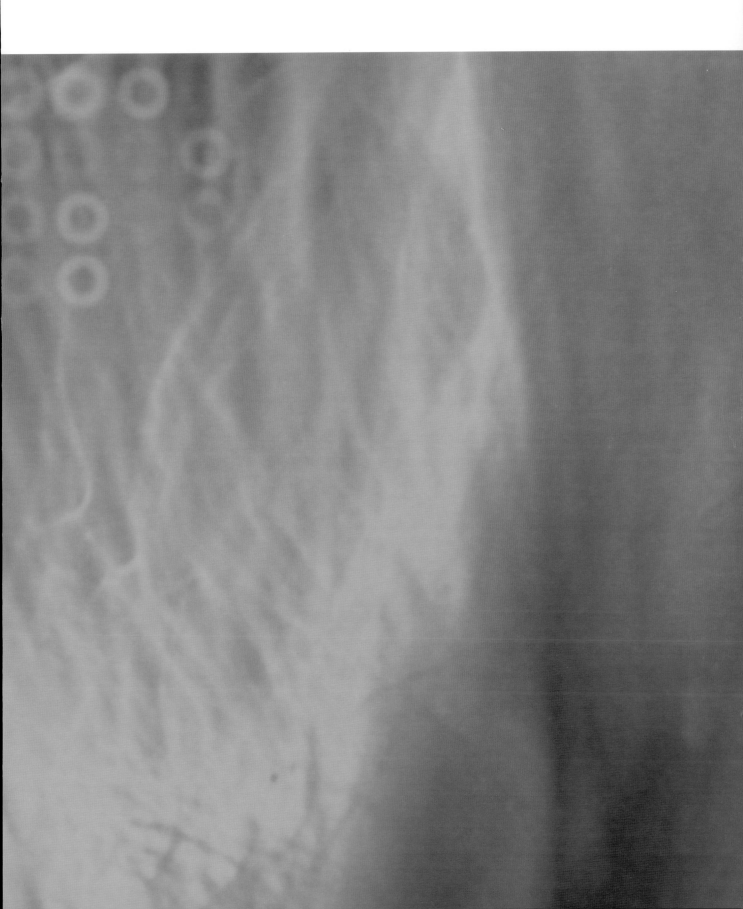

chapter six | Correlates of Differential County Admission Rates

An important objective of this and of the previous surveys has been the documentation of regional disparities in admission rates to higher education. The findings from the present study, as described in the previous chapter, are explored further in this chapter. First, an attempt is made to find an explanation for the differential county admission rates. In addition, some of the implications of these differential rates are explored.

The main focus of the chapter is on a multivariate analysis of factors related to varying county admission rates. Three groups of variables are examined as possible predictors of county admission rates. The variables used involve measures of the distance from the nearest college, the pattern of participation at second-level and some socio-economic characteristics of the population of each county. In all thirteen variables were chosen as possible predictors of differential admission rates. Initially these variables are individually correlated with county admission rates, following which multiple regression is used to ascertain which variables, considered separately and collectively, best account for differences in county admission rates.

In addition to the thirteen variables taken into account in the regression analysis, three other correlates are considered in this chapter: level of socio-economic group inequality, proportion of students in receipt of financial aid and level of prior academic attainment. These variables cannot be considered as predictors and may more appropriately be viewed as possible consequences of the pattern of admission to higher education. Before proceeding with this analysis the county admission rates are disaggregated by gender and differences in these data on the basis of this classification are briefly discussed.

County Admission Rates by Gender

Before examining possible correlates of county admission rates it is necessary to take account of the implications of the findings already presented. It has been demonstrated in the previous chapter that in addition to the variability between counties in the overall rate of admission to higher education the pattern of variability differs markedly between the various higher education sectors. For example, there was no correlation between the county admission rates to the university sector and institute of technology sectors $(r = .01)$[1]. The pattern becomes further differentiated when gender is introduced as a variable. The correlation between overall male and female admission rates was .74. Thus, in any attempt to explain differential county admission rates it is desirable to carry out separate analysis by gender and sector. For the purpose of this analysis we are primarily concerned with admission rates to the university and the technological sectors. Data in respect of the admission to the Colleges of Education and the heterogeneous 'Other Colleges' sector are not included in the multivariate analysis. The numbers admitted to these sectors are small and our experience in the earlier surveys has been that we have failed to account for inter-county variation in admission rates to these sectors. However these data are included in Table 48 which shows the rates of admission to the different sectors by county and gender.

The differentiation by gender reveals a number of interesting findings. First, we note that while, as previously reported (see Chapter 2), females constituted a slight majority (52.7%) of higher education entrants to the country as whole, the female majority is more pronounced when we look at differences between the male and female admission rates. The female admission rate exceeds the male rate by more than seven percentage points. This is explained by the slightly larger size of the male cohort (36,976 versus 34,832). With the exception of Leitrim the female rate of admission exceeds the male rate in all counties. The female differential is largest (+17%) in Carlow and exceed fifteen percentage points in four other counties: Kilkenny, Longford, Wexford and Sligo. The female advantage is smallest in Dublin, Donegal and Waterford.

Looking separately at the university sector females have higher rates of admission in all counties. The largest differentials in favour of females were found in Clare, Cork, Cavan, Laois and Wexford while the smallest differentials were found in Donegal, Mayo and Leitrim. Turning to the Institute of Technology sector we note that, for the country as a whole the gender differential favours males. This male majority is reproduced in seventeen counties. In the remaining counties females are in the majority although in most cases the gender differentials are quite small in this sector, exceeding five percentage points in only three counties. For two of these, Cork (+9%) and Tipperary (+7%) males are in the majority while in the case of Kilkenny (+5%) females have the highest admission rate. In each of the other sectors females have higher admission rates. Predictably, given the size of the female differential of nine to one in the Colleges of Education sector this majority is reproduced in all counties. Although the female advantage in the 'Other Colleges' sector is more modest it is reproduced on all counties with the exception of five.

TABLE 48   RATES OF ADMISSION TO HIGHER EDUCATION BY COUNTY, GENDER AND HIGHER EDUCATION SECTOR

County	Universities		Institutes of Technology		Colleges of Education		Other Colleges		All Higher Education	
	Male	Female	Male	Female	Male	Female	Male	Female	Male	Female
Carlow	0.120	0.211	0.240	0.264	0.000	0.039	0.004	0.019	0.364	0.533
Dublin	0.154	0.219	0.167	0.128	0.002	0.016	0.034	0.035	0.357	0.398
Kildare	0.142	0.226	0.205	0.180	0.001	0.022	0.023	0.031	0.371	0.459
Kilkenny	0.125	0.209	0.184	0.235	0.005	0.041	0.015	0.009	0.329	0.494
Laois	0.112	0.210	0.215	0.194	0.005	0.022	0.003	0.013	0.335	0.439
Longford	0.158	0.271	0.255	0.267	0.003	0.028	0.003	0.009	0.419	0.575
Louth	0.091	0.154	0.278	0.286	0.003	0.016	0.013	0.014	0.385	0.470
Meath	0.137	0.218	0.265	0.219	0.001	0.030	0.018	0.022	0.421	0.489
Offaly	0.104	0.162	0.225	0.236	0.003	0.016	0.006	0.008	0.338	0.422
Westmeath	0.160	0.207	0.286	0.288	0.001	0.016	0.014	0.009	0.461	0.520
Wexford	0.116	0.212	0.236	0.255	0.005	0.031	0.005	0.020	0.362	0.518
Wicklow	0.148	0.225	0.194	0.168	0.004	0.019	0.035	0.029	0.381	0.441
Clare	0.194	0.315	0.222	0.213	0.002	0.035	0.003	0.018	0.421	0.581
Cork	0.198	0.315	0.258	0.172	0.001	0.021	0.003	0.012	0.460	0.520
Kerry	0.206	0.255	0.280	0.260	0.002	0.039	0.007	0.007	0.495	0.561
Limerick	0.213	0.289	0.237	0.202	0.002	0.029	0.011	0.024	0.463	0.544
Tipperary	0.166	0.254	0.273	0.203	0.002	0.047	0.011	0.016	0.452	0.520
Waterford	0.117	0.186	0.257	0.226	0.004	0.014	0.007	0.013	0.385	0.439
Galway	0.225	0.303	0.295	0.264	0.007	0.030	0.004	0.008	0.531	0.605
Leitrim	0.170	0.214	0.360	0.244	0.004	0.031	0.008	0.026	0.542	0.515
Mayo	0.167	0.210	0.342	0.310	0.008	0.065	0.005	0.008	0.522	0.593
Roscommon	0.139	0.230	0.293	0.271	0.007	0.051	0.005	0.010	0.444	0.562
Sligo	0.163	0.216	0.299	0.330	0.007	0.071	0.013	0.017	0.482	0.634
Cavan	0.120	0.224	0.264	0.239	0.000	0.042	0.009	0.012	0.393	0.517
Donegal	0.077	0.115	0.249	0.226	0.001	0.028	0.001	0.004	0.328	0.373
Monaghan	0.102	0.153	0.239	0.248	0.007	0.048	0.016	0.008	0.364	0.457
State	0.158	0.234	0.233	0.201	0.003	0.027	0.016	0.020	0.410	0.482

Predictors of County Admission Rates

The first group of variables examined as possible predictors of variation in admission rates were measures of the distance of individual counties from the nearest college. In the two previous national surveys these variables proved to be important predictors. The distance of each county from the nearest University, and the nearest Institute of Technology were calculated. The measurement was based on the average road distance from the three largest urban centres in each county to the nearest town or city which had a University, or an Institute of Technology. In the case of towns, which had a third-level college, rather than using zero, a distance of seven miles was assigned[2].

Three variables were used to describe the pattern of participation in second-level education in each county. These were the retention rate to Leaving Certificate level, the proportion of post-primary enrolments in Secondary schools and the proportion of post-primary enrolments in Vocational schools. In respect of the latter two variables it has already been established (see Chapter Four, above) that retention rates and transfer rates to higher education differ by school type. Secondary schools have higher retention and transfer rates while Vocational schools have lower retention and transfer rates. Thus it was felt that the proportion of post-primary enrolments in each county might help to explain the differential rates of admission to higher education.

The relevance of examining retention rates at second-level as possible determinants of higher education participation appears self-evident since completion of the post-primary cycle is a prerequisite for admission to higher education. In recent years the Department of Education and Science has introduced a pupil tracking system, which facilitates the measurement of retention for each school. The author was given access to these data, aggregated at the level of county in which schools were located. However, it could not be assumed that the county in which schools are located corresponded with students' county of permanent residence. Many students attend schools outside their own county. This is especially prevalent in the case of boarding schools and where schools are located close to county boundaries. Thus, it was necessary to modify the county school retention figures to take account of this inter-county movement of students. The survey population, which included about half of the Leaving Certificate enrolments in 1997/98, was used to estimate this movement of students. In respect of the study population, students' county of permanent residence and the county in which their schools were located were known. An examination of the correlation between both distributions provided the basis for adjusting the school retention data by county to provide a more accurate estimate of the retention level by county of permanent residence.

Three of the socio-economic variables used in this analysis are based on the socio-economic group and social class classifications, which have already been used in this report. In Chapter two we have reported on the social class and socio-economic group differentials in participation rates. For the purpose of this analysis we have calculated the percentage of the population, under 15 years in 1996, in each county belonging to the two 'Highest Social Classes' (Professional Workers and Managerial and Technical classes) and the 'Lowest Social Classes' (Semi Skilled and Unskilled classes)[3]. In addition, given the unique profile of the farmers' socio-economic group we also include a variable based on the percentage of the relevant population from the Farmers' socio-economic group in each county. These three variables, which are highly predictive of higher education admissions at an individual level of analysis, are included here to see if they have any predictive power at an aggregate level.

Five additional indicators of the socio-economic characteristics of each county were also used. The first involves a measure of the income per capita in each county in 1997. These data on income pre capita by county, which were recently published by the Central Statistics Office (CSO, 2000), provide a more appropriate measure of this variable than that which was available in our earlier surveys (Clancy, 1995: 127). The next indicator used was the proportion of the population living in urban areas. Both this variable and income per capita have been found to be related to higher education participation rates in studies in other countries (Pike, 1970). The level of youth unemployment in each county was also included in the analysis as it is often suggested that depressed labour conditions encourage young people to stay in the educational system. The number of young persons under twenty-five years on the live register in each county in Summer 1998 was established and expressed as a proportion of the 15-24 age cohort. The final two socio-economic indicators used were chosen to reflect the educational attainment of the adult population in each county. The proportion of the population, whose education had ceased, who had left school under the age of fifteen and the proportion who had left at age twenty or over was calculated from the 1996 Census.

Multivariate Analysis

Each of the thirteen predictor-variables was first correlated with the male and female admission rate in each of the two sectors. These zero-order correlations are presented in Table 49. An inspection of these correlations suggests that at least one of the distance variables, one of the variables chosen to represent the pattern of participation at second-level and several of the socio-economic variables may help to predict the rates of admission to higher education. There is a strong negative correlation between distance from university and the rate of admission for both males and females to the university sector. While Distance from Institute of Technology is not significantly related to the rate of admission to the IT sector we note that, in the case of females, distance from a university is positively correlated with rate of admission to the IT sector.

Turning to the variables that describe the pattern of participation at second level we note that retention rate to Leaving Certificate correlates positively with the rate of admission to both university and IT sector for males and females. Furthermore, the proportion of post-primary enrolments in vocational schools is negatively related to the male rate of admission to university and while the direction of the relationship is the same for females and for both males and females in the IT sector, these relationships are not statistically significant.

TABLE 49   CORRELATION BETWEEN PREDICTOR VARIABLES AND RATES OF ADMISSION TO HIGHER EDUCATION

	University Sector		Institute of Technology Sector	
	Male	Female	Male	Female
Distance from University	-.524★★	-.564★★	.371	.619★★
Distance from Institute of Technology	-.160	-.012	.015	-.116
Retention Rate to Leaving Certificate	.493★	.443★	.492★	.392★
Proportion of Post-Primary Enrolments in Secondary Schools	.275	.211	.038	.327
Proportion of Post-Primary Enrolments in Vocational Schools	-.396★	-.334	-.276	-.326
Proportion of Population in Farming	.111	.146	.473★	.478★
Proportion of Population in Higher Social Classes	.528★★	.575★★	-370	-.424★
Proportion of Population in Lower Social Classes	-.433★	-.432★	.058	.119
Income Per Capita	.237	.215	-.433★	-561★★
Proportion of Population in Urban Areas	.068	.086	-545★★	-.549★★
Youth Unemployment Rate	-.423★	-.461★	.056	.172
Proportion of Population who left School Under 15 yrs.	-.388	-.443★	.401★	.414★
Proportion of Population who left School at Age 20 or over	.599★★	.495★	-.257	-.396★

In relation to the socio-economic variables we note that several of these variables are significantly associated with the rate of admission to university and the IT sector for both males and females. For the university sector the proportion of the population in higher social classes and the proportion of the population who left school at age 20 or over are positively associated with the rate of admission. In contrast there is a negative association between rate of admission and the proportion of population in lower social classes, the youth unemployment rate and for females the proportion of the population which left school under 15 years. In the case of the rate of admission to the Institute of Technology sector the positive predictors are proportion of the population in farming and the proportion that left school under 15 years. In contrast, income per capita, the proportion of the population in urban areas and for females the proportion of population in higher social classes and proportion who left school at age 20 or over are negatively associated with rate of admission.

However these correlations allow us to examine only the relationship between pairs of variables. Since many of the predicted variables chosen are themselves highly inter-correlated (see Appendix Table A23) some form of multivariate analysis is necessary. Alternatively we run the risk of positing a causal link between variables where the relationship may be merely a statistical artifact. Multiple regression was carried out to attempt to assess the separate and collective contribution of the predictor variables to variation in county admission rates to higher education.

The choice of variables to be entered into the regression equations was determined by a number of factors. First, on substantive grounds it was considered desirable that each of the three groups of variables should be represented. Thus, it was decided that each regression model should have at least one distance from college variable, one post-primary participation variable and one socio-economic variable. Second, the choice of predictor variables from within each group was initially influenced by the zero-order correlations reported in Table 49 above. Third, account had to be taken of the problem of multicollinearity, which exists when two or more independent variables are highly inter-correlated[4]. This problem is particularly acute in the case of some of the socio-economic variables. For example, the proportion of the population living in urban areas was very highly correlated with income per capita ($r = +.87$) and the proportion of the population in farming ($r = -.77$). These variables were in turn strongly associated with some of the distance variables (see Table A23). Guided by these considerations a number of regression models were calculated for each criterion variable. Table 50 summarises the four regression models chosen to provide the best fit for these data.

The first of the regression models summarised in Table 50 seeks to explain inter-county variability in male admission rates to university. In this regression equation four variables accounted for seventy-four per cent of the variance in county admission rates[5]. While this equation includes two socio-economic variables, one second-level school variable and one distance variable, only three of these variables make an independent statistically significant contribution to the explained variance. The proportion of the population which ceased full-time education at age twenty or over makes the largest contribution to the explained variance in county admission rates suggesting that when we simultaneously take into account the effect of the other three variable in the model, those counties, which have a high proportion of the adult population with an advanced education, have high male rates of admission to university education. The proportion of the population in farming makes the second largest contribution to the explained variance. This finding from the multivariate analysis was unexpected in view of the absence of any significant relationship in the bivariate analysis. However, it proved to be quite a robust finding emerging as highly significant in all regression models (on university admission rates) when it was included. What is evident is that distance from college acts as a suppressor variable when we look at the relationship between county admission rates and the proportion of the population in farming.[6] The retention rate to Leaving Certificate level also makes a significant contribution to the explained variance. Finally, while not statistically significant ($p<.07$), the model suggests that those counties, which are located further from a university, tend to have lower rates of admission to university for males.

TABLE 50 REGRESSION ANALYSIS OF DISTANCE FROM COLLEGE, POST-PRIMARY SCHOOL PARTICIPATION AND SOCIO-ECONOMIC VARIABLES ON MALE AND FEMALE UNIVERSITY AND INSTITUTE OF TECHNOLOGY PARTICIPATION RATES

	University Sector		Institute of Technology Sector	
	Male Beta	Female Beta	Male Beta	Female Beta
Distance from University	-.344 (-1.912)	-.699** (-4.387)	-	.427** (2.922)
Distance from Institute of Technology	-	-	-.374 (-1.922)	-.141 (-1.155)
Retention Rate to Leaving Certificate	.331** (2.704)	.271* (2.157)	.234 (1.308)	.323** (3.043)
Proportion of Post-Primary Enrolments in Secondary Schools	-	-	-	.559** (4.075)
Proportion of Population in Farming	.509** (3.363)	.527** (3.541)	-	-
Proportion of Population in Higher Social Classes	-	.303* (2.117)	-	-
Proportion of Population in Urban Areas	-	-	-.653** (-3.023)	-
Proportion of Population who left School Under 15 yrs.	-	-	-	.464** (2.897)
Proportion of Population who left School at Age 20 or over	.632** (3.426)	-	-	-
R Square (adjusted)	.74	.72	.39	.73
F	18.447 P< .001)	17.144 P< .001)	6.370 P< .001	14.414 P< .001)

The regression model chosen to explicate female admission rates to university education accounted for seventy-two per cent of inter-county variance. This model also includes two socio-economic variables, one distance and one second-level school variable. Three of the variables in the model are similar to those that serve to explain male admission rates although there is some variation in their relative importance within each model. In addition, one of the socio-economic variables (proportion of population who left school at age twenty or over), which served as the best predictor of male admission rates, is replaced by proportion of the population in higher social classes in the model, which best explains female admission rates. The best predictor of female admission rates is distance from a university, followed by proportion of population in farming. Finally as was the case in the first model, retention rate to Leaving Certificate helps to explain the level of female admissions to university.

Turning to an examination of inter-county variability in admission rates to technological education the third model reported in Table 50 examines the situation in respect of males. We have had least success in explaining variance in male admission rates to the IT sector. The optimum chosen model accounts for only thirty-nine per cent of the variance. The best single predictor is proportion of the population in urban areas. Counties with a low percentage of the population living in urban areas have higher male rates of admission to the Institute of Technology sector. Two other variables make some contribution to the explained variance in this model although neither is statistically significant at the .05 level. Distance from an Institute of Technology is negatively related to male admission rates to the IT sector while retention rate to Leaving Certificate level is positively associated with admission rates for males in this sector.

The fourth model presented in Table 50 seeks to predict female rates of admission to the Institute of Technology sector. Unlike the situation with respect to males in this sector, our data provide much greater explanatory power; five variables account for seventy-three per cent of the variance. The best single predictor is the proportion of post-primary enrolments in secondary schools. Those counties, which have a higher proportion of enrolments in secondary schools, have higher female rates of admission rates to the IT sector. A second post-primary school variable, retention rate to Leaving Certificate level, also makes a significant contribution to the explained variance in this sector. One socio-economic variable, proportion of the population who left school under the age of 15, emerges as a significant predictor. This model includes the two distance variables. Of these the most important is distance from university. Counties that are distant from a university have higher female rates of admission to the Institute of Technology sector. And finally, although not statistically significant, our explanatory model suggests that counties, which are distant from an IT, have somewhat lower female rates of admission to this sector.

Distance from College

In view of the fact that this is the fourth national survey it is of interest to compare the findings from the present study with the earlier ones on the importance of distance from college as a predictor of admission rates by county. In each of the previous surveys a multivariate analysis confirmed that distance from university was an important predictor of the rate of admission to university for both males and females. Counties, which are distant from a university, had lower rates of admission to university. The present analysis confirms this finding, emphatically in the case of females, and while the direction of the relationship is the same for males it falls just short of being statistically significant at the .05 level.

In contrast to the consistency of findings in respect of distance from university the present study fails to find a significant link between distance from an Institute of Technology and the rate of admission to the IT sector. This absence of a relationship is evident both in the zero order (Table 49) and multivariate analysis although both of our regression models suggest an inverse negative relationship which in the case of males is close to being statistically significant (Table 50). This finding replicates those from the 1992 study although for both males and females in 1980 and for females in 1986 there was a statistically significant inverse relationship between distance from an IT and admission rates to this sector.

While distance from a technological college does not account for the rate of admission to this sector, it is of interest to note that distance from a university is positively associated with the rate of admission to the IT sector. This relationship was evident, for both males and females, from the zero order relationships and for females it was confirmed at a statistically significant level in the multivariate analysis. This finding is consistent with those from two of the three earlier surveys, the exception being 1992. The link between distance from university and the rate of admission to the IT sector suggests that, at least for females, different forms of higher education may be substitutable for one another depending on the opportunity cost of take-up.

Table 51 enables us to explore further the link between accessibility of colleges and the differential take-up of different forms of higher education. This table shows for each county the proportionate distribution of higher education entrants by sector. We note that four of the five counties with the highest proportion of their entrants in the university sector, Cork (52%), Limerick (50%), Dublin (49%) and Galway (46%) each have a university located within the county. The exception to this generalisation is Clare, which is adjacent to both Limerick and Galway. However while Dublin, Cork and Limerick also have a technological institute located in the county it is noticeable that these counties have the lowest proportionate representation of entrants in the technological sector. Thus, it would appear that, at least in some counties, where both facilities are available locally, the university sector attracts a disproportionate share of entrants. This is not, of course, a universal trend, as the data for Galway testify. Here the technological sector attracted a higher proportion of entrants than the university sector.

In contrast to the clear link between location of universities and the proportion of higher education entrants admitted to the university sector the situation is less clear cut with respect to admission to the technological sector. In addition to the

TABLE 51   PROPORTIONATE DISTRIBUTION OF NEW ENTRANTS TO HIGHER EDUCATION BY SECTOR AND COUNTY

County	University	Institutes of Technology	Colleges of Education	Other Colleges	Total	
					%	N
Carlow	.367	.566	.041	.026	100	387
Dublin	.492	.393	.024	.091	100	7,118
Kildare	.438	.471	.025	.066	100	1,189
Kilkenny	.404	.511	.055	.030	100	634
Laois	.413	.531	.035	.021	100	433
Longford	.429	.531	.029	.012	100	343
Louth	.286	.661	.022	.031	100	833
Meath	.388	.535	.032	.044	100	1,110
Offaly	.349	.608	.025	.017	100	518
Westmeath	.373	.585	.018	.024	100	675
Wexford	.372	.559	.041	.028	100	984
Wicklow	.454	.440	.028	.077	100	865
Clare	.507	.435	.037	.021	100	966
Cork	.521	.443	.023	.014	100	3,999
Kerry	.436	.513	.038	.013	100	1,319
Limerick	.498	.437	.031	.035	100	1,665
Tipperary	.432	.490	.050	.027	100	1,360
Waterford	.366	.588	.022	.024	100	786
Galway	.464	.494	.032	.010	100	2,147
Leitrim	.361	.575	.032	.032	100	252
Mayo	.339	.585	.064	.012	100	1,275
Roscommon	.365	.563	.057	.015	100	542
Sligo	.340	.565	.069	.026	100	609
Cavan	.376	.556	.045	.023	100	487
Donegal	.274	.678	.041	.007	100	962
Monaghan	.309	.597	.063	.031	100	457
State	.438	.489	.033	.040	100	31,915

low proportion of entrants in the IT sector from Dublin, Cork and Limerick which we have already remarked upon, it is noticeable that only two (Donegal and Louth) of the four counties with the highest proportion of entrants in the technological sector have an Institute of Technology located in the county. However, Table 51 provides some evidence to support the link between proximity and admission rates in the IT sector. Very many counties with disproportionate numbers of entrants in the IT sector have have an Institute of Technology located within the county (e.g. Waterford, Westmeath, Mayo, Carlow) or in an adjacent county (e.g. Monaghan, Leitrim, Roscommon).

While we have not included the Colleges of Education sector in the multivariate analysis it is clear form Table 48 above that accessibility of a college does not encourage admission to this sector. Sligo is the only one of the six counties with the highest proportion of entrants in this sector to have any locational advantage vis-‡-vis Colleges of Education. We have previously argued (Clancy, 1988) that one of the factors which has differentiated the Colleges of Education from other higher education sectors has been the long tradition of recruitment (especially into primary teaching) from Western counties. Table A24 (Appendix) allows us to assess the extent to which this tradition has persisted into the 1990s at a time of growing opportunities for higher education outside this sector. When we compare the distribution of 1998 entrants to the five colleges, which educate national teachers, with the pattern that existed in 1963 and 1986 we note a substantial change in the origin of students. The percentage of students from Leinster had greatly increased from a mere nineteen per cent in 1963 to thirty-four per cent in 1998. This increase has occurred at the expense of Connaught and the three Ulster counties. In 1963 almost forty-two per cent of entrants into the Primary Teacher Training came from these eight counties. This had declined to twenty-eight per cent by 1998. Although Connaught and Ulster still contribute more than their proportionate share of entrants into primary teaching (28% versus 21% into all of higher education) this dominance has greatly declined since the 1960s. It is of interest to note that there has been little change in the percentage of recruits into colleges of education from Munster. This apparent stability has been accompanied by some changes between counties. For example, Tipperary now has the highest rate of admission to colleges of education within Munster, ahead of Kerry and Clare and more than twice the rate for Cork, counties which have traditionally contributed disproportionately to the teaching profession (see Table 36 above).

Finally in relation to admission rates and college location, it is of interest to note that in respect of the more heterogeneous 'Other Colleges' sector distance from college does appear to influence rate of admission. With eight of the twelve colleges in this sector located in Dublin it is significant that Dublin had the highest proportion of its higher education entrants in this sector. Furthermore the two counties with the next highest rates of admission in this sector were the adjacent counties of Wicklow and Kildare.

Post-primary School Variables

Three of the predictor variables included in this analysis represent the pattern of participation at second-level. The multivariate analysis revealed that one of these variables, retention rate to Leaving Certificate level, contributed significantly to the explained variance in the rate of admission to the university sector and to the Institute of Technology sector. This finding applies to both male and female admission rates, although the independent effect of this variable is not statistically significant in the case of male rates of admission to the IT sector, when the other variables are entered into the equation. Counties with a high retention rate to Leaving Certificate level had a high rate of admission to higher education. An additional finding of the multivariate analysis, which applied only to females in the IT sector, was that counties, which had a high proportion of post-primary enrolments in secondary schools, had a high female rate of admission to the Institute of Technology sector.

The significance of Leaving Certificate retention rate as a predictor of admission rates to higher education in both sectors is an important finding of this study. The uniformity of this finding mirrors the findings from the 1986 study although in 1992 retention rates were important predictors only in the IT sector while in 1980 their effect was limited to male university admission rates.

It is of interest to explore further the relationship between retention rate at Leaving Certificate level and county admission rate to higher education. Figure 4 presents a crosstabulation between admission rate to higher education and estimated retention rate to Leaving Certificate level. For the purpose of the crosstabulation both variables have been trichotomised. If there was a perfect relationship between the two variables all counties would be located in the cells on the diagonal. Seventeen counties were thus located. In a comparable analysis in the earlier studies sixteen countries were thus located in 1992, thirteen in 1986 and eight in 1980 suggesting that over time the rate of admission to higher education is becoming more dependent on the retention rate to the end of the senior cycle.

FIGURE 4 RATES OF ADMISSION TO HIGHER EDUCATION IN 1998 BY RETENTION RATES TO LEAVING CERTIFICATE LEVEL

		Admission Rates to Higher Education 1998		
		High	Medium	Low
Estimated Retention Rates to Leaving Certificate Level 1998	High	Leitrim Mayo Longford Sligo Kerry Clare Galway	Westmeath	
	Medium		Carlow Cork Cavan Tipperary Meath	Laois Kildare Kilkenny
	Low	Roscommon Limerick	Wexford Louth	Waterford Wicklow Dublin Donegal Monaghan

141

We note from Figure 4 that seven of the counties with highest rates of admission to third-level education also had high retention rates to Leaving Certificate level. Furthermore, five of the counties which had lowest rates of admission also had low retention rates to Leaving Certificate level. The most interesting feature of Figure 4 is the identification of those counties that are located off the diagonal. Five counties are located to the right of the diagonal. In these instances the relative rates of admission to higher education are lower than the relative retention rates to Leaving Certificate level. Offaly represents the most extreme deviation. It is estimated that it is amongst those counties with the highest retention rates to Leaving Certificate level, yet as have already noted it had the third lowest[7] rate of admission to higher education. The other four counties, whose relative ranking on admission rates were lower than that the retention rates were Westmeath, Laois, Kildare and Kilkenny. A characteristic, which is common to all of these counties is that with the exception of Westmeath, none has a third level college.

The four counties that are located left of the diagonal reflect a discrepancy in the opposite direction. For these counties their relative ranking on rates of admission to higher education was higher than their relative ranking on retention rates. In two instances, Roscommon and Limerick, the discrepancy was quite marked. Although both counties were estimated to be amongst those with the lowest retention rates they were amongst those with the highest rates of admission to third-level. While Limerick has a clear locational advantage with a full range of third-level colleges, which facilitate access, this is not the case for Roscommon. Similarly, while proximity to a third level college may also help to account for Louth's position this does not help to explain the situation for Wexford whose rate of admission is higher than would be predicted on the basis of its relatively low retention rate. This analysis demonstrates how the interaction of separate independent variables may help to account for differential rates of admission to higher education. Notwithstanding the exception which we have noted, this analysis suggests the following generalisations. A relatively high retention rate to Leaving Certificate level is normally a necessary condition for achieving high admission rates to higher education. However, if a county is locationally disadvantaged this potential may not be realised. Similarly locational advantage can compensate for modest levels of retention at second level in achieving relatively high third-level admission rates.

Socio-economic Variables

A number of socio-economic variables were examined as possible predictors of county rates of admission to higher education. As discussed above because of the high inter-correlation between these variables it was necessary to limit the number that could be entered simultaneously into the regression models. In all five of these variables made a contribution to the explained variance in county rates of admission to higher education. In the case of admission rates to university education the impact of the proportion of the population engaged in farming was especially striking, in view of the fact that this zero-order correlation was not significant. What emerged is that when the other three variables in these equations were taken into account, counties with a high proportion of the population engaged in farming had a significantly higher rate of admission to university education for both males and females. In the case of male admission rates to university the single best predictor was the proportion of the population who left school at age twenty or over. The higher the educational profile of the adult population the higher the male admission rate to university. The explanatory power of this variable with respect to male university admission rates was matched by a closely related variable in the case of female admission rates to this sector. The larger the proportion of the population in the higher social classes the higher the female rate of admission to university education.

The socio-economic variables were less important in predicting the rate of admission to the IT sector. In respect of both models reported in Table 50 above only one socio-economic variable contributed at a statistically significant level to an explanation of rate of admission in this sector. In the case of males the proportion of the population in urban areas was the best single predictor of admission rates to the IT sector. The larger the proportion of the population living in urban areas, the lower the male admission rate to the Institute of Technology sector. In the case of female admission rates to the IT sector the proportion of the population who left school under fifteen years of age emerged as an important predictor.

In reporting on the relative predictive power of aggregate-level socio-economic variables it is necessary to be conscious of the problem of the ecological fallacy, i.e. the impossibility of inferring conclusions about relationships between variables at the individual level on the basis of correlations at the aggregate level (see Robinson, 1950). For example, the finding that aggregate income per capita by county is negatively related to the rate of admission to technological education does not allow us to conclude that family or individual income is negatively associated with rate of admission to higher education. Indeed, the findings reported in Chapter 3 above on the socio-economic background of higher education entrants are strongly suggestive of a positive relationship at the individual level between family income and rate of admission. However, the analysis in the present chapter is concerned with an attempt to explain inter-county variability, not intra-county variability. In respect of the latter, socio-economic variables measured at the individual level may have entirely different predictive power.

One of the variables not included in the multivariate analysis, although it is closely related to the socio-economic characteristics of the different counties, was the proportion of students in receipt of financial aid. Our main interest here is in the proportion of entrants in receipt of means tested maintenance grants. Thus in Table A25 the percentages in receipt of Higher Education Grants, VEC Scholarships and ESF Grants are combined. As discussed in Chapter 3, above, those designated as having no financial aid includes the majority of students for whom no tuition fees are charged. The pattern revealed is one of considerable variability. While, for the country as a whole, thirty-five per cent of entrants were in receipt of means tested aid this percentage varied from sixty-two per cent in Mayo to a mere sixteen per cent in Dublin. Apart from Mayo, the percentage of entrants in receipt of means tested financial aid exceeded fifty per cent in Leitrim, Roscommon and Donegal (55% in each), Galway (53%) and Cavan (52%).

Only two other counties apart from Dublin, Kildare (24%), and Wicklow (27%) had less than thirty per cent of entrants in receipt of means tested financial aid while in three other counties (Limerick, Meath and Cork) the percentage was less than thirty-one per cent. Although not statistically significant, there was a positive relationship between the proportion of entrants in receipt of financial aid and the county rate of admission to higher education (r = .33). This is illustrated by the fact that four of the six counties with highest levels of entrants on means tested financial aid had highest admission rates, the exceptions were the two border counties of Donegal and Cavan. Similarly the three counties with lowest levels of financial aid were amongst those with lowest rate of admission to higher education. The variability in the percentage of students in receipt of financial aid is, of course, related to the distribution of family income. The correlation between the percentage of entrants in receipt of means tested financial aid and income per capita was r = -.81. Notwithstanding the strong correlation at this aggregate level existing student support schemes have been criticised on the basis of the criteria used to determine eligibility at the individual level.[8] Whatever the causes of variability in the distribution of means tested student aid, the main rationale for the existence of student support schemes has been to reduce inequalities in access to higher education. We now turn to examine variation by county in the levels of socio-economic inequality in access to higher education.

Socio-Economic Group Inequality

We have described above the summary measures that we calculated to characterise the social class and socio-economic characteristics of the population of each county. We have calculated the percentage of the population in the two higher social classes, the two lower social classes and the farming socio-economic group. We have also noted how the percentage from the farming social group and to a lesser extent the percentage from the higher social classes have served as predictors of admission rates. Our concern here is not with prediction but rather with outcomes. Thus analogous to the strategy, which we used for the country as whole, to measure the degree to which each social class and socio-economic group was 'over-represented' or 'under-represented' in higher education we have calculated for each county the participation ratios of the higher social class, the lower social classes and the farmers' socio-economic group. In each county the percentage of entrants from each of these categories was expressed as a proportion of the percentage of children under the age of fifteen years in each of these class and socio-economic group categories.

The results of this analysis are presented in Table 52, which also includes a social class inequality index for each county. This index was derived by dividing the participation ratio of the higher social class groups by the participation ratio of the lower social class groups. The index is a measure of the differential probability of being admitted to higher education by a member of the higher social classes compared to a member of the lower social classes. For example, if we look at the situation in respect of Co. Carlow we note that the participation ratio of the higher social classes 1.45 signifying that these groups had forty-five per cent more places in higher education than would be warranted on the basis of their proportionate size in the population. The participation ratio of the lower social classes was 0.43 indicating that these groups had fifty-seven per cent fewer places than their proportionate size would warrant. Thus, the differential probability was in excess of three and a third indicated by a score of 3.39 on the non-farm social class inequality index.

County	Social Class Participation Ratios		Social Class Inequality Index	Farmer Socio-Group Economic Participation Ratio
	Higher Social Classes	Lower Social Classes		
Carlow	1.45	0.43	3.39	1.35
Dublin	1.60	0.46	3.44	2.50
Kildare	1.29	0.69	1.85	1.88
Kilkenny	1.26	0.73	1.72	1.59
Laois	1.29	0.62	2.09	1.87
Longford	1.07	0.61	1.77	1.88
Louth	1.26	0.85	1.47	1.95
Meath	1.26	0.62	2.04	1.52
Offaly	1.37	0.62	2.22	1.71
Westmeath	1.19	0.68	1.75	1.92
Wexford	1.34	0.74	1.81	1.80
Wicklow	1.53	0.60	2.54	2.14
Clare	1.26	0.54	2.32	1.80
Cork	1.25	0.71	1.78	3.49
Kerry	1.25	0.67	1.86	1.43
Limerick	1.23	0.59	2.08	1.83
Tipperary	1.27	0.66	1.92	1.61
Waterford	1.38	0.71	1.94	1.63
Galway	1.13	0.73	1.54	1.50
Leitrim	0.95	0.79	1.21	1.51
Mayo	0.96	0.90	1.07	1.55
Roscommon	1.06	0.54	1.96	1.77
Sligo	1.08	0.82	1.32	1.76
Cavan	1.21	0.79	1.54	1.54
Donegal	1.14	0.96	1.18	1.16
Monaghan	1.08	0.86	1.25	1.18
All Counties	1.31	0.66	1.98	1.77

We note from Table 52 that the level of social class inequality for the country as a whole was 1.98. However, the degree of inequality on this measure varies considerably by county. The highest level of inequality was found in Dublin (3.44) and Carlow (3.39). Other counties with high scores on this index included Wicklow (2.54), Clare (2.32), and Offaly (2.22). The counties with the lowest social class inequality scores were Mayo (1.07), Donegal (1.18), Leitrim (1.21), Monaghan (1.25) and Sligo (1.32). Since two of these are border counties it is probable that these scores underestimate the true level of non-farm socio-economic group inequality because of the exclusion from these calculations of those who enrolled in universities in Northern Ireland[9]. Notwithstanding this caveat the distribution of scores on this index reveals a regional pattern. Most of the counties with high levels of social class inequality are from Leinster while the counties from Connaught and Ulster exhibit lower level of social class inequality.

In examining the variations by county in the levels of social class inequality a central concern was to explore the possible links between enrolment rates and levels of inequality. It has long been a central assumption shared by liberal educationalists and policy makers that the expansion of schooling can increase opportunity and reduce inequality. This belief has been used to justify increased provision. The evidence presented in Table 52 provides some modest support for this hypothesis. Although not statistically significant, the correlation between the degree of social class inequality and rate of admission to higher education ($r = -.33$) reveals that there is a tendency for counties with high rates of admission to have somewhat lower scores on the inequality index. Thus we note that five of the counties with highest levels of social class inequality (Dublin, Wicklow, Offaly, Laois and Waterford) are amongst those classified as having lowest levels of admission to higher education. Similarly, four of the counties with highest levels of admission (Mayo, Leitrim, Sligo and Galway) have lowest levels of social class inequality. However, there are many exceptions to this trend. For example two of the counties with highest levels of inequality (Clare and Limerick) are amongst those with highest admission rates while three of those with lowest levels of inequality also are amongst those with low rates of admission to higher education[10].

Our exploration of the relationship between socio-economic group disparities and the rate of admission to higher education has thus far been limited to the two social class groupings. Although these class categories include farmers differentiated by farm size it is of interest to look separately at the participation ratios of the Farmers' socio-economic group (Table 52, final column). It is clear that the participation ratio of the Farmers' group varies significantly by county. A clear regional pattern is evident. Nine of the twelve Leinster counties have participation ratios which exceed the average for all counties. By comparison none of the counties of Connaught and Ulster have participation ratios which exceed the average. While these regional differences are clearly reflect income differences there are some anomalies. Meath is one of the Leinster counties which has a low participation ratio for the farmers' group. Carlow and Offaly also belong to this category although the latter may reflect the income profile. While no recent county-level income per capita data are available for the farming sector these data, at the aggregate level, seem to lend support to the generalisation made earlier in our analysis of the individual level data that class differences within the farming sector mirror the social class differences which are evident between the other social groups.

Academic Attainment of Entrants

The final correlate of differential county admission rates to higher education which was examined in this study was the level of prior academic attainment of new entrants. This variable is relevant in any attempt to estimate the adequacy of existing provision and the potential for future expansion in higher education enrolment. A relevant question is whether the level of prior academic attainment of new entrants decreases as the rate of admission rises. Some commentators argue that as larger proportions of the age cohort are enrolled in higher education this inevitably involves reaching down into the lower ability bands to fill the quota of places. An adequate test of this proposition would require knowledge of the distribution of ability and attainment level in each county in addition to the data that we have on the academic attainment of new entrants.

In the absence of more comprehensive data the present analysis is limited to an examination of the distribution of new entrants by level of prior academic attainment (Table 53). To provide summary measures of the relationship between academic attainment of entrants and county admission rates the proportion of new entrants with two or more subjects and the proportion with five or more subjects at grade C or higher on Higher level papers was correlated with higher education admission rates. There was no correlation between level of academic attainment of entrants and county admission rates. For two or more honours the correlation was $r = .08$ while for five or more honours the correlation was $r = .04$. The absence of a significant relationship is illustrated by the fact that of the nine counties with the highest levels of educational attainment (those with the highest percentage of entrants with five or more honours), four counties were amongst those having highest admission rates, three were classified as having lowest admission rates and two had medium levels of admission. The nine counties with lowest levels of academic attainment (those with the highest percentages of entrants having less than two subjects at honours level) were similarly distributed among the counties with admission rates classified as 'high', 'medium' and 'low'. Thus there is no support for the general proposition that for the country as a whole we have reached an ability threshold, which limits the scope for further expansion in higher education enrolments.

TABLE 53   LEVEL OF PRIOR ACADEMIC ATTAINMENT OF NEW HIGHER EDUCATION ENTRANTS BY COUNTY

County	Number of Subjects with Grade C or Higher on Higher Level Papers								
	0%	1%	2%	3%	4%	5%	6%	7%	8+%
Carlow	6.3	9.2	13.5	18.6	14.3	10.3	16.6	10.0	1.1
Dublin	4.3	7.8	9.6	11.8	12.8	16.5	21.3	14.1	1.9
Kildare	6.3	9.8	12.6	13.1	14.2	15.4	18.1	9.5	1.0
Kilkenny	3.9	9.2	9.0	15.4	14.2	14.4	17.9	15.2	0.7
Laois	3.8	12.5	13.5	13.3	14.5	12.3	18.3	11.0	0.8
Longford	9.8	14.4	11.8	10.1	13.7	13.4	16.3	9.2	1.3
Louth	15.0	17.7	14.1	10.2	10.6	9.5	12.9	8.7	1.3
Meath	6.5	11.0	12.8	13.9	11.7	13.6	18.6	11.2	0.8
Offaly	8.4	15.6	15.0	10.8	11.2	12.1	16.5	9.5	0.9
Westmeath	11.8	14.9	10.3	10.6	12.3	13.2	17.5	8.9	0.5
Wexford	8.1	11.6	13.4	12.3	14.8	14.8	16.1	8.0	0.8
Wicklow	5.0	9.4	12.4	9.7	15.1	18.2	18.5	10.9	0.9
Clare	4.2	9.0	12.8	12.0	12.5	14.6	21.4	12.4	1.1
Cork	2.4	6.2	10.7	11.9	12.8	16.5	21.9	15.0	2.6
Kerry	5.7	10.0	14.0	12.4	13.0	14.2	18.9	11.2	0.6
Limerick	4.6	9.2	13.6	12.7	11.8	15.2	19.7	12.2	1.0
Tipperary	3.6	9.5	12.8	12.6	11.6	14.8	19.9	14.4	0.7
Waterford	4.7	8.5	11.0	15.2	16.9	13.8	18.1	11.0	0.9
Galway	6.2	9.3	12.3	11.9	14.5	15.7	18.7	10.4	1.1
Leitrim	7.2	15.3	16.7	16.2	12.2	14.0	12.6	5.0	0.9
Mayo	8.3	11.5	12.7	12.3	12.8	14.7	17.5	8.9	1.3
Roscommon	10.4	12.7	15.0	10.8	13.3	14.0	14.8	8.5	0.4
Sligo	12.5	11.2	14.2	12.4	11.8	12.5	17.4	7.5	0.4
Cavan	7.1	11.5	15.1	12.9	12.2	12.4	17.5	10.6	0.7
Donegal	14.3	17.7	16.7	12.0	10.5	10.5	11.6	6.7	0.1
Monaghan	8.0	14.3	12.6	15.0	13.3	14.0	13.5	9.2	0.2
All Counties	6.0	9.9	12.0	12.3	12.9	14.9	18.9	11.8	1.3

While the data presented in Table 53 does not support any overall generalisation on the relationship between county admission rates and the academic attainment of entrants, the pattern revealed for some counties is of particular interest. Higher education entrants from Cork had the highest level of educational attainment, with fewer than nine per cent having less than two 'honours' and an impressive fifty-six per cent having five or more subjects with 'honours'. Entrants from Dublin had the second highest level of educational attainment with fifty-four per cent having five or more subjects at honours level. The counties with lowest levels of attainment may be of more interest for policy makers, since those with a high proportion of entrants with less than two honours may have a lower potential for further enrolment growth given existing levels of output from the second level system. Three of the four border counties (Louth, Donegal and Monaghan) are in this category. And while it is possible that the exclusion from this table of those attending colleges in Northern Ireland may account for the lower percentage of high achievers, it is significant that Monaghan, Louth and Donegal are the three counties with lowest retention levels at second level. The other counties with a high percentage of entrants with lower levels of attainment are less homogeneous. These include three counties from Connaught (Sligo, Roscommon and Leitrim) and three further counties from Leinster (Westmeath, Longford and Offaly). Five of these counties (excepting Roscommon) have high retention rates to Leaving Certificate level and four of them (Sligo, Leitrim, Roscommon and Longford) already have high admission rates to third level. It is perhaps among this latter group of counties that we may be approaching an ability threshold, which may operate as a constraint on further enrolment growth at third level.

Finally, it is of interest to compare these findings on the academic attainment of entrants with those reported in the previous study. The findings relating to Cork replicate those from 1992 when it also had the highest level of educational attainment, suggesting that there is still a substantial pool of talented students who are not being catered for within the present system. The continuity with respect to Dublin is also striking. Two of the three previous surveys (1980 and 1986) found that Dublin has the lowest proportion of students with less than two honours while it was the fourth lowest in 1992. Thus our present finding that in 1998, second only to Cork, it had the highest level of attainment among entrants represents a consistent pattern which has shown little change over the past two decades. This consistency is reflected by the percentage with five or more honours and the percentage with less than two honours. This pattern is complemented by the consistency of its low admission rate and the low retention rate to Leaving Certificate. All of these combine to emphasise its unique position of disadvantage in Irish higher education.

Footnotes

1. The correlation between university admission rate and admission rate to colleges of education was .11 while the correlation between the technological admission rate and the admission rate to colleges of education was .55.

2. The urban centres chosen for measurement purposes served as an approximation for the total population hinterland. Since the ratio of the largest to smallest values was substantial a logarithmic transformation was carried out before proceeding with the multivariate analysis.

3. We have chosen to limit our measure of the lowest social classes to the two manual classes even though our findings reported in Chapter 3 show that the Non Manual class has a lower participation ratio than the Semi Skilled class. Most international research suggests that the critical divide between social classes, in terms of education, is that based on the Non-Manual/Manual distinction.

4. This is the problem of multicollinearity which exists when two or more independent variables are inter-correlated. In such cases the statistical estimation techniques used in regression analysis are incapable of sorting out the independent effect of each on the dependent variable. Where independent variables correlate at or in excess of $r=.80$ they may be suspected of exhibiting multicollinearity (see Bryman and Cramer, 1990).

5. The Beta coefficients of these predictor variables are shown in the first column of this table together with the associated T values, which allow us to assess their statistical significance.

6. While the zero order relationship between proportion of the population in farming and male and female admission rates was .11 and .15, respectively, the partial correlation between these variables rises to .58 and .69 when distance from college is introduced as a control. Similarly, when we control for proportion of the population in farming the relationship between distance from college and male and female admission rates rises (from $- .34$ and $-.70$) to $- .72$ and $- .80$.

7. After we take into account those who went to colleges in Northern Ireland it was the second lowest.

8. For a review of these issues see Report of Advisory Group on Student Support Schemes, 1993.

9. It will be recalled from Chapter 5 that the great majority of students from the Republic of Ireland who enrolled in Northern Ireland colleges entered the university sector and that univesity entrants tend to come from higher socio-economic groups (see Chapter 3).

10. This latter finding may be less significant since two of these are border counties with significant flows of students into Northern Ireland colleges.

chapter seven | Conclusion

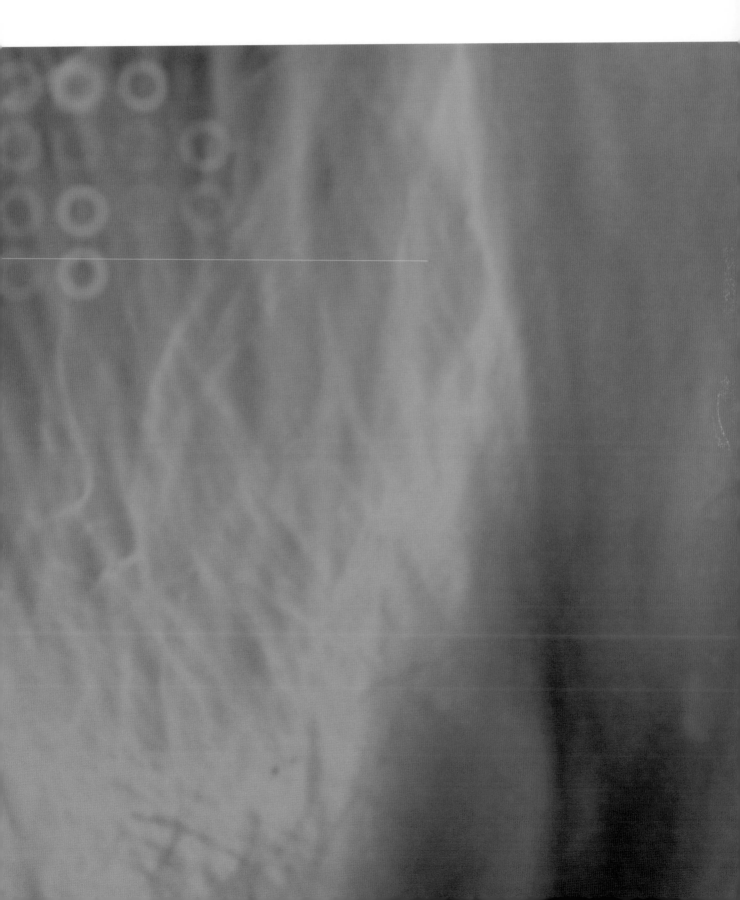

This study has examined the pattern of access to higher education in the Republic of Ireland in 1998. It is the fourth in a series of national surveys carried out at six-year intervals and thus facilitates an analysis of changes in the pattern of participation over a period of eighteen years. The present chapter summarises the main research findings. In addition, the chapter includes some discussion of the implications of the research findings. However, as discussed in the introduction, although the study is policy-oriented it does not seek to make far-reaching policy recommendations, its main aim is to add to the knowledge base which informs decision making. The author's position on the relationship between research and policy-making was discussed elsewhere (Clancy, 1988: 68), where Weiss's (1986) description of the 'enlightenment function' of research for policy-making was endorsed. It was argued that policy implications do not arise directly from the findings of empirical research and that value judgements will always influence the choice of policy options.

Summary

A total of 32,724 students were admitted as new entrants on the first year of an undergraduate programme to forty-three colleges of higher education in the Republic of Ireland in Autumn 1998. Forty-eight per cent of entrants were admitted to Institutes of Technology, with a further forty-five per cent admitted to the Universities. Three per cent of entrants were admitted to the Colleges of Education while a further four per cent were admitted to the heterogeneous 'Other Colleges' sector. The increase in the level of admission to higher education represents the continuation of a long-term trend. The increase in admissions between 1992 and 1998 was thirty per cent by comparison with an increase of forty-seven per cent between 1986 and 1992 and an increase of twenty-eight per cent between 1980 and 1986.

All sectors contributed to the enrolment growth between 1986 and 1992. Admissions to the Institute of Technology sector increased by almost a third, while the universities increased by almost a quarter. The 'Other Colleges' sector grew by fifteen per cent and while the Colleges of Education remains the smallest sector its enrolment increased by a factor of two and a half over the six-year period.

Technology was the field of study which enrolled the largest percentage (26%) of new entrants. More than a fifth (21%) were admitted to courses in Commerce, with a further seventeen per cent in the Humanities and twelve per cent entering courses in Science. A comparison of the distribution of entrants by field of study with previous national surveys reveals relative stability in the disciplinary balance over the past eighteen years. With the exception of Education in the period 1980-92 all fields of study participated in the enrolment growth. Looking at the entire period of almost two decades and focussing only on those fields of study that enrol large percentages of students we found that the Humanities (+171%),

Commerce (+157%) and Technology (+153%) all recorded growth rates somewhat in excess of the average for all fields of study (+145%). For the more recent period 1992-98, with the exception of Combined Studies, a recently introduced category, and Medical Sciences, the growth of which was influenced by the inclusion of Nursing Studies, the largest increases were recorded for Education, Hotel, Catering & Tourism, and Technology.

While female enrolments have been growing at a faster rate in recent years this is the first survey to record a female majority (53%) among entrants. This has removed an anomaly which has persisted for many years, whereby females have had higher retention rates to Leaving Certificate level, yet until now, this did not translate into higher rates of admission to third level. In 1998 the representation of females among higher education entrants fully reflects their proportionate representation among Leaving Certificate students. The distribution of entrants by gender was differentiated by sector and field of study. Females constituted a majority (58%) of entrants to the university sector and a preponderance (90%) of entrants to the Colleges of Education. In contrast, they formed a smaller percentage (45%) of entrants to the IT sector. Education emerged to be the most sex-typed field of study with males constituting only seventeen per cent of entrants. This is followed closely by Technology and Medical Science (including Nursing). Females constituted twenty-two per cent of entrants into Technology while the males constituted a similar percentage of entrants into Medical Sciences. Several other fields of study also reflected considerable gender imbalance, with significant females majorities in Social Science (75%), Hotel, Catering & Tourism (73%) and the Humanities (68%), In contrast, there was greater gender balance in Agriculture, Commerce and Science.

Fifty-five per cent of new entrants were enrolled on degree level courses with the remainder on Certificate or Diploma level programmes. This differentiation by level of programme is closely linked to the type of college attended, with the vast majority of sub-degree programmes concentrated in the Institute of Technology sector. The distinction between degree level and sub-degree level programmes refers only to the level of programmes on which students embark. Because of the cumulative nature of the NCEA award structure an increasing number of Certificants go on to study for Diplomas while many Diploma recipients subsequently go on to study for degrees.

Half of the new entrants were aged eighteen at the time of entry to higher education. A further nineteen per cent were aged seventeen while twenty-one per cent were aged nineteen. The remaining ten per cent were aged twenty or over. Less than five per cent of entrants could be classified as 'mature students', being aged twenty-three or over at the time of entry. While the age distribution is broadly similar to that recorded in 1992 there is evidence that recent entrants are somewhat older. The reduction (from 31% in 1992 to 19% in 1998) in the number of entrants aged seventeen or under is quite significant and represents a continuing trend since 1980 when forty-four per cent of entrants were in this age group. However, there is much less change at the other end of the age range. Between 1992 and 1998 there has only been a small increase in the percentage of 'mature students' (from 2.5% to 4.5%). Similarly, over the same six-year period, there has only been a three per cent increase in the percentage of entrants aged twenty or over (from 6.9% to 9.9%).

An important aim of this study was to examine the social background of entrants to higher education. It examines three main characteristics of parents of higher education entrants; principal economic status, socio-economic status and social class. In addition to reporting the findings from the 1998 college entry cohort the study also reports on the changes over time in respect of these characteristics. It compares the findings on socio-economic status with those from 1980, 1986 and 1992 while a comparison with the findings from the 1992 study is made in respect of principal economic status and social class.

An analysis of the principal economic status of parents revealed that eighty-three per cent of fathers were in employment, nine per cent were unemployed and almost seven per cent were retired. A comparison of the distribution of the principal economic status of fathers with the appropriate national distribution of 'ever-married' males revealed that young people whose fathers were unemployed were significantly 'under-represented' in higher education. While nine per cent of higher education entrants had fathers who were unemployed, eighteen per cent of ever married males aged 45-54 in the national population were unemployed [1].

In contrast with the situation of fathers, only forty per cent of mothers of higher education entrants were employed. Almost fifty-three per cent were classified as being on 'home duties', while less than five per cent were unemployed. A comparison with the national distribution of ever married females aged 45-54 revealed that young people, whose mothers were employed, were 'over-represented', while those on 'home duties' were 'under-represented' in higher education [2].

In Ireland to date, most analysis of the social background of higher education entrants is based on the occupations of parents as classified into one of the socio-economic groups used in the Census of Population. In the analysis of the 1996 Census of Population, the Central Statistics Office introduced a new classification system for socio-economic groups. This new classification system is used in this report. The study found large differences between socio-economic groups in levels of participation in higher education. Fifty-eight per cent of higher education entrants came from four socio-economic groups, (Higher Professional, Lower Professional, Employers and Managers and Farmers) although these groups constituted only thirty-seven per cent of the relevant population. In contrast, the other six socio-economic groups (Non-Manual, Manual Skilled, Semi-Skilled, Unskilled, Own Account Workers and Agricultural Workers) were seriously 'under-represented'; forty-one per cent of entrants came from these groups although they constituted sixty-three per cent of the relevant age cohort. The Higher Professional group was most strongly represented in higher education, taking almost twice the number of places, which its proportionate size in the population would warrant. This yields a participation ratio of 1.94. The representation of the Farmers group was also striking; it emerged as the second highest group, with a participation ratio of 1.77. It accounted for almost seventeen per cent of higher education entrants, although it accounts for only nine per cent of the relevant national population. In contrast, entrants from the Agricultural Workers and Unskilled groups had only a third of the higher education places, which their proportionate size in the population would warrant.

Information on the socio-economic status of mothers was available for thirty-nine per cent of entrants. Of these, almost forty per cent were from the Non-Manual group while thirty-two per cent were from the Lower Professional group. The percentages of mothers in these groups are significantly higher (by a factor of four and three, respectively) than for the comparable distribution of fathers. In contrast, mothers of higher education entrants were significantly less likely than fathers to come from the Employers and Managers, Higher Professional, Manual Skilled, Own Account Workers and Farmers groups.

The third measure of social background used in this study was that of social class. Although this ordinal social class scale is not long in use, the adoption of a new occupational classification system by the Central Statistics Office has also necessitated changes in this scale. A comparison of the distribution of higher education entrants with the national population confirmed the findings in respect of socio-economic groups. With one exception, the higher the social class the higher the participation ratio. Two social classes were 'over-represented': Professional Workers (participation ratio, 1.64) and the Managerial and Technical class (1.22). The main deviation from the common hierarchical ranking on the two distributions is in respect of the Non-Manual class. Its participation ratio is lower than that of the Skilled Manual and the Semi-Skilled. The participation ratio of the Skilled Manual is 1.0; its representation among higher education entrants corresponds exactly with its proportionate size in the national population of young people. The social class with the lowest representation was the Unskilled, with a participation ratio of 0.46, while the other 'under-represented' classes were the Non Manual (0.79) and the Semi-Skilled (0.82).

One of the advantages of the use of the social class scale is that it allows for the disaggregation of the Farmers' social group into one of five classes. It emerged that the class differences in admission rates, found in the non-farm sector, were replicated within the farming sector. Students from larger farms were 'over-represented' while those from smaller farms were 'under-represented'.

An important finding from the previous national surveys was that selectivity in overall levels of participation in higher education was complemented by further selectivity by sector and field of study. The present study replicates the finding that the more prestigious the sector and field of study, the greater the social inequality in participation levels. The Higher Professional and Employers and Managers groups had their strongest representation within the university sector, while students from the Manual Skilled, Semi-Skilled and Unskilled had their lowest representation in this sector. The three manual (Skilled, Semi-Skilled and Unskilled) groups, the Other Agricultural and Own Account Workers groups have their highest proportionate representation in the Institute of Technology sector.

There was further differentiation within the university sector. The Higher Professional group was the most strongly represented in Medicine, Law, Veterinary Medicine and Dentistry. In contrast, the Semi-Skilled and Unskilled groups had their lowest representation in Architecture, Veterinary Medicine, Equestrian Studies, Medicine, Economics and Social Studies and Law.

The distribution of financial aid is related to the socio-economic background of entrants. The groups with the highest percentage of students in receipt of financial aid were the Unskilled Manual (78.6%) and the Agricultural Workers group (75.6%). In contrast, only thirteen per cent of the Higher Professional group and eighteen per cent of the Lower Professional group were in receipt of financial aid. The distribution of financial aid amongst the Farmers' group was related to the farm size. For those with 200 acres or more, twenty-five per cent were in receipt of financial aid, while this rose to seventy-three per cent for those with less than thirty acres.

A major objective of this study is to examine trends over time in levels of inequality in access to higher education. However, such comparisons have been complicated by changes introduced by the Central Statistics Office in the classification of socio-economic groups and social classes. In addition to using the new classification system, this study also recoded data on parents' occupation in terms of the 'older' socio-economic and social class categories to facilitate an analysis of change over time. Our main comparison is based on fathers' socio-economic group since it is only in respect of this variable that we have data from all four surveys.

Drawing on the results of the four national surveys, we have calculated estimates of the percentages of each socio-economic group entering higher education. While acknowledging that these percentages are 'estimates', and hence subject to a margin of error, they provide a reasonable measure of the changes in equality of access to higher education. Since the overall rate of admission to higher education in Ireland has risen from twenty per cent in 1980 to forty-four per cent in 1998, it is not surprising that, most social groups experienced a progressive increase in the proportion going on to higher education.

Furthermore, the highest proportionate increase occurred for those lower socio-economic groups, which had very low participation rates in 1980. For the Unskilled Manual group the 1998 estimate is twenty-one per cent, compared with a mere three per cent in 1980. The proportionate increase for the Other Agricultural Occupations group is also impressive, rising from six per cent in 1980 to thirty-four per cent in 1998. The rates for the other three groups, which were 'under-represented' in 1980, have also increased significantly, if less dramatically. In 1980 each of these groups had a participation rate of nine per cent; the 1998 estimate is thirty-two per cent, thirty-one per cent and twenty-three per cent, respectively, for the Skilled Manual, Other Non-Manual and Semi-Skilled groups.

At the other end of the spectrum, the progressive increase in the estimated participation rate of those groups, which were already 'over-represented' in 1980, is striking. In all four surveys, the Higher Professional group has had the highest participation rate. And while our 1998 estimate of ninety-seven hundred per cent is clearly an overestimate it would appear that the higher education participation rate of this group must be close to saturation level, having risen progressively from an estimated fifty-nine per cent in 1980. The group with the second highest participation rate is the Employers and Managers group. The 1998 estimate is an impressive eighty-one per cent, having increased in each successive survey from forty-two per cent in 1980. The participation rate of the Farmers group is the third highest, having reached an estimated seventy-two per cent in 1998. Here, also, the pattern is one of continuing improvement, with the increase between 1992 and 1998 (from 53% to 72%) being especially noteworthy.

By comparison with the former eight groups, the performance of three socio-economic groups (Lower Professional, Salaried Employees and Intermediate Non-Manual) reveals a pattern of very modest improvement. Indeed in the case of the Salaried Employee's group the 1998 estimated participation rate is still below the 1980 estimate, although there is evidence of improvement (from 48% to 53%) between 1992 and 1998. There is no obvious explanation as to why the Salaried Employees group should not have participated in the general increase in admission rates over the entire period covered by these studies. However, as noted in the report on the 1992 study, it is necessary to keep in mind, that even at present levels, this group is one of those 'over-represented' in higher education.

The pattern of change for the Lower Professional group is broadly similar to that of the Salaried Employees group. While it continues to be 'over-represented', and while it has improved its participation rate between 1992 and 1998, the rate of increase over the longer period is modest. Finally, the Intermediate Non-Manual group, which joined the 'under-represented' in the 1992 study is also 'under-represented' in the present study. The 1998 estimate is that less than one-third of this social group entered higher education.

While our main indicator of changes in the social background of higher education entrants is in respect of socio-economic status, it is also possible to look at changes in the principal economic status and social class of parents over the more recent period 1992 to 1998. Our main interest in principal socio-economic status of parents centres on the incidence of employment and unemployment. While the findings from the 1998 survey are broadly similar to those from 1992, there is some evidence that the situation of those coming from families where the father is unemployed has disimproved relative to those whose fathers are in employment. While Census figures show little change between 1991 and 1996 in the incidence of unemployment among ever-married males aged 45-54, there was a decline (from 10.9% to 8.9%) in the percentage of higher education entrants coming from families where the father was unemployed. The main change in respect of the principal economic status of mothers was the significant increase in the percentage of those in employment (from 25.5% to 40.3%) and the decline in the percentages on 'home duties'.

To monitor change in the pattern of access to higher education by social class it was necessary, as in the case of socio-economic groups, to revert to the use of the 'old' social class scale. To compare the findings from the 1992 and 1998 studies we have estimated the percentage of each social class entering higher education in each year. And while, as in the case of the comparison by socio-economic group, it is necessary to keep in mind that these participation rates are 'estimates', to which the same caveats apply, we believe that these estimates provide a clear picture of the changing patterns of admission to higher education by social class. The main finding is one of considerable continuity. The rank order of the social classes in terms of their participation rates is common for the two studies. In both, the higher the social class, the higher the levels of participation in third level education. Since the overall rate of admission increased from thirty-six per cent in 1992 to forty-four per cent in 1998, it is of interest to note that all social classes participated in this increase. However, the rate of increase is not uniform. Two of the Manual groups have registered especially large increases. The Skilled Manual group shows the largest absolute increase, from twenty-eight to thirty-eight per cent, while the Unskilled Manual group registers the largest proportionate increase, rising from twelve per cent to twenty-one per cent. In contrast, the Semi-Skilled group registered only a small increase from twenty-two to twenty-four per cent. The other group to show a small rate of increase was the Other Non Manual group, which increased from thirty-eight to forty-one per cent. Both of the Professional groups showed significant increases of six and eight per cent, respectively, for the Higher and Lower Professional groups.

To complement our analysis of the pattern of access to higher education, this report also includes an analysis of data from the three most recent School Leavers Surveys. It has been found that differential participation and performance at second level serve as proximate determinants of access to higher education. This aspect of the report replicates work done by the Technical Working Group (1995), which supported the Steering Committee on the Future Development of Higher

Education. The ESRI provided data from the three most recent School Leavers Surveys, carried out in 1996, 1997 and 1998. These data relate to school leavers from the school years 1994/95, 1995/96 and 1997/98. They allow us to examine the inter-relationship between the principal socio-economic status of school leavers (based on fathers' occupation), educational level, attainment, and destination upon leaving school.

An analysis of the data from the School Leavers Survey allows us to delineate three second-level transitions, which relate directly to access to higher education. The first crucial transition is whether students continue in school to take the Leaving Certificate. While overall, almost eighty-one per cent of school leavers have taken the Leaving Certificate and less than four per cent left before taking the Junior Certificate, the second level retention rate varies by social group. Only seven per cent of the two Professional groups failed to make the transition to Leaving Certificate, by comparison with thirty-five per cent of the Unskilled Manual group.

The second 'transition' relates to the level of achievement of those school leavers who stay to complete the Leaving Certificate. To progress to higher education it is not enough to sit the Leaving Certificate; it is also necessary to reach a satisfactory level of performance. We found that the pattern of attainment is strongly influenced by socio-economic group; the higher the school leavers' socio-economic group the higher the level of attainment. For example, more than half the students from Higher Professional (55.9%) and Lower Professional (51.1%) groups have 'honours' in five or more subjects. This is true of just twelve and fourteen per cent, respectively, of those from Unskilled and Semi-Skilled Manual backgrounds. In contrast, these latter socio-economic groups are 'over-represented' among those with lower levels of attainment. For the Unskilled and Semi-Skilled Manual groups, the incidence of those who failed to get at least five passes is twice the average for all groups.

The third transition, which we document is in respect of those who have both survived to Leaving Certificate level and achieved a minimum attainment threshold in this examination. The socio-economic differentials evident at this transition are closely related to level of attainment. In general, for those with modest levels of attainment the percentages going on to higher education are lowest for the manual groups. For those with just a pass Leaving Certificate and those with just one honour, the percentages from the Unskilled Manual group entering higher education are just nine and eight per cent, respectively. This compares with more than thirty per cent for the Higher Professional group. However, for those with better Leaving Certificates the socio-economic differentials in the transition to higher education are not significant. This absence of significant socio-economic group differentials is most marked for those with the highest level of attainment (5 or more honours).

Because of our concern with monitoring changes in levels of inequality in access to higher education, we have compared these findings from the most recent School Leavers Surveys with those from a similar analysis, which relate to the late 1980s and early 1990s. The overall patterns are very similar. However some interesting trends are evident. In relation to the first transition, the main change over the period is an improvement in the retention rates among the lower socio-economic groups. There has been an increase of thirteen per cent in the numbers from the Semi-Skilled and Unskilled Manual groups who leave school with Leaving Certificate level of education.

In respect of the second transition, which relates to the level of achievement in the Leaving Certificate, while there is some improvement in the overall level of achievement, there is no clear pattern in the changes in performance by socio-economic group. The third transition relates to the transfer to higher education from that cohort which has both survived to Leaving Certificate level and achieved a minimum attainment threshold in this examination. There has been an increase of twelve per cent in the numbers going on to higher education and while this increase is more marked for those with high levels of attainment it is also significant for those with only a pass Leaving Certificate. However, there has only been a minimal change in the transfer rate from the Higher Professional and Employers and Managers groups, perhaps because the rates for these groups were already close to saturation in the early 1990s.

Our analysis of the School Leavers Surveys complements our own study of the pattern of participation in higher education, since it is clear that the social group differentials in third-level participation find their origins in differential patterns of participation and performance through the second level system. Furthermore, in a special analysis of the situation of the Semi-Skilled and Unskilled Manual groups we found that the estimate of the rate of transfer into higher education, using the School Leavers Survey data, serves to validate our own estimates from the 1992 and 1998 surveys.

This is the first survey to be carried out since the introduction of 'free fees' for the vast majority of undergraduate students. The main exception relates to those students who attend private colleges. With the elimination of tuition fees for the majority of students our analysis of the pattern of financial aid focused on the receipt of means-tested maintenance grants. Overall, thirty-six per cent of entrants were in receipt of means-tested financial aid. The percentage was highest in the Institute of Technology sector at forty-five per cent; twenty-seven per cent of university entrants were in receipt of aid, while the rates for the colleges of Education and 'Other Colleges' were twenty-seven and sixteen per cent respectively. Because of the changes in the student funding regime direct comparison is not possible with earlier studies. However, it is of interest to note the reduction in the percentage who qualified for means-tested aid fell from fifty-one per cent in 1992 to thirty-five per cent in the present study.

Predictably, the pattern of financial aid is related to the socio-economic background of entrants. The groups with the highest percentages in receipt of means-tested aid were the Unskilled (78%) and Agricultural Workers (74%). In contrast, the percentage of students in receipt of such aid from the white-collar groups was much lower, ranging from nine per cent for the Higher Professional group to thirty-two per cent for the Non-Manual group. Fifty-seven per cent of entrants from the Farmers socio-economic group were in receipt of means-tested aid; this was higher than the rate for the Skilled Manual group (55%) and only one per cent lower than the rate for the Semi-Skilled group (58%).

Turning to an analysis of the educational background of entrants we found that seventy-two per cent of entrants came from Secondary schools, a further fourteen per cent attended Vocational schools, eleven per cent attended Community schools while the remainder came from Comprehensive schools or other, mainly private non-recognised schools. Linking these data on school background with aggregate enrolment data for state-aided schools we have estimated a transfer rate for each school type. Overall, the 1998 new entrants represented over fifty-four per cent of the Leaving Certificate class of 1997/98. The overall transfer rate for secondary schools was sixty per cent; the rate for fee-paying secondary schools was seventy-one per cent compared with fifty-nine per cent for non-fee paying secondary schools. In contrast, the transfer rate for vocational schools was thirty-eight per cent. The transfer rate for comprehensive schools (57%) was broadly similar to that of non-fee paying secondary schools while the rate for community schools was fifty per cent.

An analysis of the level of prior academic attainment of entrants revealed a wide range of attainment levels. Six per cent of entrants had no subject with 'honours' (i.e. Grade C or higher on a Higher level paper) while a total of fifteen per cent had less than two honours, thus falling below the minimum matriculation requirement for university entry. In contrast sixty per cent of entrants had four or more honours while thirteen per cent had seven or more subjects with this level of attainment. Significant differences were evident in the level of attainment of entrants to the different third level colleges. The modal level of attainment of entrants to the universities and colleges of education was six honours. The largest percentage (42%) of entrants to the Institutes of Technology two or three subjects with honours, a pattern which was broadly similar to that found in the 'Other Colleges' sector where forty-four per cent of entrants had this level of attainment.

A comparison of the levels of attainment of 1998 entrants with those reported in the previous national surveys revealed an interesting pattern. The findings for the present cohort are broadly similar with those from the 1992 study. While the percentage of entrants with less than two honours has risen from four per cent in 1992 to six per cent in 1998 the percentages with six or more honours has increased over the period from twenty-eight per cent in 1992 to thirty-two per cent by 1998. This broad similarity of findings between the last two surveys stands in contrast to that which we have reported previously. In the report on the 1992 survey we noted a continuing rise in the level of attainment of new entrants between 1980 and 1992. It is clear that this continuing rise in attainment has been halted.

In addition to reporting on the level of attainment of entrants we also examined the pattern of subject specialisation at second level, comparing the college entry cohort with the total Leaving Certificate cohort and examining the link between the pattern of subject specialisation at second level and third level field of study. In respect of the latter we found that students with more than three Language subjects in the Leaving Certificate were more likely to study Law, Humanities and Combined Studies while those with more Leaving Certificate Science subjects were disproportionately represented in Medical Science, Science and Agriculture. The take-up of Leaving Certificate Business subjects was also linked to field of study destinations. This was most evident in respect of those who entered Commerce who tended to have significantly more Business subjects at Leaving Certificate level but was also a feature of those who entered Social Science and Combined Studies. Although the overall level of take-up of Technical subjects at Leaving Certificate level was low, especially for females, predictably, the highest level of take-up was associated with those who enrolled to study Technology. Students who enrolled to study Education and Art and Design were also somewhat more likely to have studied Leaving Certificate Technical subjects. Finally, the take-up of subjects from the heterogeneous 'other subjects' group (Home Economics, History, Geography, Art and Music) was also linked with third level field of study. Students who entered programmes in Art and Design, Hotel, Catering and Tourism, and the Humanities had significantly higher take-up rates in these subjects.

An important feature of this study is the comprehensive analysis of national and county participation rates. Following the pattern of the three earlier national surveys the focus was on the rate of admission, calculated on the basis of the flow of new entrants. It is our view that the rate of admission provides the most sensitive indicator of trends in participation. It was found that the national rate of admission to higher education was forty-four per cent. This represents a significant increase on the 1980 rate of twenty per cent, the 1986 rate of twenty-five per cent and the 1992 rate of thirty-six per cent.

Rates of admission varied significantly by county. Galway had the highest rate of admission with an impressive fifty-seven per cent of the age cohort enrolled in higher education. Seven other counties had rates of admission in excess of fifty per cent. These were in descending order: Mayo, Sligo, Leitrim, Kerry, Limerick, Roscommon and Clare. Before taking account of the flow of students into colleges in Northern Ireland Donegal had the lowest rate of admission at thirty-five per cent. Three other counties had admission rates of less than forty per cent. These were in ascending order, Dublin, Offaly and

Laois. Other counties with relatively low rates of admission were Monaghan, Kilkenny, Wicklow, Kildare and Waterford, all of which had admission rates of forty-one per cent. A clear regional pattern is evident. The eight counties with admission rates in excess of fifty per cent are all from the West, the five Connaught counties, Kerry, Limerick and Clare. In contrast, the counties with the lowest rates are two of the three Ulster counties (Donegal and Monaghan), Dublin and other Eastern and South-East counties and the Midland counties of Laois and Offaly. In general, these findings on the relative ranking of counties are very similar to those found in the previous national surveys.

The foregoing description of the rates of admission to higher education relates only to those students who were admitted to colleges in the Republic of Ireland. However, information was also collected on those students from the Republic who were new entrants to full-time higher education in Northern Ireland. The inclusion of these students in our analysis increased significantly the admission rates in some counties: Donegal (+10.5%), Monaghan (+8.1%) and Louth (+3.2%). In addition three other counties (Sligo, Cavan and Leitrim) increased their admission rate by at least one per cent. After these additions Monaghan and Donegal now joint the other border counties of Cavan and Louth with 'medium' admission rates. The net effect of the inclusion of data from colleges in Northern Ireland is to sharpen the regional differentiation in admission rates. Dublin now has the lowest overall rate of admission to higher education and all of the counties in the lower third of the ranking now come from the East, Midlands and South East. These are in ascending order Dublin, Offaly, Laois, Kilkenny, Waterford, Wicklow, Kildare, Wexford and Carlow.

A separate analysis was made of intra-county differences through an examination of admission rates by postal district in Dublin. This analysis revealed very large variability by district. For example, five of the districts in the south of the city had admission rates in excess of fifty per cent. These ranged from seventy-seven per cent in Dublin 18 to fifty-six per cent in Dublin 16. Only one of the districts in the North city (Dublin 3) had an admission rate in excess of fifty per cent. In contrast, there were very low admission rates in Dublin 10 (7%), Dublin 17 (8%) and the North Inner City (9%). Other districts with admission rates of less than half the average for Dublin City and County were Dublin 22 (13%), Dublin 11 (14%) and Dublin 20 (17%). The variability in admission rates, which reflects the socio-economic patterning of the population, replicates closely the findings from our earlier studies in respect of higher education entrants in 1978 and 1992.

A further aspect of the variability in admission rates in Dublin was the differential take-up of degree and sub-degree courses in the different districts. In general the ratio of degree to sub-degree admission rates was significantly higher in the affluent parts of the city. In contrast, this ratio was less than half the average for Dublin in Postal districts 1, 17, 24, and 22.

In summary, areas of Dublin with a high concentration of lower socio-economic groups tended to have low admission rates to higher education and for those who were admitted they were significantly more likely to enrol on sub-degree courses.

Having provided evidence of major regional disparities in rates of admission to higher education an attempt was made to explain some inter-county differences. Three groups of variables were examined as possible predictors of differential admission rates: these variables were distance from the nearest college, pattern of participation at second level and some socio-economic variables. For the purpose of this analysis county admission rates were disaggregated by gender and sector. A multivariate analysis found that each group of variables possessed some explanatory power in respect of county admission rates to the university and Institute of Technology sectors.

In respect of distance from college the present analysis replicated the findings of the two previous national surveys that rates of admission to university education are negatively related to distance from the nearest university college. Counties, which are distance from a university, had a lower rate of admission to university education. This finding was most emphatic in respect of females and while the direction of the relationship is the same for males it falls short of being statistically significant. In contrast, distance from an Institute of Technology is not an important predictor of the county rate of admission to the IT sector. Although our multivariate analysis reveals a weak inverse relationship it is not statistically significant. This finding is broadly similar to those from the 1992 study. However distance from a university is positively associated with the rate of admission to the IT sector. This latter finding is consistent with those from two of the three earlier surveys, the exception being 1992. The link between distance from university and the rate of admission to the IT sector suggests that, especially for females, different forms of higher education may be substitutable for one another depending on the opportunity cost.

These differential findings are illustrated by the fact that three (Galway, Cork and Limerick) of the four counties with highest rates of admission to the university sector have a university in the county. Furthermore, while Dublin, Cork and Limerick have at least one Institute of Technology they have the lowest proportionate representation of entrants in the technological sector. When we look at the nine counties with highest rates of admission to the IT sector we notice that while six of these counties have an Institute of Technology located within the county only one of the nine has a university.

Three of the predictor variables included in this analysis represent the pattern of participation at second-level. An important finding of the study was that retention rate to Leaving Certificate level contributed significantly to the explained variance in the rate of admission to the university sector and to the Institute of Technology sector. Counties with a high retention rate to Leaving Certificate level had a high rate of admission to higher education. When this finding was compared with those from the earlier surveys there was some evidence that over time the rate of admission to higher education in a county is becoming more dependent on the retention rate to the end of the senior cycle. An additional finding of the multivariate analysis, which applied only to females in the IT sector, was that counties, which had a high proportion of post-primary enrolments in secondary schools, had a high female rate of admission to the Institute of Technology sector.

In all five socio-economic variables made a significant contribution to the explained variance in county admission rates to higher education. In the case of admission rates to university education the proportion of the population engaged in farming proved to be a very important predictor for both males and females. Counties which had a high proportion of the population engaged in farming had higher rates of admission to university. The educational attainment of the adult population also helped to predict the rate of admission to university education. Counties with a high proportion of the population whose full-time education ceased at age twenty or over had higher male rates of admission to university education. The explanatory power of this variable with respect to male admission rates was matched by a closely related variable in case of female rates of admission. The larger the proportion of the population in the higher social classes the higher was the female rate of admission to university education.

The socio-economic variables were less important predictors of the rate of admission to the Institute of Technology sector. For males, the best predictor of the rate of admission was the proportion of the population living in urban areas. The larger the proportion of the population living in urban areas, the lower was the rate of admission to the Institute of Technology sector. In the case of female admission rates to the IT sector the proportion of the population who left school under fifteen years of age emerged as an important predictor. The lower the educational level of the adult population the higher was the rate of admission to the IT sector.

In addition to the thirteen variables included in the multivariate analysis as possible predictors of county admission rates, three other correlates of differential admission rates were also examined. A social class inequality index was calculated for each county and this was correlated with the rate of admission to higher education. Although not statistically significant, there was a modest inverse relationship between these variables revealing a tendency for counties with high rates of admission to have lower levels of social class inequality. Variability by county in the distribution of financial aid was also examined. There was considerable variability in the distribution of financial aid by county, ranging from a mere sixteen per cent in Dublin to sixty-two per cent in Mayo. Although not statistically significant, there was a weak positive relationship between the percentage of entrants in receipt of aid and the county rate of admission to higher education.

Finally, variability by county in the distribution of entrants by level of prior academic achievement was examined. There was no relationship between county admission rates and the proportion of entrants with low levels of academic achievement. This suggests that, with the possible exception of a few counties, for the country as a whole we have not reached an ability threshold, which limits the scope for further expansion in higher education enrolments.

Discussion

In our introduction we have already drawn attention to the remarkable increase in higher education participation rates in Ireland and internationally over the past half century. From a comparative perspective Ireland's performance, which ranks ahead of many European countries, represents a significant achievement in public policy. The large increase in the admission rate, from twenty per cent in 1980 to more than forty-four per cent in 1998, was partly fuelled by rising retention rates at second level. However it also reflects a significant increase in the transfer rate by Leaving Certificate students into higher education. New entrants to higher education in 1998 accounted for fifty-four per cent of the 1997/98 Leaving Certificate cohort. This compares with a transfer rate of about a third in 1980.

While our admission rate is now broadly in line with the average for Western Europe[3] it is appropriate to ask whether there is still scope for further growth. This question has been considered by the Steering Committee on the Future Development of Higher Education (1995) and more recently by the Review Committee on Post Secondary Education and Training Places (1999). The former report set an enrolment target of 121,000 for 2010/11, representing an increase of some 30,000 over the existing 1994/95 stock enrolment figures. The Review Committee did not query this target and suggested that the appropriate strategic objective for Ireland must be to first achieve and then maintain a position within the top quarter of OECD countries in terms of the participation of the population in post second-level education and training, and in the quality of that education and training. This objective stems from an analysis of the changing international environment and the growing consensus that advanced education and training are critical for sustaining national competitive advantage (Porter, 1990). In this context it is of interest to note the achievements and ambitious targets set by many other countries. For example, the OECD reports that by 1995 in Japan sixty-three per of the 18-year-old cohort were already enrolled in some kind of tertiary institution while Finland has declared that at least sixty per cent of the age cohort will participate in tertiary education by the early 21st century. Thus the OECD (1999: 9) survey team argues that a new paradigm is emerging 'whereby participation in some form of tertiary education may be expected to be the norm in our society'. In contrast with the situation two decades ago when 'universal' was taken to be fifty per cent of the age cohort, now it may be eighty per cent or more.

In terms of the progress achieved in respect of these targets is of interest to note that the enrolment growth achieved between 1994/95 and 1998/99 was ahead of that projected by the Steering Committee. While stock enrolments in the IT sector were almost 2,000 below that projected, the university sector was more than 4,000 ahead of the projections. When we compare the educational attainment of the Irish population against the OECD benchmarks we note that, while in respect of third level attainment, Ireland is about average for the population aged 25-64, it is above the average, although still not in the first quarter, for the 25-34 age cohort. However, it is significant that in relation to completion of second level education Ireland remains below the average for both the 25-64 and 25-44 age cohort. While the differences in educational attainment between the different age cohorts reflect the recency of the rapid expansion of post-compulsory education, they underline the particular challenge which we have yet to face in respect of redressing the generational inequality in access to higher education. Our findings, that less than five per cent of entrants were aged twenty-three or over, testify to the magnitude of this task. The Steering Committee recommended that the percentage of 'mature' students should increase from 1,100 (3.7%) in 1993/94 to about 2,200 (6.2%) in 2000 to about 5,600 (16%) by 2010. It would appear that on the basis of current trends (1,450 matures in 1998) that this target is unlikely to be met with existing policies.

This lack of progress has been recognised by the Action Group on Access (2001: 81-100) which proposes a wide range of policy initiatives in this area. This group seeks to broaden the policy agenda to include specific enrolment targets for part-time as well as full-time mature students, which should be met within the lifetime of the National Development Plan 2000-2006. Although existing data in this area are inadequate the Action Group estimates that most (82%) part-time entrants to higher education are mature. Taking both part-time and full-time students into account it is estimated that mature students accounted for about twenty-two per cent of total entrants in 1998. Its recommended targets for the duration of the National Development Plan are that this be increased to twenty-six per cent in 2003 and thirty per cent by 2006. Within this overall target it suggests separate targets for full-time mature students of seven and ten per cent, respectively, for 2003 and 2006.

It is because of the our very poor provision for mature students, by comparison with other Western countries (Clancy, 1999), that both the Steering Committee and the Review Committee have recommended relatively ambitious enrolment targets notwithstanding the substantial decline in the age cohort which has begun to effect the size of the conventional college entry age cohort. It should not simply be a matter of expediency that colleges are now willing to extend a welcome to mature students to offset the decline in the eighteen year old cohort. Social justice considerations should impel us to tackle the generational inequalities. By a happy coincidence such action is also justified by instrumental considerations since the speed of social and technological change dictate that we plan higher education as an integral part of life long learning with strong links to the community and the labour market as well as to secondary schooling.

In our last report we raised some questions, which arise in any decision to plan for increased provision of higher education places: (1) which sector should provide these places? (2) what level of programmes should be provided i.e. degree level or sub-degree level? and (3) in what fields of study should the places be provided? These are important policy questions that have attracted little public debate in Ireland. Decisions in these areas involve delicate judgements about the intrinsic value of different educational experiences, an assessment of the requirements of the labour market and a related knowledge about the labour market experience of different graduates. The issue of optimum resource utilisation is also relevant with a need to adjudicate on the conflicting claims of those who argue for a greater concentration of resources versus those who advocate a greater dispersal in programme provision. International comparisons of developments in other higher education systems can also be relevant. The latter comparisons point to the fact that Ireland currently has one of the highest concentrations of entrants on sub-degree programmes in Western Europe (OECD, 1999b). While this may suggest that there is a greater need for extra provision on degree level courses it gives no guidance on whether these are best provided on ab initio degree programmes or on add-on degree programmes. The latter judgment requires an assessment in terms of quality, cost effectiveness and accessibility of the different types of degree. After a preliminary review of some of these issues the report of the Technical Working Group (1995) in its Interim Report to the Steering Committee on the Future Development of Higher Education suggested that there was a need for a specially commissioned review of this policy issue. This has not happened to date.

However, in the absence of such a review some changes are evident at least in relation to the first of these questions. As we have already noted, enrolment growth in the university sector has run ahead of projections while growth in the IT sector is somewhat lower than that projected. This may reflect some change in client demand, a trend that is also reflected in the changing points requirements in the different sectors. The change in client demand may have been influenced by the abolition of undergraduate fees in the university sector. This policy change altered the pricing policy for different forms of higher education. The Institute of Technology sector lost the pricing advantage which its sub-degree programmes had vis-a-vis degree level programmes. Under the European Social Fund grant scheme all sub-degree programmes were tuition free prior to the general abolition of undergraduate fees. A related factor, which of course may not be known to potential students, is the evidence on the economic returns to education. Barrett et al (1999) have reported increasing returns to degree qualifications over the period 1987 -'94 while returns to non-degree third level certificates and diplomas fell in relative terms.

A unique feature of Irish life is the emergence in recent years of labour market shortages in some areas. This situation is being monitored by an Expert Group on Future Skills Needs. Of particular concern in the technology area is the decline in the number of Leaving Certificate students taking science subjects, especially Physics and Chemistry. This is evident in our analysis over the three most recent surveys. For example, while the percentages taking Biology has shown little change the percentages of Leaving Certificate students taking Chemistry and Physics have declined from twenty per cent and nineteen per cent respectively in 1984, to twelve and sixteen per cent respectively in 1998. This supply side constraint is reflected in the educational profile of higher education entrants. In 1986 about a third of higher education entrants had taken Chemistry (35%) and/or Physics (33%). By 1998 this had dropped to seventeen per cent for Chemistry and twenty-two per cent for Physics. Thus, while higher education entrants are much more likely than the total Leaving Certificate cohort to have studied Chemistry and/or Physics the decline in the take-up of these subjects is likely to operate as a constraint on recruitment into certain forms of higher education. This can operate both as an absolute constraint where certain subjects may be defined as perquisites for some courses but it also operates as a filtering mechanism influencing choice of field of study.

Our discussion linking the future expansion of higher education with the need to make greatly improved provision for mature student, the majority of whom are likely to wish to study part-time, points to a limitation of this research. The scope of our study, like that of the earlier surveys, has been limited to full-time students. A further limitation of the study is that it does not deal with students with a disability. This issue is the subject of a separate study, the initial findings of which were published in November 2000 (AHEAD, 2000). In addition, the limited provision for students with disabilities was also one of the concerns of the Action Group on Access (2001) which made a series of policy recommendations in this area. The Action Group was also concerned with the issue of students from socio-economically disadvantaged backgrounds, which has been a special focus of this study and of previous national surveys.

Our study of the social background of higher education entrants can be viewed within the context of a substantial body of international research, which has sought to study the relationship between levels of socio-economic inequality and expanding enrolments. Perhaps the most robust finding from this literature is that whereas the proportion of all social classes attending higher levels of education has increased the relative advantage associated with higher class origins persists. For example, in a thirteen-country study, Shavit and Blossfield (1993) report that only two countries, Sweden and the Netherlands, have achieved a significant equalisation among socio-economic groups. This conclusion is based on an analysis of relative chances of different social groups attaining a specific educational level. While, in most countries, the working class have increased their absolute chances of going on to some form of higher education, class inequalities measured in relative terms have remained relatively stable in recent decades.

While the research literature offers a variety of ways of quantifying changes in levels of inequality, such as simple odds and percentage differences (Ambler and Neathery, 1999) and odds ratios (Barry, 1999), there is no statistical tool which can substitute for critical judgement on this matter. For example, if we compare the changes, between 1980 and 1998, with respect to the six socio-economic groups which were 'over-represented' in 1980, and the five groups which were 'under-represented', we find that in 1980, thirty-five per cent of the former and eight per cent of the latter group entered higher education. This was at a time when the overall rate of admission was twenty per cent. By 1998, when the overall rate had risen to forty-four per cent, the rate for the six higher socio-economic groups was fifty-nine per cent versus twenty-nine per cent for the lower socio-economic groups. A comparison of the relative odds of entering higher education for the two subgroups has changed from more that four to one in 1980 to two to one in 1998, suggesting that there was a significant reduction in inequality. However, the percentage difference between the two groups has slightly increased over the period, from twenty-seven per cent in 1980 to thirty per cent in 1998. The use of odds ratios, an approach which has become popular in recent years, also gives an equivocal answer[4]. While a comparison of the 1980 and 1998 data shows a reduction in inequality, this reduction has not been continuous; the odds ratios for 1992 and 1998 suggest that inequality actually increased in the most recent period. However, if the same technique is applied to the data on estimated participation rates by social class, comparing the three highest with the three lowest social classes, the reduction in the odds ratio suggests a continuing decline in inequality between 1992 and 1998[5].

Thus, there is no magic statistical tool which allows for an unambiguous answer to the question of whether or not the dramatic expansion in provision and take-up of higher education places has resulted in a reduction in inequality by social group. It is a matter of individual judgement to assess whether the increase in the participation rate of the five 'under-represented' social groups, from eight per cent in 1980 to twenty-nine per cent in 1998, is more significant, than the change in the representation of the 'over-represented' groups, from thirty-five per cent to fifty-nine per cent. It is our view that an assessment of change requires us to take account of changes both in absolute and relative participation rates. Thus, in looking at changes in the situation of the two lowest socio-economic groups (Semi-Skilled and Unskilled Manual) we need to acknowledge the significance of the increase from six to twenty-two per cent. By any standards, the change from almost seventeen to one to about four and a half to one in the probability of accessing higher education represents a significant improvement, irrespective of how other groups may have fared over the period.

However, in a society with growing credential inflation, a focus on relative inequalities is also apposite. Educational credentials, as Hirsch (1977) reminds us, are 'positional goods' where the value of a qualification is partly a function of its scarcity. In this context we have to take account of the competition between groups to achieve the most highly valued credentials. Hence, it is not enough to monitor the absolute increases in access to higher education from historically 'under-represented' groups, we must also compare this rate of progress with that achieved by other social groups. This focus on relative inequalities also legitimates our decision to disaggregate between different types of higher education. The social selectivity by sector and field of study, which we have reported, reflects another increment of this competition to ascend the hierarchy to the scarcest and most highly valued credential.

An important contribution to the international literature on the relationship between expansion and changing levels of inequality is that made by Rafterty and Hout (1993). Arising out of their analysis of the relationship between inequality and expanded educational provision in Ireland over the period 1921-75, they advance the hypothesis of maximally maintained inequality. This hypothesis suggests that in the absence of growth in educational systems there will be no redistribution of educational opportunity among social classes. Growth will enhance the educational chances of formerly disadvantaged groups mainly through the principle of non-selection, whereby more and more students pass on to advanced levels of schooling. Relative inequalities between classes are likely to change only when demand for advanced schooling from the privileged class is saturated.

In the absence of greatly expanded provision, it is unlikely that there would have been any significant reduction in class inequalities. Our analysis suggests that the demand for third level places from the Higher Professional group has now reached saturation level and that the demand from the Employers and Managers group must be approaching this level. This suggests that as provision increases or as the size of the college going age cohort decreases there will be scope for further reductions in inequality.

However, the maximally maintained inequality hypothesis may be unduly pessimistic. It has, as Shavit and Blossfeld report, been possible for at least some societies to achieve a reduction in inequality before saturation of attendance by privileged groups has been achieved. The possibility of making such progress may, as in the case of Sweden and the Netherlands, be linked to a more general policy of equalisation of socio-economic conditions in the wider society or it may follow from specific policy interventions in education. In respect of the latter it is worth noting that an important consequence of increased provision is to lessen the degree of competition for places since it well established that access by competition to a scarce resource always tends to favour the privileged (Reid, 1991). Some policy initiatives can alter the terms under which competition takes place. For example, one of the initiatives recommended by the Steering Committee on the Future Development of Higher Education (1995) and more recently by the Action Group on Access (2001) and which is now in place in some colleges, is to reserve some places for students from disadvantaged backgrounds. The entry requirements and admission procedure for these places differ from those for the general intake. Since this and other policy initiatives have been the subject of a several recent reviews (Osborne and Leith, 2000; Skilbeck and Connell, 2000; Action Group on Access, 2000) they will not be discussed further in this report .

Finally, in relation to the problems of students from socio-economically disadvantaged backgrounds, it is necessary to recognise one of the paradoxes of higher education policy with respect to equality of access. Our analysis of data from the most recent School Leavers' Surveys confirms our view that it is likely that some of the most fruitful areas for policy intervention lie outside the higher education system. The socio-economic differentials which we have identified at each of the educational transitions suggest that effective policies aimed at increasing retention rates to Leaving Certificate and facilitating higher attainment levels at this level will be especially effective in reducing socio-economic group inequalities in access to higher education. The broadening of the policy agenda to encompass initiatives at second level does not, of course, imply that policy makers at third level sector can abdicate their responsibility to tackle inequalities. Policies which facilitate completion and enhanced attainment at second level are viewed as complements, not alternatives to third level initiatives. Furthermore, it is essential to keep in mind the more positive aspect of Raftery and Hout's maximally maintained inequality thesis. The policy of increasing the number of places at third level has the potential to further reduce inequality in higher education.

The existence of large regional differentials in admission rates constitutes a further dimension of inequality in participation in higher education. The delineation of these geographical differentials constitutes an important dimension of this and of the previous national surveys. A striking feature of this analysis is the degree of consistency between the findings of the three studies both in relation to variability in the overall levels of participation and in relation to differential participation rates by sector.

There was also considerable consistency of findings in respect of our attempts to explain differential participation rates by county in university education. Proximity to a university emerged as a good predictor of university admission rates by county. However this relationship did not manifest itself in the case of county rates of admission to the IT sector, where distance from a university emerged as a positive predictor rather than the expected inverse relationship with distance from an Institute of Technology and the county rate of admission in this sector. This finding reveals the complex interaction between distance from college and higher education sector.

Although differences in overall levels of participation represent the most visible form of regional inequality, account must also be taken of differences in participation by sector. A feature of the expansion of higher education has been the growing differentiation within the third level sector. While the emergence of a mainly short-cycle non-university sector has provided a major expansion of opportunity for groups which were traditionally excluded from higher education, there is a danger that institutional differentiation will ensure that the more prestigious programmes, usually of longer duration, in the more prestigious colleges will remain the cultural possession of traditionally advantaged groups. While it is probable that abolition of undergraduate fees may have made university programmes more attractive to some groups, where parental income lies above the grant eligibility threshold, the availability and adequacy of the maintenance grant is crucial, especially for the majority of students for whom university attendance requires living away from home. What is essential is that a concern for equality of opportunity requires us to monitor not just the overall admission levels but also the differentiation within the third level sector.

It is clear that part of the regional inequalities in participation in higher education is due to differences in retention rate to Leaving Certificate level. Our analysis which suggests that the relationship between retention to Leaving Certificate level and third level admission rates has become stronger over the period covered by these surveys lends further support to the argument that intervention at first and second level will be necessary if we are to eliminate inequalities in access to higher education.

Dublin, with twenty-six per cent of the college entry age cohort, still occupies a unique position in the context of regional disparities in participation in higher education. Its consistent designation as one of the counties with the lowest admission rate runs counter to the situation in other countries where the large urban centres tend to have the highest levels of participation (Richardson, 1981). Dublin's low admission rate is accounted for by an especially low participation rate in the technological sector. The low participation rate is complemented by having the lowest percentage of entrants in receipt of means tested financial aid and the highest level of social class inequality.

While the county has been the main unit of analysis in our examination of regional variations in admission rates, the analysis of variability by postal districts in the Dublin area reveals that counties are not homogeneous regions. The enormous disparities in admission rates, as reflected in an almost eleven fold difference between admission rates in Dublin 18 and Dublin 10, mirror the socio-economic patterning of the population.

It has been suggested in a series of reports (Clancy and Benson, 1979; Clancy, 1988, and Technical Working Group, 1995) that part of the difficulty in the Dublin area relates to deficiencies in provision, especially in relation to sub-degree courses. The establishment of Tallaght Institute of Technology represented the first step in addressing this deficiency. The evolution of the Dun Laoghaire College of Art and Design into the Dun Laoghaire Institute of Art, Design & Technology also represents an improvement in provision. Since this survey was carried out a further college has been opened in Blancharstown, which should help to redress the deficiency.

As already indicated for the country as a whole, the provision of additional third-level places in Dublin will not of itself eliminate inequalities in participation. Dublin shares with most of the other counties with low admission rates the distinction of having relatively low retention rates to Leaving Certificate level. Problems of early leaving and of low attainment levels tend to be heavily concentrated in certain areas of the city and county. This concentration is itself linked with areas of high unemployment and economic disadvantage. Thus, initiatives in the wider sphere of economic and social policy will be necessary before we can eliminate educational disadvantage.

While, as already suggested, much of the problem of early leaving and under-achievement is linked to socio-economic disadvantage, it is also the case that we cannot discount the importance of cultural factors. The high admission rates from Western counties, which are linked to high retention rates at second level, reflect a cultural orientation in many families, which, despite meagre resources, foster and realise high educational aspirations. The high levels of social segregation and polarisation which occur both in housing and in education in large urban areas inhibit the development of high aspirations for many working class children.

A concern with gender differentials constitutes an additional focus for the analysis of inequalities in participation in higher education. As we have already noted this is no longer an area of concern as far as aggregate enrolments are concerned. The situation in Ireland now corresponds to the average for all EU countries. The remaining gender inequalities relating to differentiation by field of study have proved more resistant to change. The under-representation of females in the technological sector is now matched by the under-representation of males in Medicine (following the inclusion of Nursing Studies students) and surpassed by the under-representation of males in Education. We have noted that there has been less progress in the movement of males into fields of study traditionally dominated by females than in respect of the movement of females into areas traditionally dominated by males. The third-level field of study destinations are of course strongly linked to choice of subjects at second level. Thus, change at this level will be necessary if we are to reduce significantly gender inequalities in higher education.

The patterns of continuity and change in access to higher education over the past two decades, which we have documented in this study, represent a microcosm of the changing Ireland. In part this is a story of progress. The growth of a mass higher education system has offered a diverse range of opportunities to an increasingly large percentage of the young population. These educational opportunities, for which the state has progressively assumed most of the cost, have fuelled the growth of the economy and yielded an impressive private dividend to the individuals who participated. However, the distribution of these opportunities has, like the distribution of wealth, been extremely uneven. Furthermore, in an apparent paradox, as more and more people participate in higher education the implications of non-participation are becoming more acute. While education has not a complete monopoly over the process of status attainment, its role is becoming more critical. For these reasons educational policy has become a central element of overall public policy. While this has been readily acknowledged in respect of the parameters of economic policy there has been a slower recognition of its salience for social policy. While there has been a widespread recognition that education is a determinant of economic success for the individual as well as for society generally, policy makers have been slower to acknowledge that economic circumstances and other features of the opportunity structure crucially condition the individual's capacity to avail of educational opportunities. Much of this report has been concerned with documenting the consequences of this unequal competition. While it has not been our remit to offer particular policy proposals it is hoped that we have contributed to the knowledge base, which will stimulate public debate and inform decision making.

Footnotes

1. As noted above (Chapter 3, footnote 3) the unemployment rate for males in this age cohort is significantly greater than for all ever married males aged 15 or over (10.7%). However, the unemployment rate for females in this age cohort differs little from that of the total cohort of ever-married males.

2. As noted above (Chapter 3, footnote 4) we use the term 'under-represented' and 'over-represented' in this report to describe the situation where there are significant departures from proportionality in the distribution of higher education places between different social groups. It should be noted that the use of the term 'over-represented', with respect to a particular group, does not indicate that we believe it is necessary or appropriate to effect a reduction in the absolute level of representation of this group. The achievement of greater equity can be effected by an increase in the representation of the group or groups which are currently 'under-represented'.

3. In spite of the plethora of comparative statistics produced by the OECD in its annual *Education at a Glance* series it is has not been possible to calculate a rate of admission for each country. The problem arises from the danger of 'double counting' where the same students frequently enroll in different sectors of higher eduction. Admissions to tertiary-type A and tertiary-type B cannot be added together to give an overall rate (OECD, 2000: 152).

4. One of the advantages in the use of the odds ratio is that it takes account of both the differences in the percentages going on to higher education and those not going on to higher education. Comparing the six 'over-represented' and the five 'under-represented' socio-economic groups we noted that in 1980 the relative odds of progressing to higher education was 35/8 = 4.38. However, the relative odds of not progressing to higher education was 92/65 = 1.42. The odds ratio, which is the product of the two odds, is 6.22 (4.38 x 1.42). By 1998 the relative odds of progressing was 2.03 (59/29), a reduction of 54%, while the relative odds of not progressing had increased to 1.73 (71/41), an increase of 22%. This gives an odds ratio of 3.51 (2.03 x 1.73) and represents a reduction of 39% over the eighteen year period. This can be taken as an indicator of degree of the reduction in inequality. The relevant calculations for each of the four surveys, are reproduced below allowing us to monitor changes in each indicator between different survey years.

	Odds of progressing to higher education	Odds of not progressing to higher education	Odds Ratio
1980	4.38	1.42	6.22
1986	3.91	1.56	6.10
1992	2.08	1.52	3.16
1998	2.03	1.73	3.51

We can also calculate odds ratios for the data on estimated participation rates for the different social classes (Table 27). If we compare the three highest and three lowest social classes, in 1992, the odds of progressing to higher education were 2.22 (51/23) while the odds of not progressing were 1.57 (77/49), giving an odds ratio of 3.49. In 1998 the odds of progressing were 1.87 (56/30) while the odds of not progressing were 1.59 (70/44), giving an odds ratio of 2.97. This suggests a reduction of inequality of fifteen per cent over the six-year period.

5. There is no unanimity amongst researchers on what conclusions we can draw from existing research data, as illustrated in the international literature by exchanges between Hellevik (1997) and Marshall and Swift (1999) In the Irish context Smyth (1999) has challenged our conclusions from the 1992 study and argues that educational expansion has not resulted in any significant reduction in equality in recent years (p.282). It is proposed, in a separate paper, to address the discrepancy between her findings based on an analysis of the School Leavers Surveys and our findings.

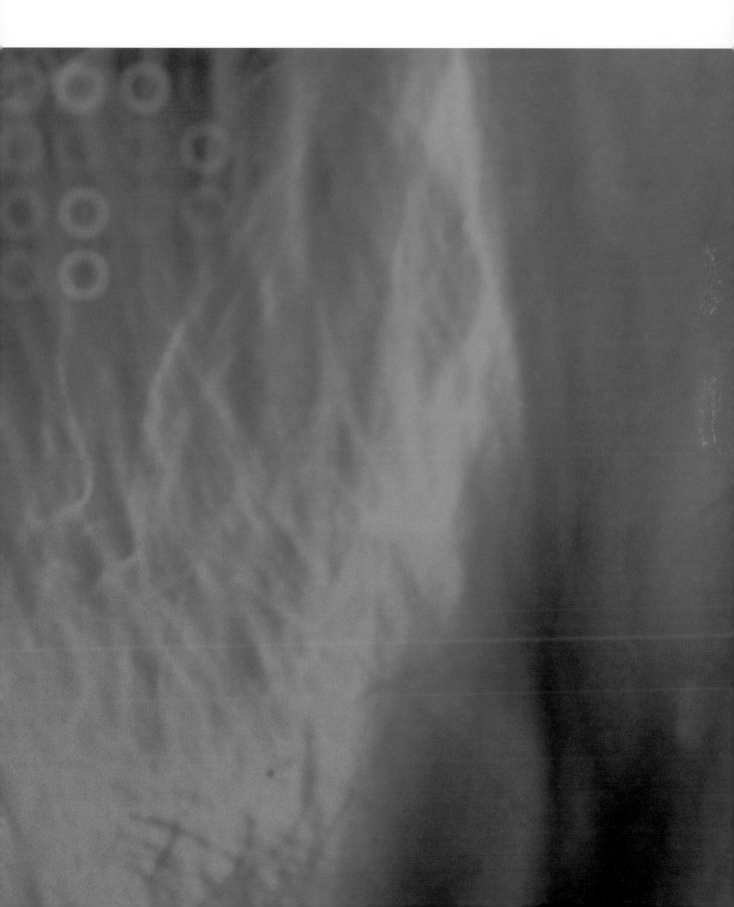

references

Action Group on Access 2001 *Report of the Action Group on Access to Third Level Education*, Dublin, Stationery Office.

Advisory Committee on Third-Level Student Support 1993 *Third-Level Student Support*, Dublin, Stationery Office.

AHEAD 2000 *Students with Disabilities in Higher Education: Initial Findings of the Survey on Provision for Students with Disabilities in Higher Education for the Academic Year 1998/99.* Dublin, Higher Education Authority.

Amber, J. and Neatherly, J. 1999 *"Education Policy and Equality: Some Evidence from Europe"*, Social Science Quarterly, Vol 80, No. 3.

Barrett, A, Callan, T. & Nolan, B. 1999 *"Returns to Education in the Irish Youth Labour Market"*, Journal of Population Economics, 12, pp.313-326.

Barry, F. 1999 *"Editorial Introduction"*, The Economic and Social Review, Vol. 30, No.3.

Bryman, A. and Cramer, D. 1990 *Quantitative Data Analysis for Social Scientists*, London, Routledge.

Callan, T. and Harmon, C. 1997 *The Economic Return to Schooling in Ireland, UCD Working Paper, WP97/23*, Dublin, UCD Centre for Economic Research.

Clancy, P. 1982 *Participation in Higher Education*, Dublin, Higher Education Authority.

Clancy, P. 1988 *Who Goes to College?* Dublin, Higher Education Authority.

Clancy, P. 1994 "Expanding Enrolments in Higher Education – some trends and implications" *in The Role of The University in Society,* Dublin, The National University of Ireland.

Clancy, P. 1995 *Access to college: Patterns of Continuity and Change,* Dublin, Higher Education Authority.

Clancy, P. 1999 "Participation of Mature Students in Higher Education" in Higher Education the Challenge of Lifelong Learning, (eds.) T. Fleming, T. Collins and J. Coolahan, Centre for Educational Policy Studies, NUI, Maynooth.

Clancy, P. and Benson, C. 1979 *Higher Education in Dublin: A Study of Some Emerging Needs,* Dublin, Higher Education Authority.

Clancy, P. and Brannick, T. 1990 *"Subject Specialisation at Second Level and Third Level Field of Study: Some Gender Differences" Irish Educational Studies,* Vol. 9.

Eurostat 2000 *Eurostat Yearbook: A Statistical Eye on Europe,* Luxembourg, European Commission.

Hannan, D., Smyth, E., McCullagh, J., O'Leary, R. and McMahon, D. 1996 *Coeducation and Gender Equality: Exam Performance, Stress and Personal Development,* Dublin, Oak Tree Press.

Helleick, O. 1997 *"Class Inequality and Egalitarian Reform", Acta Sociologica,* 40, pp.377-397.

Hirsch, F. 1977 *The Social Limits to Growth,* London, Routledge.

Investment in Education, 1965 Report of the Survey Team Appointed by the Minister for Education, Dublin, Stationery Office.

Jallade, J.P. 1992 *Access to Higher Education in Europe: Problems and Perspective,* Strasbourg, Council of Europe.

Jallade, J.P. 1993 *"Participation in and Access to Higher Education" in European Commission, Responses to the Memorandum on Higher Education in The European Community,* Brussels, Task Force Human Resources, Education, Training and Youth.

McManus, R. and Brady, J. 1994 *"Recent Trends in the Irish Urban System with Particular Reference to Dublin and Cork", Acta Universitatis Carolinae Geographica,* No.1.

Marshall, G. & Swift, A. *"On the Meaning and Measurement of Inequality", Acta Sociologica,* 42, pp.241-250.

NESC 1999 *Opportunities, Challenges and Capacity for Choice,* Dublin, National Economic and Social Council.

Nolan, B., O'Connell, P.J. & Whelan, C.T. (eds.) *2000 Bust to Boom? The Irish Experience of Growth and Inequality,* Dublin, Institute of Public Administration.

O'Hare, A., Whelan, C.T. and Commins, P. 1991 "The Development of an Irish Census-Based Social Class Scale", *The Economic and Social Review, Vol. 22.*

OECD 1972 *Development of Higher Education 1950-67:* Analytic Report, Paris, Organisation for Economic Co-operation and Development.

OECD 2000 *Education at a Glance: OECD Indicators,* Paris, Organisation for Economic Co-operation and Development.

OECD 1999a *Redefining Tertiary Education,* Paris, Organisation for Economic Co-operation and Development.

OECD 1999b *Educational Policy Analysis 1999,* Paris, Organisation for Economic Co-operation and Development.

Osborne, R. & Leith, H. 2000 *Evaluation of the Targeted Initiative on Widening Access for Young People from Socio-Economically Disadvantage Backgrounds,* Dublin Higher Education Authority.

Pike, R.M. 1970 *Who Doesn't Get to University and Why: A Study of Accessibility to Higher Education in Canada,* Ottawa.

Porter, M. 1990 *The Competitive Advantage of Nations,* London, Macmillan Press.

Raftery, A.E. and Hout, M. 1993 "Maximally Maintained Inequality: Expansion, Reform, and Opportunity in Irish Education, 1921-75", *Sociology of Education, Vol. 66.*

Reid, E. 1991 "Access and Institutional Change", in T. Schuller (ed.) *The Future of Higher Education,* Buckingham, SRHE/Open University Press.

Report of Review Committee on Post Secondary Education and Training Places, Dublin, Higher Education Authority.

Richardson, J. 1981 "Geographical Bias" in *'Is Higher Education Fair?'* (ed.) D. Warren Piper, London, Society for Research in Higher Education.

Robinson, W.S. 1950 "Ecological Correlations and the Behaviour of Individuals", *American Sociological Review, Vol. 15.*

Shavit, Y. and Blossfeld, H.P. (eds.) 1993 *Persistent Inequality: Changing Educational Attainment in Thirteen Countries,* Boulder, Westview Press.

Skilbeck, M. with Connell, H. 2000 *Access and Equity on Higher Education: An International Perspective on Issues and Stratgeies,* Dublin, Higher Education Authority.

Smyth, E. *"Educational Inequalities among School Leavers in Ireland 1979-1994", The Economic and Social Review,* 30, 3, pp.267-284.

Steering Committee on the Future Development of Higher Education, 1995 *Report*, Dublin, Higher Education Authority.

Technical Working Group, 1995 *Interim Report of the Steering Committee's Technical Working Group,* Dublin, Higher Education Authority.

Teichler, U. 1988 *Changing Patterns of Higher Education Systems,* London, Jessica Kingsley.

appendix a | Additional Tables

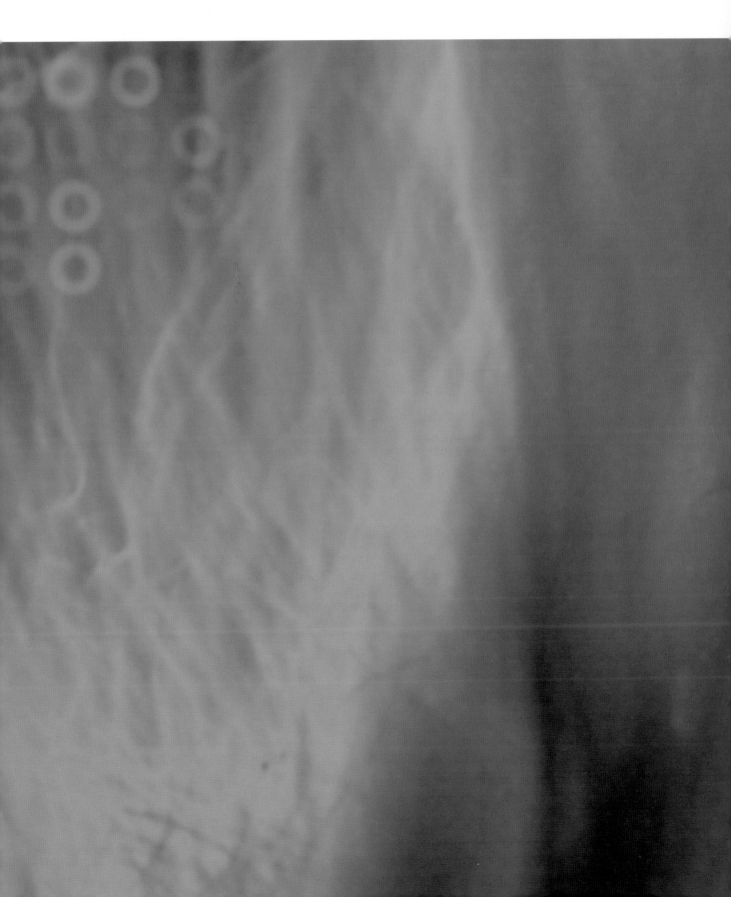

TABLE A1 NUMBER OF NEW ENTRANTS TO FULL-TIME HIGHER EDUCATION IN 1998 BY GENDER, COLLEGE AND COLLEGE TYPE

College	Male%	Female%	Total%	Total N
UNIVERSITY SECTOR				
University College Dublin	42.4	57.6	100	3685
University College Cork	36.8	63.2	100	2568
NUI, Galway	40.9	59.1	100	1857
Trinity College Dublin	39.3	60.7	100	1870
NUI, Maynooth	39.2	60.8	100	1140
Dublin City University	41.9	58.1	100	1260
University of Limerick	50.6	49.4	100	2041
Royal College of Surgeons in Ireland	49.3	50.7	100	201
TOTAL	41.8	58.2	100	14,622
COLLEGES OF EDUCATION				
St. Patrick's, Drumcondra	12.0	88.0	100	418
Mary Immaculate, Limerick	9.0	91.0	100	294
St. Catherine's, Blackrock	-	100.0	100	29
Froebel College, Blackrock	20.7	79.3	100	29
Mater Dei Institute of Education	21.2	78.8	100	66
St. Mary's Marino	14.3	85.7	100	49
Church of Ireland, Rathmines	6.9	93.1	100	30
St. Angela's, Sligo	5.2	94.8	100	77
St. Nicholas, Montessori College	-	100.0	100	34
Montessori College, AMI	3.7	96.3	100	27
TOTAL	**10.5**	**89.5**	**100**	**1053**

College	Male %	Female%	Total%	Total N
Institutes of Technology				
Athlone	50.3	49.7	100	1117
Carlow	56.8	43.2	100	903
Cork	63.7	36.3	100	1725
Dublin	55.6	44.4	100	2945
Dun Laoghaire Institute of Art, Design & Technology	50.5	49.5	100	195
Dundalk	56.3	43.7	100	1119
Galway	55.7	44.3	100	1699
Letterkenny	50.7	49.3	100	761
Limerick	58.4	41.6	100	1134
Sligo	45.0	55.0	100	917
Tallaght	57.0	43.0	100	740
Tralee	56.9	43.1	100	824
Waterford	50.9	49.1	100	1604
TOTAL	**55.2**	**44.8**	**100**	**15,683**
OTHER COLLEGES				
National College of Art and Design	19.7	80.3	100	143
Dublin Business School	67.6	32.4	100	105
American College Dublin	33.3	66.7	100	114
National College of Ireland	44.6	55.4	100	249
Shannon College of Hotel Management	56.8	43.2	100	44
Milltown Institute	50.9	49.1	100	55
HIS College	19.4	80.6	100	62
LSB College	38.6	61.4	100	154
Griffith College Dublin	54.1	45.9	100	137
Mid-West Business Institute	58.3	41.7	100	12
Skerry's Business College	9.7	90.3	100	31
Portobello College Dublin	64.1	35.9	100	260
TOTAL	45.7	54.3	100	1366
TOTAL ALL COLLEGES	**47.4**	**52.6**	**100**	**32,724**

TABLE A2   DISTRIBUTION OF NEW ENTRANTS BY FIELD OF STUDY TO HEA-SECTOR COLLEGES

College	% Arts	% Education	% Art & Design	% Social Science	% Economic & Social Studies	% European Studies	% Communication & Information Studies	% Commerce	% Law	% Science	% Engineering	% Architecture	% Medicine	% Dentistry	% Veterinary Medicine	% Agricultural Science & Forestry	% Food Science & Technology	% Equestrian	% Combined Studies	Total %	Total N
UCD	39.2	0.0	0.0	3.9	0.0	0.0	0.0	12.1	3.4	12.6	7.5	1.4	8.7	0.0	2.0	5.5	0.0	0.0	3.8	100	685
UCC	33.6	0.0	0.0	4.8	0.0	0.0	0.0	16.0	3.3	19.5	6.0	0.0	9.8	1.6	0.0	0.0	3.9	0.0	1.4	100	2568
NUIG	37.5	0.0	0.0	0.0	0.0	0.0	0.0	16.8	3.1	21.7	13.4	0.0	7.4	0.0	0.0	0.0	0.0	0.0	0.2	100	1857
TCD	29.6	0.0	0.0	2.0	11.8	2.0	0.0	0.0	4.5	18.2	13.3	0.0	12.0	1.6	0.0	0.0	0.0	0.0	5.0	100	1870
NUIM	68.3	0.0	0.0	0.0	0.0	0.0	0.0	0.0	0.0	31.7	0.0	0.0	0.0	0.0	0.0	0.0	0.0	0.0	0.0	100	1140
DCU	8.0	0.0	0.0	0.0	0.0	0.0	4.3	38.4	0.0	22.3	9.9	0.0	13.3	0.0	0.0	0.0	0.0	0.0	3.8	100	1260
UL	14.7	6.9	0.0	0.0	0.0	6.5	0.0	16.0	0.0	6.9	34.1	0.0	3.1	0.0	0.0	0.0	0.0	3.0	8.7	100	2041
RCSI	0.0	0.0	0.0	0.0	0.0	0.0	0.0	0.0	0.0	0.0	0.0	0.0	100.0	0.0	0.0	0.0	0.0	0.0	0.0	100	201
NCAD	0.0	0.0	100.0	0.0	0.0	0.0	0.0	0.0	0.0	0.0	0.0	0.0	0.0	0.0	0.0	0.0	0.0	0.0	0.0	100	143
All Colleges	32.1	1.0	1.0	2.1	1.5	1.2	0.4	13.4	2.4	16.9	11.9	0.3	7.9	0.5	0.5	1.4	0.7	0.4	3.4	100	14,765

Field of Study	Construction Studies %	General Engineering %	Science %	Art & Design %	Computer Studies %	Business, Administrative and Secretarial Studies %	Hotel, Catering and Tourism %	Education %	General Studies %	Total %	Total N
St. Patrick's College of Education	0.0	0.0	0.0	0.0	0.0	0.0	0.0	68.2	31.8	100	418
Mary Immaculate College of Education	0.0	0.0	0.0	0.0	0.0	0.0	0.0	100.0	0.0	100	294
Church of Ireland College of Education, Rathmines	0.0	0.0	0.0	0.0	0.0	0.0	0.0	100	0.0	100	30
St. Mary's College of Education, Marino	0.0	0.0	0.0	0.0	0.0	0.0	0.0	100	0.0	100	49
St. Angela's College of Education	0.0	0.0	67.5	0.0	0.0	0.0	0.0	32.5	0.0	100	77
St. Catherine's College of Education	0.0	0.0	0.0	0.0	0.0	0.0	0.0	100	0.0	100	29
Froebel College of Education	0.0	0.0	0.0	0.0	0.0	0.0	0.0	100	0.0	100	29
Mater Dei Institute Dublin Institute of	0.0	0.0	0.0	0.0	0.0	0.0	0.0	100	0.0	100	66
DIT	5.7	23.7	10.6	5.8	1.3	36.4	12.2	0.2	4.2	100	2945
Athlone IT	3.2	25.1	8.1	2.6	8.2	40.7	5.6	0.0	6.4	100	1117
Carlow IT	0.0	20.4	6.8	2.7	39.5	30.7	0.0	0.0	0.0	100	903
Cork IT	6.7	38.4	12.5	3.1	13.7	17.6	4.1	0.0	3.9	100	1725
Dun Laoghaire IADT	0.0	0.0	0.0	62.1	19.0	19.0	0.0	0.0	0.0	100	195
Dundalk IT	8.8	18.5	7.5	0.0	18.1	42.1	0.0	0.0	5.0	100	1119
Galway IT	7.8	19.1	11.2	4.9	11.8	22.7	21.4	0.0	1.2	100	1699
Letterkenny IT	5.1	19.8	9.7	9.1	16.6	29.6	0.0	0.0	10.1	100	761
Limerick IT	18.4	24.2	7.5	12.6	13.8	23.5	0.0	0.0	0.0	100	1134
Sligo IT	6.3	7.5	13.6	13.4	10.4	35.1	8.1	0.0	5.6	100	917
Tralee IT	6.4	27.7	17.2	0.0	9.3	37.9	0.0	0.0	1.5	100	824
Waterford IT	10.3	10.7	8.3	1.7	17.8	32.8	9.4	0.0	9.0	100	1604
Tallaght	0.0	27.8	15.8	0.01	6.6	33.9	0.0	0.0	5.8	100	740
Skerries	0.0	0.0	0.0	0.0		61.3	0.0	0.0	38.7	100	31
National College of Ireland	0.0	0.0	0.0	0.0	0.0	100.0	0.0	0.0	0.0	100	249
Shannon College of Hotel Management	0.0	0.0	0.0	0.0	0.0	0.0	100.0	0.0	0.0	100	44
DBS	0.0	0.0	0.0	0.0	0.0	91.4	0.0	0.0	8.6	100	105
ACD	0.0	0.0	0.0	0.	0.0	27.2	7.0	0.0	65.8	100	114
LSB College	0.0	0.0	0.0	0.0	13.6	39.6	5.8	0.0	40.9	100	154
Griffith College	0.0	0.0	0.0	0.0	43.1	21.9	0.0	0.0	35.0	100	137
St Nicholas, Montessori	0.0	0.0	0.0	0.0	0.0	0.0	0.0	100.0	0.0	100	34
Portobello College	0.0	0.0	0.0	0.0	30.0	44.2	0.0	0.0	25.8	100	260
Milltown Institute	0.0	0.0	0.0	0.0	0.0	0.0	0.0	0.0	100.0	100	55
Montessori, AMI	0.0	0.0	0.0	0.0	0.0	0.0	0.0	100.0	0.0	100	27
HSI Limerick	0.0	0.0	0.0	0.0	0.0	35.5	37.1	0.0	27.4	100	62
Mid-West Limerick	0.0	0.0	0.0	0.0	0.0	100.0	0.0	0.0	0.0	100	12
All Colleges	6.2	19.3	8.7	4.7	12.2	30.7	6.5	6.4	5.3	100	18,303

TABLE A4   DISTRIBUTION OF NEW ENTRANTS BY LEVEL OF STUDY AND BY COLLEGE

COLLEGE	Degree	Sub-Degree	TOTAL	
	%	%	%	N
UNIVERSITIES				
University College Dublin	96.3	3.7	100	3685
University College Cork	93.2	6.8	100	2568
NUI, Galway	94.9	5.1	100	1857
Trinity College Dublin	95.7	4.3	100	1871
NUI, Maynooth	100	–	100	1140
Dublin City University	86.7	13.3	100	1260
University of Limerick	95.3	4.7	100	2041
Royal College of Surgeons in Ireland	100	–	100	201
INSTITUTES OF TECHNOLOGY				
Athlone	3.8	96.2	100	1117
Carlow	1.4	98.6	100	90.3
Cork	15.5	84.5	100	1725
Dublin	37.8	62.2	100	2945
Dun Laoghaire	–	100	100	195
Dundalk	–	100	100	1119
Galway/Mayo	9.1	90.9	100	1699
Letterkenny	–	100	100	761
Limerick	13.5	86.5	100	1134
Sligo	4.1	95.9	100	917
Tallaght	–	100	100	740
Tralee	–	100	100	824
Waterford	34.7	65.3	100	1604
COLLEGES OF EDUCATION				
St. Patrick's, Drumcondra	100	–	100	418
St. Nicholas, Montessori College	–	100	100	34
St. Catherine's, Blackrock	100	–	100	29
Froebel College, Blackrock	100	–	100	29
Mater Dei Institute of Education	100	–	100	66
St. Mary's Marino	100	–	100	49
Church of Ireland, Rathmines	100	–	100	29
St. Angela's, Sligo	32.5	67.5	100	77
Montessori College, AMI	–	100	100	27
Mary Immaculate, Limerick	100	–	100	294
OTHER COLLEGES				
National College of Art and Design	21.0	79.0	100	143
Dublin Business School	78.1	21.9	100	105
National College of Ireland	53.4	46.6	100	249
Shannon College of Hotel Management	–	100	100	44
Milltown Institute	70.9	29.1	100	53
American College, Dublin	86.0	14.0	100	114
HSI College	–	100	100	62
LSB College	63.0	37.0	100	154
Griffith College, Dublin	82.5	17.5	100	137
Mid-West Business Institute	–	100	100	12
Skerries Business College	–	100	100	31
Portobello College, Dublin	61.5	38.5	100	260
TOTAL ALL COLLEGES	**17,903**	**14,821**	**100**	**32,724**

192

TABLE A 5 DISTRIBUTION OF NEW ENTRANTS BY AGE AND GENDER

AGE	MALE %	FEMALE %	TOTAL %
Under 17	0.1	0.1	**0.1**
17	18.0	20.1	**19.1**
18	49.5	50.7	**50.1**
19	21.9	19.9	**20.8**
20	4.2	3.4	**3.8**
21	1.2	1.0	**1.1**
22	0.7	0.4	**0.5**
23-25	0.6	0.7	**0.6**
26-30	2.0	1.6	**1.8**
31-40	1.2	1.1	**1.2**
Over 40	0.8	1.1	**0.9**
Total %	**100**	**100**	**100**
Total N	**15,428**	**17,101**	**32,530**

TABLE A6 DISTRIBUTION OF NEW ENTRANTS TO HIGHER EDUCATION BY AGE AND COLLEGE

COLLEGE	Under 17	17	18	19	20	21	22–25	26–30	31–40	Over 40	Total %	Total N
Universities												
UCD	0.2	17.3	53.5	22.5	4.0	0.6	0.9	0.4	0.3	0.3	100	3619
UCC	0	15.5	50.7	22.5	4.4	0.9	0.9	1.9	1.4	0.6	100	2566
NUIG	0.2	24.4	51.3	18.3	2.3	0.6	1.5	0.6	0.3	0.4	100	1856
TCD	0.1	13.8	57.6	19.2	1.5	0.4	2.7	1.5	1.8	1.2	100	1872
NUIM	0.2	21.6	46.7	19.1	2.5	0.5	1.8	2.5	2.4	2.7	100	1132
DCU	0.2	21.3	53.3	15.4	2.5	0.8	2.5	1.7	2.0	0.1	100	1260
UL	0.2	22.0	51.8	17.7	2.9	0.7	1.8	1.1	1.0	0	100	2038
R.C.S.I.	0	7.0	19.4	27.4	10.9	7.0	21.4	6.5	0.5	0	100	201
Institutes of Technology												
Athlone	0	23.6	45.4	19.2	4.4	1.7	2.4	1.3	0.9	1.2	100	1116
Carlow	0.1	19.5	50.4	20.6	3.3	1.4	3.2	0.6	0.6	0.3	100	903
Cork	0.1	15.1	51.2	23.6	3.5	1.4	3.0	1.1	0.8	0.2	100	1725
Dun Laoghaire	0	4.6	40.2	28.4	7.2	3.6	5.1	5.6	3.1	2.1	100	194
DIT	0.1	17.6	53.0	22.4	3.9	0.7	1.3	0.5	0.4	0.2	100	2939
Dundalk	0.1	27.8	47.3	17.1	3.7	0.4	2.3	0.4	0.5	0.2	100	1648
Galway	0	16.6	44.1	24.3	5.9	2.2	3.8	1.6	1.0	0.4	100	739
Letterkenny	0.1	26.4	45.9	17.6	3.9	2.2	1.9	1.4	0.5	0.3	100	1134
Limerick	0	20.1	53.2	18.9	3.3	1.0	2.3	0.5	0.4	0.7	100	916
Sligo	0.1	24.1	46.6	20.3	3.2	1.2	1.7	1.3	1.1	0.1	100	740
Tallaght	0.3	21.4	47.8	22.2	4.1	0.9	1.2	0.3	0.1	0	100	824
Tralee	0	21.2	50.6	19.3	3.4	1.2	2.3	0.7	0.6	0.6	100	1604
Waterford	0	21.0	49.8	21.6	3.6	1.3	1.3	0.4	0.7	1.3	100	15,596

DISTRIBUTION OF NEW ENTRANTS TO HIGHER EDUCATION BY AGE AND COLLEGE

COLLEGE	Under 17	17	18	19	20	21	22-25	26-30	31-40	Over 40	Total %	Total N
Colleges of Education												
Mary Immaculate	0	17.2	58.6	20.3	1.0	0	1.4	1.0	0.3	0	100	290
St Patrick's	0	23.9	42.4	14.5	2.2	0.7	5.3	2.7	3.9	4.6	100	415
Mater Dei	0	30.3	43.9	24.2	0	0	0	0	1.5	0	100	66
Marino	0	16.3	63.3	20.4	0	0	0	0	0	0	100	49
St Nicholas, Montesorri	0	2.9	44.1	26.5	8.8	5.9	6.3	2.9	2.9	0	100	34
Mount Mill	0	0	25.9	33.3	14.8	7.4	14.8	3.7	0	0	100	27
St Angela's	0	19.5	37.7	24.7	9.1	2.6	2.6	2.6	1.3	0	100	77
Church of Ireland	0	10.3	69.0	20.7	0	0	0	0	0	0	100	29
Freobel	3.4	24.1	34.5	37.9	0	0	0	0	0	0	0	29
St Catherine's	0	6.9	48.3	31.0	6.9	0	0	3.4	3.4	0	100	29
Other Colleges												
NCAD	0	7.1	33.6	32.9	11.4	3.6	3.6	2.9	2.9	2.1	100	140
NCI	0	12.4	49.8	22.1	5.2	1.6	2.6	2.4	1.2	1.6	100	249
Milltown	0	14.5	36.4	16.4	3.6	1.8	3.6	7.3	7.3	9.1	100	55
ACD	0	12.7	33.6	20.0	7.3	5.5	10.9	7.3	0.9	1.8	100	110
Griffith	0.8	8.3	31.1	29.5	10.6	9.8	11.8	1.5	2.3	1.5	100	132
LSB	0	14.4	49.7	22.9	8.5	2.0	2.0	0	1.7	0	100	153
Portobello	0	13.6	42.8	25.3	1.05	3.5	2.3	1.2	0.4	0.4	100	257
HIS Limerick	0	18.0	45.9	24.6	8.2	1.6	0	0	1.6	0	100	61
Mid West Limerick	0	25.0	41.7	33.3	0	0	0	0	0	0	100	12
DBS	0	5.8	42.7	22.3	9.7	4.9	7.7	1.9	0	0	100	103
Skerries	0	16.1	45.2	38.7	0	0	0	0	0	0	100	31
Shannon	0	11.6	51.2	23.3	9.3	2.3	2.3	0	0	0	100	43
TOTAL ALL COLLEGES	30	6199	16,305	6772	1229	549	1746	336	303	204	-	32,530

TABLE A7   AGE AT OCTOBER 1, 1998, OF NEW ENTRANTS BY FIELDS OF STUDY TO HEA-SECTOR COLLEGES

Field of Study	% Under 17 Years	% 17 Years	% 18 Years	% 19 Years	% 20 Years	% 21 Years	% 22-25 Years	% 26-30 Years	% 31-40 Years	% Over 40 Years	Total %	Total N
Arts	0.1	16.9	49.5	22.4	4.1	0.8	1.8	1.6	1.4	1.5	100	4,730
Education	0.0	13.5	59.6	17.0	2.1	0.0	3.5	3.5	0.7	0.0	100	141
Art & Design	0.0	1.7	33.6	32.9	11.4	3.6	3.6	2.9	2.9	2.1	100	140
Social Science	0.0	11.2	49.0	20.4	4.3	1.0	3.0	3.3	5.9	2.0	100	304
Economic & Social Studies	0.0	12.7	62.7	16.8	2.3	0.5	0.9	1.4	1.8	0.9	100	220
European Studies	0.0	17.1	47.1	28.2	4.7	0.6	1.8	0.0	0.6	0.0	100	170
Communication & Information Studies	0.0	9.3	74.1	16.7	0.0	0.0	0.0	0.0	0.0	0.0	100	54
Commerce	0.2	22.2	58.1	16.6	1.9	0.3	0.5	0.2	0.1	0.1	100	1,978
Law	0.3	16.8	56.1	23.1	1.1	0.0	0.6	1.1	0.0	0.9	100	351
Science	0.1	23.0	56.4	17.3	1.5	0.5	0.6	0.4	0.1	0.1	100	2,490
Engineering	0.1	23.1	54.9	18.2	1.8	0.4	0.8	0.4	0.3	0.0	100	1,750
Architecture	0.0	17.6	56.9	15.7	2.0	0.0	3.9	2.0	0.0	2.0	100	51
Medicine	0.3	10.3	33.7	24.4	7.5	2.9	10.7	5.0	3.9	1.2	100	1,297
Dentistry	0.0	12.7	35.2	33.8	11.3	1.4	5.6	0.0	0.0	0.0	100	71
Veterinary Medicine	0.0	2.8	51.4	25.0	8.3	1.4	7.0	4.2	0.0	0.0	100	72
Agriculture Science & Forestry	0.0	21.1	60.3	14.2	2.0	0.0	1.0	0.5	1.0	0.0	100	204
Food Science & Technology	0.0	15.0	60.0	20.0	3.0	0.0	0.0	2.0	0.0	0.0	100	100
Equestrian	0.0	9.7	33.9	30.6	14.5	1.6	6.4	0.0	3.2	0.0	100	62
Combined Studies	0.6	20.9	57.3	17.5	2.2	0.0	0.4	0.4	0.6	0.0	100	497
TOTAL	0.1	18.5	51.8	20.2	3.3	0.8	2.1	1.3	1.1	0.7	100	4,682

TABLE A8 AGE AT OCTOBER 1, 1998, OF NEW ENTRANTS BY FIELDS OF STUDY TO NON -HEA SECTOR COLLEGES

Field of Study / Age	% Construction	% General Engineering	% Science	% Art & Design	% Computers Studies	% Business, Administrative & Secretarial Stuies	% Hotel, Catering & Tourism	% Education	% General Studies	Total %	Total N
Under 17 years	0.1	0.1	0.1	0.1	0.1	0.0	0.0	0.1	0.1	0.1	11
17 years	22.0	21.4	20.6	10.3	19.6	20.1	16.7	20.0	16.1	19.5	3,465
18 Years	48.2	50.1	51.4	41.5	44.3	50.3	52.5	51.0	43.8	48.7	8,670
19 Years	21.9	20.0	20.2	29.3	20.9	21.4	21.4	20.4	21.9	21.3	3,791
20 Years	3.7	3.6	3.8	6.5	5.1	4.1	4.0	2.0	4.9	4.2	733
21 Years	1.6	1.2	1.1	2.9	1.7	1.2	1.3	0.6	2.4	1.4	250
22-25 Years	1.4	2.2	1.7	4.4	4.8	1.6	2.5	3.5	2.9	2.4	434
26-30 Years	0.6	0.8	0.6	2.4	1.7	0.4	0.9	1.4	2.5	1.0	174
31-40 Years	0.4	0.5	0.6	1.3	1.2	0.4	0.5	0.8	2.6	0.8	132
Over 40 Years	0.2	0.3	0.1	1.3	0.6	0.4	0.2	0.2	2.9	0.6	96
TOTAL %	100	100	100	100	100	100	100	100	100	100	-
TOTAL N	1,073	3,448	1,570	841	2,181	5,525	1,114	869	1,135	-	17,756

(a)   School Type by Fathers' Socio-Economic Group

Fathers' SEG	Secondary Fee Paying %	Secondary Non-Fee Paying %	Vocational %	Compre-hensive %	Community %	Other %
Data Available	8.6	61.9	13.7	2.6	10.6	2.6
Data Not Available	8.3	61.0	13.5	2.6	10.7	3.9

(b)   Type of Financial Aid by Fathers' Socio Economic Group

Father's SEG	Grant %	ESF %	Other %	None %
Data Available	16.2	20.0	4.4	60.4
Data Not Available	12.7	22.3	3.0	61.9

(a)   College Type by Fathers' Socio-Economic Group

Fathers' SEG	University %	IOTs %	Col. of Ed. %	Other %
Data Available	48.2	47.4	3.7	0.7
Data Not Available	41.0	54.1	2.6	2.3

(c)   Selected Fields of Study (University Sector) by Fathers' Socio-Economic Group

Fathers' SEG	Law./Medicine/Dentistry/Architecture %
Data Available	6.0
Data Not Available	1.9

(a) Higher Education Entrants

Fathers' Principal Economic Status	Mothers' Principal Economic Status					
	At Work %	Unemployed/ Unable to work %	Home Duties %	Retired %	Other %	TOTAL %
At Work	33.9	2.2	42.6	0.4	0.7	**79.7**
Unemployed/ Unable to Work	2.3	1.6	4.3	0.0	0.1	**8.5**
Home Duties	0.4	0.0	0.7	0.0	0.0	**1.2**
Retired	1.6	0.2	3.9	0.6	0.0	**6.3**
Other	1.2	0.4	1.1	0.0	1.6	**4.3**
TOTAL %	**39.5**	**4.4**	**52.7**	**1.0**	**2.5**	**100.0**

Total N = 19,843

(b)   Labour Force Survey: Couples

Males' Principal Economic Status	`Females' Principal Economic Status					
	At Work %	Unemployed/ Unable to work %	Home Duties %	Retired %	Other %	TOTAL %
At Work	33.9	2.2	42.6	0.4	0.7	**79.7**
Unemployed/ Unable to Work	2.3	1.6	4.3	0.0	0.1	**8.5**
Home Duties	0.4	0.0	0.7	0.0	0.0	**1.2**
Retired	1.6	0.2	3.9	0.6	0.0	**6.3**
Other	1.2	0.4	1.1	0.0	1.6	**4.3**
TOTAL %	**39.5**	**4.4**	**52.7**	**1.0**	**2.5**	**100.0**

Total N = 19,843

TABLE A11 CROSS CLASSIFICATION OF PARENTS OF HIGHER EDUCATION ENTRANTS AND OF COUPLES WITH EITHER PARTNER AGED 40-54 FROM 1997 LABOUR FORCE SURVEY: BOTH PARTNERS WORKING

(a) Higher Education Entrants

Fathers' Social Class	Mothers' Social Class						
	1	2	3	4	5	6	Total
1 Higher Professional	7.5	14.4	7.1	0.2	2.2	0.5	**31.9**
2 Lower Professional	1.9	16.8	6.9	0.1	2.6	0.8	**29.0**
3 Other Non Manual	0.9	7.3	5.4	0.1	2.2	0.7	**16.4**
4 Skilled Manual	0.6	4.7	4.5	0.4	3.3	1.2	**14.7**
5 Semi-Skilled Manual	0.2	1.5	1.7	0.1	1.5	0.7	**5.7**
6 Unskilled Manual	0.1	0.7	0.7	-	0.5	0.2	**2.2**
Total	11.2	45.4	26.3	0.8	12.4	4.0	100.0

(b) Labour Force Survey: Couples

Males' Social Class	Females' Social Class						
	1	2	3	4	5	6	Total
1 Higher Professional	5.4	8.5	5.4	0.2	2.2	0.6	**22.2**
2 Lower Professional	1.4	10.1	4.9	0.2	2.3	0.6	**19.6**
3 Other Non Manual	0.7	3.6	4.6	0.3	2.3	0.8	**12.4**
4 Skilled Manual	1.2	4.9	6.8	1.2	6.5	3.1	**23.7**
5 Semi-Skilled Manual	0.7	5.3	3.6	0.5	5.4	2.2	**17.6**
6 Unskilled Manual	0.0	0.7	0.8	0.2	0.2	1.4	**4.4**
Total	9.4	33.1	26.2	2.4	20.4	8.5	100.0

SOCIO-ECONOMIC STATUS OF NEW ENTRANTS BY COLLEGE

Socio-Economic Group / College	% Employers & Manager	% Higher Professionals	% Lower Professionals	% Non-Manual	% Manual Skilled	% Semi-Skilled	% Unskilled	% Own Account Workers	% Farmers	% Agricultural Workers	Total %	Total N
Universities												
U.C.D.	26.0	20.4	12.7	9.9	8.0	4.4	0.9	4.3	13.1	0.2	100	1907
U.C.C.	22.9	13.5	11.9	7.8	12.2	6.9	2.1	6.5	15.4	0.8	100	1595
NUIG	20.6	12.8	14.1	8.2	8.9	6.4	2.9	6.9	18.7	0.5	100	1145
T.C.D.	27.0	24.4	15.1	9.3	6.6	2.9	0.7	5.1	8.5	0.3	100	1162
NUIM	19.1	7.4	11.3	12.9	12.9	7.8	4.2	9.6	14.1	0.6	100	665
D.C.U.	31.5	9.6	12.4	10.6	11.2	6.2	1.9	5.2	10.7	0.6	100	726
U.L.	20.6	8.1	10.3	9.9	9.4	5.9	2.0	6.9	25.3	1.4	100	1228
R.S.C.I.	31.8	40.9	18.2	0.0	4.5	0.0	0.0	0.0	4.5	0.0	100	22
Institutes of Technology												
Athlone	14.3	2.2	5.1	9.8	21.1	7.0	4.7	9.4	25.4	1.0	100	511
Carlow	19.6	3.5	5.8	7.1	20.0	11.5	5.4	9.4	15.9	1.7	100	479
Cork	18.6	6.6	7.6	9.3	17.3	11.5	2.7	7.2	18.5	0.7	100	969
Dublin	28.4	8.7	10.0	10.5	14.8	6.7	2.6	7.2	10.4	0.8	100	1639
Dun Laoghaire	35.1	11.7	11.7	11.7	9.1	2.6	1.3	13.0	3.9	0.0	100	77
Dundalk	18.3	4.2	7.1	9.3	21.6	12.3	6.7	8.7	11.1	0.7	100	578
Galway	15.7	4.5	7.5	7.8	17.9	9.4	3.9	8.4	24.3	0.6	100	822
Letterkenny	14.7	5.2	4.1	10.1	18.0	13.7	8.0	7.5	16.2	2.6	100	388
Limerick	16.6	4.9	6.5	9.5	17.4	8.9	5.2	11.4	19.4	0.1	100	674
Sligo	13.9	2.2	7.5	9.0	13.1	9.0	6.3	10.6	28.2	0.2	100	510
Tallaght	22.9	6.9	10.7	12.9	22.6	8.0	3.0	10.7	2.2	0.0	100	363
Tralee	13.1	3.0	4.2	7.3	20.4	9.6	4.7	7.5	29.5	0.7	100	427
Waterford	17.9	6.0	6.4	8.5	17.3	10.5	4.3	7.5	19.7	1.8	100	866

TABLE A12   SOCIO-ECONOMIC STATUS OF NEW ENTRANTS BY COLLEGE

Socio-Economic Group / College	% Employers & Manager	% Higher Professionals	% Lower Professionals	% Non-Manual	% Manual Skilled	% Semi-Skilled	% Unskilled	% Own Account Workers	% Farmers	% Agricultural Workers	Total %	Total N
Colleges of Education												
St. Patrick's	21.0	4.5	15.7	8.6	14.6	6.0	2.6	7.5	19.1	0.4	100	267
St. Catherine's	1.8	0.0	17.6	17.6	11.8	5.9	5.9	0.0	29.4	0.0	100	17
Froebel	10.0	10.0	10.0	10.0	25.0	10.0	5.0	10.0	10.0	0.0	100	20
Church of Ireland	13.0	8.7	4.3	13.0	4.3	0.0	0.0	17.4	34.8	4.3	100	23
Mater Dei Institute	9.8	3.9	3.9	9.8	9.8	5.9	7.8	5.9	43.1	0.0	100	51
Marino	23.3	6.7	26.7	10.0	10.0	6.7	3.3	0.0	13.3	0.0	100	30
St. Angela's	7.1	0.0	7.1	0.0	7.1	7.1	0.0	7.1	64.3	0.0	100	14
Mary Immaculate	16.1	8.0	11.6	8.9	13.8	6.7	1.3	6.3	26.8	0.4	100	224
Other Colleges												
National College of Ireland	33.0	12.0	8.0	7.0	16.0	9.0	0.0	12.0	3.0	0.0	100	100
NCAD	13.9	13.9	20.1	17.3	14.8	9.6	4.3	0.0	6.1	0.0.	100	115
Milltown	23.8	9.5	4.8	19.0	9.5	9.5	0.0	14.3	9.5	0.0	100	21
TOTAL ALL COLLEGES	**21.6**	**10.1**	**10.2**	**9.4**	**13.6**	**7.5**	**3.1**	**7.2**	**16.6**	**0.7**	**100**	**17,635**

TABLE A13 SOCIO-ECONOMIC STATUS OF NEW ENTRANTS BY FIELD OF STUDY IN HEA SECTOR COLLEGES

Field of Study \ Socio-Economic Group	Employers & Managers	Higher Professional	Lower Professional	Non-Manual	Manual Skilled	Semi-Skilled	Unskilled	Own Account Workers	Farmers	Agricultural Workers	Total %	Total N
Total N	2044	1279	1087	819	828	482	165	510	1761	51	-	8564
Total %	23.9	14.9	12.7	9.6	9.7	5.6	1.9	6	20.6	0.6	100	-
% Combined Studies	27.7	19.5	9.9	8.3	6.6	5.9	2.3	7.3	12.2	0.3	100	303
% Equestrian	24.2	6.1	6.1	9.1	0.0	3.0	0.0	9.1	42.4	0.0	100	33
% Food Science & Technology	11.8	6.5	12.9	9.7	9.7	3.2	2.2	6.5	36.6	1.1	100	93
% Agricultural Science & Forestry	8.9	4.8	6.2	4.8	4.8	4.1	0.0	3.4	62.3	0.7	100	146
% Veterinary Medicine	15	27.5	10.0	2.5	5.0	2.5	0.0	2.5	35.0	0.0	100	40
% Dentistry	21.6	27.0	16.2	5.4	2.7	5.4	0.0	5.4	16.2	0.0	100	37
% Medicine	23.2	39.3	11.8	6.5	6.5	2.4	0.8	5.7	13.4	0.4	100	246
% Architecture	12.9	22.6	25.8	6.5	9.7	0.0	0.0	3.2	19.4	0.0	100	31
% Engineering	22.9	16.4	15.8	9.4	8.0	4.0	1.3	5.4	15.7	1.0	100	1169
% Science	22.8	13.5	12.6	10.6	10.9	5.5	2.2	6.4	14.9	0.6	100	1632
% Law	27.7	28.8	13.1	7.9	6.8	3.1	0.5	3.1	8.9	0.0	100	191
% Commerce	27.1	15.2	11.2	8.7	8.2	5.7	1.5	5.8	16.0	0.6	100	1318
% Communication & Information Studies	26.3	7.9	23.7	7.9	5.3	7.9	2.6	5.3	10.5	2.6	100	38
% European Studies	25.5	11.2	9.2	8.2	16.3	6.1	1.0	0.1	15.3	1.0	100	98
% Economic & Social Studies	39.2	19.6	10.8	10.1	6.1	3.4	0.0	4.7	4.7	1.4	100	148
% Social Science	27.6	11.5	8.0	9.2	17.2	8.6	2.3	7.5	8.0	0.0	100	174
% Education	14	5.8	17.4	7.0	7.0	9.3	0.0	7.0	32.6	0.0	100	86
% Art & Design	13.9	13.9	20.0	17.4	14.8	9.6	4.3	0.0	6.1	0.0	100	115
% Arts	23.8	13.3	12.7	10.2	11.1	6.7	2.7	6.4	12.6	0.5	100	2666

TABLE A14 SOCIO-ECONOMIC STATUS OF NEW ENTRANTS BY FIELD OF STUDY IN NON-HEA SECTOR COLLEGES

Socio-Economic Group	% Construction Studies	% General Engineering	% Science	% Art & Design	% Computers Studies	% Business, Administrative & Secretarial Stuies	% Hotel, Catering & Tourism	% Education	% General Studies	Total %	Total N
Employers & Managers	16.2	17.5	16.7	22.5	19.5	21.5	22.6	17.4	18.2	19.4	1758
Higher Professional	4.3	5.9	6.1	8.9	6.0	5.1	4.7	5.9	5.3	5.6	510
Lower Professional	8.8	6.7	8.0	7.5	8.0	7.0	7.6	13.1	8.5	7.8	708
Non-Manual	8.3	9.6	8.7	10.9	10.7	8.9	8.1	9.3	10.4	9.3	845
Manual Skilled	17.9	18.6	20.9	15.5	17.5	17.0	15.0	13.4	17.2	17.3	1572
Semi-skilled	8.8	8.6	9.7	8.0	10.5	9.4	11.7	6.2	8.7	9.2	832
Unskilled	5.5	3.3	5.0	5.2	3.9	4.3	4.8	2.6	3.1	4.1	373
Own Account Workers	7.3	9.0	8.0	9.8	8.8	8.5	9.1	6.8	7.7	8.4	765
Farmers	21.9	20.0	15.2	11.8	14.5	17.6	15.5	24.8	19.6	18.0	1632
Agricultural Workers	0.8	0.9	1.6	0.0	0.6	0.8	0.9	0.5	1.2	0.8	76
TOTAL %	100	100	100	100	100	100	100	100	100	100	–
TOTAL N	599	1819	814	440	1013	2745	580	643	413	–	9071

Socio-Economic Groups	National Population Under 15 years in 1996 %	National Population Aged 13 &14 years in 1996 %
Employers and Managers	14.8	14.9
Higher Professional	5.2	4.3
Lower Professional	7.7	7.3
Non-Manual	15.0	13.8
Manual Skilled	19.1	18.8
Semi-Skilled	10.6	10.8
Unskilled	8.5	9.0
Own Account Workers	7.8	8.3
Farmers	9.4	10.9
Agricultural workers	2.0	1.9
TOTAL %	100	100
TOTAL N	766,057	122,396

TABLE A15   COMPARISON BETWEEN NATIONAL DISTRIBUTION OF THE POPULATION UNDER 15 YEARS AND THOSE AGED 13 AND 14 YEARS BY FATHERS SOCIO-ECONOMIC GROUP FROM CENSUS 1996.

TABLE A16   CHANGES BETWEEN 1991-93 AND 1996-98 IN THE PERCENTAGE DISTRIBUTION OF SCHOOLLEAVERS WHO SAT THE LEAVING CERTIFICATE BY LEVEL OF ATTAINMENT AND FATHERS' SOCIO-ECONOMIC

Fathers' Socio Economic Group	< 5 Ds %	5 passes, no hons %	1 Honour %	2-4 Hons %	5+ Hons %
Farmers	0.0	+4.7	-3.4	-2.0	+10.1
Other Agricultural	+3.9	-17.3	+3.4	+6.1	+7.5
Higher Professional	+0.3	+2.3	-4.0	+0.2	+1.4
Lower Professional	+3.4	-2.6	-5.2	-4.6	+9.2
Employers & Managers	+0.8	+1.3	-0.1	-10.7	+8.5
Salaried Employees	-0.8	-5.7	+1.8	-1.2	+5.8
Intermediate Non-Manual	0.8	-3.2	-1.8	-7.6	+13.4
Other Non-Manual	+3.2	-8.5	+3.7	-6.0	+7.6
Skilled Manual	-1.3	-10.1	-0.5	+3.1	+8.9
Semi-Skilled Manual	-2.0	-12.6	-2.8	+11.9	+4.4
Unskilled Manual	+1.2	-11.5	-0.4	+6.5	+4.1
Unknown	-11.9	-7.0	+7.4	+12.3	-0.8
TOTAL	**+0.7**	**-4.5**	**-0.8**	**-2.3**	**+6.7**

TABLE A17 EDUCATIONAL ATTAINMENT BY SUBJECT OF 1998 NEW HIGHER EDUCATION ENTRANTS AND ALL 1998 LEAVING CERTIFICATE CANDIDATES

		Higher Level					Lower Level					TOTAL	
		A %	B %	C %	D %	Other %	A %	B %	C %	D %	Other %	N	%
Languages													
English	HE	6.4	20.3	33.6	18.0	0.7	1.1	6.2	9.9	3.7	0.1	27,559	95.2
English	LC	3.2	11.0	21.7	17.2	2.0	1.0	7.8	18.7	14.4	2.9	61,304	98.9
Irish	HE	5.0	19.1	20.1	6.0	0.1	0.3	9.0	23.2	14.6	2.6	25,896	89.4
Irish	LC	2.6	10.3	12.6	5.2	0.2	0.4	8.9	26.4	25.5	7.9	57,556	92.9
French	HE	6.1	19.6	26.4	15.3	1.1	0.1	5.2	15.0	10.2	1.0	18,965	65.5
French	LC	3.5	11.6	17.4	13.2	1.8	0.1	4.0	17.3	23.5	7.6	37,085	59.9
German	HE	8.5	27.5	30.0	13.2	0.5	0.7	7.8	8.2	3.3	0.4	6,653	23.0
German	LC	5.7	18.9	23.9	13.9	1.1	0.5	9.2	14.0	9.1	3.5	11,372	18.4
Latin	HE	24.1	36.2	29.1	7.8	1.4	0.0	0.0	0.7	0.7	0.0	141	0.5
Latin	LC	22.9	32.5	28.0	9.6	2.5	0.0	0.0	1.3	3.2	0.0	157	0.3
Spanish	HE	12.8	24.2	25.4	15.4	1.0	1.0	7.5	10.3	2.0	0.6	814	2.8
Spanish	LC	8.0	15.6	18.0	15.6	1.9	0.8	8.4	17.6	10.9	3.2	1,674	2.7
Italian	HE	13.9	23.6	25.0	16.7	1.4	0.0	11.1	4.2	4.2	0.0	72	0.2
Italian	LC	11.3	16.3	16.9	15.0	3.1	0.0	8.1	18.1	9.4	1.9	160	0.3
Classical Studies	HE	6.1	23.2	38.1	23.5	5.6	0.0	0.4	0.9	1.6	0.7	570	2.0
Classical Studies	LC	3.7	16.4	27.5	25.1	11.1	0.1	0.3	1.8	5.4	8.6	1,000	1.6
Other Languages	HE★	16.7	38.9	33.3	11.1	0.0	0.0	0.0	0.0	0.0	0.0	18	0.1
Other Languages	LC	14.3	39.3	39.3	7.1	0.0	0.0	0.0	0.0	0.0	0.0	28	0.0

★ Includes Greek, Dutch, Danish and Portuguese

TABLE A17 Cont. EDUCATIONAL ATTAINMENT BY SUBJECT OF 1998 NEW HIGHER EDUCATION ENTRANTS AND ALL 1998 LEAVING CERTIFICATE CANDIDATES

		Higher Level					Lower Level					TOTAL	
		A %	B %	C %	D %	Other %	A %	B %	C %	D %	Other %	N	%
Mathematics & Sciences													
Maths	HE	7.0	12.4	9.1	3.	0.2	17.6	24.9	16.7	8.4	0.7	28,666	99.0
Maths	LC	3.3	6.1	5.1	2.3	0.5	11.1	21.2	21.0	18.4	11.0	61,969	100.0
Biology	HE	12.8	25.2	26.5	17.2	3.3	0.6	4.9	6.5	2.5	0.5	4,582	50.4
Biology	LC	7.3	14.7	17.8	15.8	6.7	0.6	6.1	13.0	11.4	6.8	30,613	49.4
Chemistry	HE	16.3	27.6	25.5	16.6	4.6	0.4	2.6	3.7	2.2	0.5	5,045	17.4
Chemistry	LC	13.0	23.4	21.4	16.6	8.2	0.4	2.6	5.1	5.5	3.7	7,325	11.8
Physics	HE	11.1	22.7	24.2	18.3	4.7	1.6	6.6	6.4	3.6	0.8	6,280	21.7
Physics	LC	7.9	17.2	18.8	18.3	7.2	1.4	6.4	8.3	8.3	6.1	9,659	15.6
Physics & Chemistry	HE	19.7	29.5	20.6	12.5	4.8	0.1	2.7	4.7	3.4	1.1	705	2.4
Physics & Chemistry	LC	14.2	21.6	16.9	11.9	6.3	0.6	3.1	7.1	7.2	11.0	1,240	2.0
Applied Maths	HE	27.8	36.2	19.4	8.3	1.9	1.9	1.4	1.3	1.0	0.8	1,175	4.1
Applied Maths	LC	24.2	31.8	20.6	10.0	4.6	1.7	1.6	2.3	1.8	1.4	1,531	2.5
Agricultural Science	HE	7.5	35.0	36.7	15.6	0.7	-	0.9	1.8	1.5	0.3	1,091	3.8
Agricultural Science	LC	3.3	20.2	28.2	19.3	3.4	0.1	2.6	10.0	9.2	3.6	2,847	4.6

TABLE A17 Cont.   **EDUCATIONAL ATTAINMENT BY SUBJECT OF 1998 NEW HIGHER EDUCATION ENTRANTS AND ALL 1998 LEAVING CERTIFICATE CANDIDATES**

		Higher Level					Lower Level					TOTAL	
		A %	B %	C %	D %	Other %	A %	B %	C %	D %	Other %	N	%
Business Studies													
Accounting	HE	14.5	25.5	23.4	15.6	4.9	5.0	6.0	3.1	1.5	0.5	5,787	20.0
Accounting	LC	9.2	16.8	17.6	14.4	7.8	5.4	9.0	7.8	5.9	6.0	9,888	16.0
Business Organisation	HE	10.6	30.3	30.4	15.4	2.0	1.8	4.6	3.4	1.3	0.1	10,099	34.9
Business Organisation	LC	4.9	15.9	19.9	15.2	4.7	2.5	9.4	12.3	10.6	4.7	24,055	38.8
Economics	HE	12.5	35.9	27.4	13.9	1.5	2.2	3.8	1.8	1.0	0.1	3,209	11.1
Economics	LC	8.2	24.6	21.7	16.3	4.8	3.4	7.6	7.1	5.3	1.1	5,394	8.7
Economic History	HE	3.4	22.5	38.6	24.6	7.9	-	0.3	0.8	0.8	1.1	378	1.3
Economic History	LC	2.5	17.2	34.1	25.5	14.9	0.2	0.7	1.8	1.4	1.6	552	0.9
Agricultural Economics	HE	11.8	27.4	33.3	24.7	2.2	-	-	-	0.5	-	186	0.6
Agricultural Economics	LC	8.2	18.9	26.4	31.8	10.4	-	0.4	1.1	1.4	1.4	280	0.5
Technical													
Technical Drawing	HE	12.4	23.4	20.8	12.9	2.0	8.0	10.8	7.0	2.3	0.4	3,260	11.3
Technical Drawing	LC	6.2	12.8	13.7	9.9	3.1	7.0	13.2	15.5	13.2	5.3	7,480	12.1
Construction Studies	HE	0.1	48.9	32.0	4.0	0.1	0.1	1.7	2.5	0.6	0.1	2,884	10.0
Construction Studies	LC	4.2	27.7	29.0	9.6	0.6	0.0	6.1	14.6	6.9	1.3	8,608	13.9
Engineering	HE	13.5	40.0	30.1	7.2	0.2	0.8	5.0	2.9	0.5	-	1,672	5.6
Engineering	LC	5.7	21.4	23.6	10.8	1.4	1.0	11.0	16.0	7.4	1.8	5,138	8.3

TABLE A17 Cont.   EDUCATIONAL ATTAINMENT BY SUBJECT OF 1998 NEW HIGHER EDUCATION ENTRANTS AND ALL 1998 LEAVING CERTIFICATE CANDIDATES

		Higher Level					Lower Level					TOTAL	
		A %	B %	C %	D %	Other %	A %	B %	C %	D %	Other %	N	%
Social Studies													
Home Econ.	HE	9.7	33.6	33.4	16.2	2.5	0.4	1.6	1.9	0.5	0.1	**9,710**	**33.5**
Home Econ.	LC	4.7	17.7	24.0	19.2	7.0	0.9	5.2	9.8	8.5	2.9	**24,336**	**39.3**
History	HE	11.1	27.6	30.0	16.4	2.2	5.9	3.2	2.1	1.1	0.3	**6,644**	**22.9**
History	LC	5.6	14.8	19.7	15.1	5.6	9.0	9.0	6.8	6.5	7.9	**14,842**	**24.0**
Geography	HE	9.0	32.6	38.6	14.2	0.9	1.1	1.8	1.3	0.4	0.0	**12,860**	**44.4**
Geography	LC	4.5	18.3	28.3	17.7	3.5	2.4	8.2	9.3	5.8	1.9	**29,689**	**47.9**
Art & Music													
Art	HE	8.3	32.0	37.6	16.1	0.9	0.6	1.9	1.9	0.7	0.1	**3,640**	**12.6**
Art	LC	3.4	15.4	26.9	20.0	3.4	1.9	8.3	12.2	7.2	1.3	**10,323**	**16.7**
Music & Musicianship A&B		10.6	40.8	38.8	7.7	0.2	-	1.0	0.9	0.1	-	**925**	**3.2**
Music & Musicainship A&B		6.6	26.5	34.0	15.7	2.0	-	2.3	6.0	5.6	1.3	**1,793**	**2.9**

| Field of Study | Number of Honours* | | | | | | | | | | | Total |
	0 %	1 %	2 %	3 %	4 %	5 %	6 %	7 %	8 %	9 %	10+ %	N
Arts	0.8	0.6	1.0	4.2	18.2	32.2	32.8	9.3	0.9	–	–	4,100
Education	–	–	–	1.6	8.6	20.3	37.5	30.5	1.6	–	–	128
Art & Design	–	3.9	24.0	16.3	14.0	16.3	17.1	8.5	–	–	–	129
Economic & Social Studies	–	–	0.5	0.5	1.1	6.3	47.9	37.4	6.3	–	–	190
European Studies	–	–	0.7	8.4	19.6	35.0	25.21	1.2	–	–	–	143
Social Science	2.7	–	1.6	1.2	3.5	26.8	52.9	10.9	0.4	–	–	257
Communications & Information Studies	–	–	–	–	1.9	3.7	61.1	31.5	1.9	–	–	54
Commerce	0.1	0.1	–	0.4	3.4	21.0	43.0	28.5	3.4	0.1	–	1914
Law	–	–	–	–	0.3	2.4	42.7	47.1	6.8	0.7	–	295
Science	0.1	–	1.9	5.7	11.4	19.8	31.1	26.5	3.2	0.3	–	2396
Engineering	–	0.1	1.3	2.7	9.3	16.7	31.0	32.8	5.6	0.2	0.1	1649
Architecture	–	–	–	–	–	–	22.7	65.9	11.4	–	–	44
Medicine	–	–	–	–	0.3	–	16.7	60.2	18.5	4.3	–	324
Dentistry	–	–	–	–	4.2	4.2	12.5	54.2	18.8	6.3	–	48
Veterinary Medicine	–	–	–	–	–	–	16.0	52.0	26.0	4.0	2.0	50
Agricultural Science & Forestry	–	0.5	0.5	12.7	20.8	32.6	24.9	8.1	–	–	–	221
Food Science & Technology	–	–	0.8	4.2	21.0	28.6	35.3	8.4	1.7	–	-1	19
Equestrian	–	2.3	11.4	15.9	13.6	34.1	22.7	–	–	–	–	44
Combined Studies	–	–	–	0.7	2.2	7.9	51.3	34.3	3.4	0.2	–	417
TOTAL	0.4	0.3	1.2	3.5	11.1	22.9	34.5	23.0	3.3	0.3	0.0	12,564

* Honours = Grade C of higher attained on a higher level paper.

FIELD OF STUDY OF NEW ENTRANTS TO NON-HEA SECTOR COLLEGES, BY LEVEL OF PRIOR ACADEMIC ATTAINMENT

	Number of Honours★									Total
Field of Study	**0**	**1**	**2**	**3**	**4**	**5**	**6**	**7**	**8+**	**Total**
	%	%	%	%	%	%	%	%	%	N
Construction Studies	7.6	19.0	23.9	24.8	12.9	6.8	3.1	1.7	0.1	**1,040**
General Engineering	12.1	22.6	27.5	18.5	10.3	4.9	2.7	1.2	0.1	**3,177**
Science	9.7	15.3	20.6	19.7	14.9	7.8	6.7	4.6	0.7	**1,465**
Art & Design	8.5	21.1	18.3	21.0	14.3	9.4	6.4	0.9	0.1	**777**
Computer Studies	11.0	18.3	21.3	20.1	17.0	8.5	3.4	0.4	-	**1,923**
Business, Administrative & Secretarial	12.5	14.6	17.9	20.7	18.2	10.9	4.6	0.7	0.0	**5,179**
Hotel, Catering & Tourism	7.7	14.4	20.3	22.6	17.4	11.3	5.6	0.7	-	**1,035**
Education	1.6	1.6	1.7	1.8	1.3	10.9	48.7	30.4	2.0	**819**
General Studies	7.5	10.9	16.9	20.8	15.1	13.9	12.6	2.3	0.1	**966**
TOTAL	**10.4**	**16.3**	**20.1**	**19.6**	**14.6**	**9.1**	**7.0**	**2.8**	**0.2**	**16,381**

★ Honours = Grade C of higher attained on a higher level paper.

Field of Study / Subject Groupings		Humanities	Education	Art & Design	Social Sciecne	Law	Commerce	Science	Technology	Medical Sciences	Agriculture	Hotel, Tourism and Catering	Combined Studies	All Disciplines
No. of Maths and Science Subjects	*1	26	19	43	23	19	35	2	19	0	0	28	28	23
	2	62	62	54	63	58	59	42	55	15	49	67	57	56
	3	11	18	3	13	20	7	50	21	68	46	6	14	19
	4+	1	2	0	1	3	0	6	4	17	4	0	1	2
Number of Languages Subjects	1	0	0	1	1	0	1	0	1	1	0	0	0	0
	2	2	1	11	5	3	5	3	7	2	1	6	1	4
	3	81	91	83	85	82	87	92	88	80	97	89	81	86
	4+	18	8	5	10	16	8	5	5	17	2	5	18	10
Number of Business Subjects	0	53	53	65	45	48	18	63	48	63	50	43	32	44
	1	41	42	34	49	44	63	35	46	34	46	52	54	48
	2	5	5	1	6	7	18	2	6	3	4	5	13	8
	3+	0	0	0	1	0	1	0	0	0	0	0	1	0
Number of Technical Subjects	0	98	98	96	99	99	99	98	91	99	99	98	98	97
	1	2	2	4	1	2	1	2	8	1	1	2	2	2
	2	0	0	0	0	0	0	0	1	0	0	0	0	0
	3+	0	0	0	0	0	0	0	0	0	0	0	0	0
Number of Other Subjects	0	6	8	1	8	13	13	22	17	39	15	3	18	13
	1	41	44	19	40	44	52	51	45	43	59	43	50	46
	2	44	43	60	45	40	32	26	33	15	24	47	29	36
	3+	9	5	21	7	3	3	2	5	3	1	7	2	5

* This includes four people who have no Science subject

Subject Groupings	Humanities	Education	Art & Design	Social Science	Law	Commerce	Science	Technology	Medical Sciences	Agriculture	Hotel, Tourism and Catering	Combined Studies	All Disciplines
No. of Maths and Science Subjects ★1	33	19	43	28	21	37	3	21	0	4	33	28	24
2	51	57	52	54	40	53	41	56	7	57	58	50	52
3	14	20	5	17	34	9	42	18	45	30	9	19	19
4+	2	4	1	2	5	1	14	5	48	9	0	3	5
Number of Languages Subjects •1	1	0	10	3	0	2	1	4	4	0	4	1	3
2	4	11	29	14	4	13	9	23	1	10	13	5	16
3	83	87	58	73	84	81	87	71	86	89	79	85	77
4+	12	3	3	10	12	4	3	2	9	1	4	9	4
Number of Business Subjects 0	38	53	62	31	42	13	55	54	61	49	39	24	43
1	46	39	34	51	39	51	39	38	38	45	48	51	43
2	13	8	4	17	16	31	5	8	1	5	12	21	13
3+	3	0	0	2	3	5	0	0	0	0	1	4	2
Number of Technical Subjects 0	86	60	47	78	88	80	75	43	91	65	72	88	62
1	12	15	27	14	9	15	19	31	8	22	22	10	23
2	2	22	22	6	2	4	6	21	1	11	5	2	12
3+	0	4	4	2	1	1	0	5	0	1	2	0	3
Number of Other Subjects 0	12	29	10	20	20	23	35	34	48	30	9	21	28
1	42	39	39	44	51	52	47	46	36	51	47	53	47
2	37	28	39	32	24	23	16	17	13	17	35	25	22
3+	9	4	2	4	5	2	2	3	3	2	9	1	3

★ This includes five people who have no Science subject

• This includes 1 person who has no Language subject

	U.C.D.	U.C.C.	NUIG	T.C.D.	D.C.U.	U.L.	NUI/St.Patrick's, Maynooth	R.C.S.I.	St. Patrick's College of Education	Mary Immaculate College of Education	Froebal	Montessori College, Milltown	St. Nicholas, Montessori	Mater Dei Institute	St. Mary's College of Education, Marino	Church of Ireland College of Education	St. Catherine's College	St. Angela's College, Sligo
Carlow	59	6	9	11	22	12	23	0	6	1	0	2	0	0	4	2	1	0
Dublin	1709	30	38	819	507	48	323	25	119	1	5	5	17	4	11	6	1	1
Kildare	156	9	32	77	61	22	162	2	17	0	0	3	1	1	4	1	2	1
Kilkenny	78	38	14	27	21	53	23	2	14	9	1	0	0	6	2	0	3	0
Laois	60	11	22	17	23	25	20	1	8	3	0	0	0	3	0	1	0	0
Longford	38	2	36	11	22	14	24	0	4	1	0	0	1	3	0	0	0	1
Louth	72	6	17	36	58	7	41	1	13	0	1	0	0	1	1	0	2	0
Meath	153	5	29	62	101	18	62	1	24	1	1	1	1	3	2	2	1	0
Offaly	52	0	39	19	22	31	17	1	8	0	0	0	1	1	1	2	0	0
Westmeath	83	6	53	24	27	31	28	0	7	0	0	0	1	1	1	1	0	2
Wexford	146	32	12	47	53	34	42	0	20	0	4	2	3	6	2	0	3	0
Wicklow	210	6	6	76	49	13	33	0	9	0	3	2	2	5	0	3	0	0
Clare	35	58	130	23	8	217	18	1	2	28	0	0	0	1	0	0	1	4
Cork	60	1645	44	42	34	237	19	1	0	74	1	1	0	5	2	2	3	2
Kerry	51	232	56	27	15	180	13	1	0	40	3	0	0	1	1	1	2	2
Limerick	61	134	51	41	9	520	13	0	1	40	0	0	1	3	0	2	0	4
Tipperary	97	138	57	43	29	205	19	0	11	40	1	3	1	2	1	3	3	3
Waterford	75	129	10	9	15	42	8	0	6	7	0	0	0	1	2	0	1	0
Galway	67	23	653	38	30	146	40	0	19	26	2	2	1	6	1	0	4	7
Leitrim	19	0	24	6	11	14	17	0	5	0	1	0	0	0	0	0	0	2
Mayo	57	3	189	33	41	76	32	1	34	11	3	3	2	6	9	0	0	14
Roscommon	24	3	97	10	12	30	20	2	10	6	1	1	1	2	1	0	0	9
Sligo	45	1	82	23	15	20	21	0	17	5	1	0	0	0	1	0	0	18
Cavan	62	2	27	24	32	7	29	0	15	1	0	0	1	1	0	0	1	3
Donegal	55	2	93	29	15	22	48	0	27	0	0	0	0	1	3	5	0	3
Monaghan	46	1	14	19	21	7	32	1	22	0	1	1	0	3	0	0	1	1
N.Ireland	46	4	17	151	5	1	5	0	0	0	0	0	0	0	0	0	0	0
Overseas	69	42	6	126	2	9	8	161	0	0	0	0	1	0	0	0	0	0
TOTAL	**3685**	**2568**	**1857**	**1870**	**1260**	**2041**	**1140**	**201**	**418**	**294**	**29**	**27**	**34**	**66**	**49**	**30**	**29**	**77**

TABLE 21b   DISTRIBUTION OF NEW ENTRANTS BY COUNTY OF PERMANENT RESIDENCE AND BY COLLEGE

County	Dublin Institute of Technology	Athlone IT	Carlow IT	Cork IT	Dundalk IT	Dun laoghaire College of Art, Design & Technology	Galway/Mayo IT	Letterkenny IT	Limerick IT	Sligo IT	Tallaght IT	Tralee IT	Waterford IT	N.C.A.D	National College of Ireland	Shannon College of Hotel Management	Milltown Institute	American College Dublin	Dublin Business school	LSB College	Griffith College	Portobello College	H S I College	Mid West Business Institute	Skerry's Business College	Total All Colleges
Carlow	39	5	118	1	2	1	6	2	3	2	1	4	35	2	2	0	1	-	1	2	1	1	0	0	0	387
Dublin	1407	44	92	20	269	128	60	39	9	24	622	11	73	68	147	7	21	38	58	84	69	159	0	0	0	7118
Kildare	190	33	116	5	14	2	24	8	9	17	62	5	75	7	12	2	4	6	8	16	9	14	0	0	0	1189
Kilkenny	45	4	77	18	5	3	11	1	14	5	3	4	134	3	4	0	0	0	0	5	3	4	0	0	0	634
Laois	32	35	68	7	1	0	20	1	9	5	2	8	47	3	2	0	1	1	0	1	4	0	0	0	0	433
Longford	25	56	3	1	6	1	20	7	1	54	0	0	8	0	2	0	0	1	0	0	1	0	0	0	0	343
Louth	76	9	5	2	423	1	11	13	3	1	1	0	6	7	6	1	2	3	2	1	1	3	0	0	0	833
Meath	234	57	19	5	152	7	25	13	6	9	11	10	46	3	16	0	1	2	2	9	4	12	0	0	0	1110
Offaly	44	128	39	3	6	1	43	0	10	10	3	11	19	0	2	0	1	0	0	2	1	2	1	0	0	518
Westmeath	64	212	10	3	8	0	25	3	14	32	3	3	18	1	3	0	2	0	0	2	3	5	0	0	0	675
Wexford	85	4	117	18	2	4	13	5	18	6	1	2	275	14	3	0	2	0	0	4	2	3	0	0	0	984
Wicklow	162	5	63	1	17	20	10	8	4	8	26	3	54	5	14	1	3	5	8	15	5	11	0	0	0	865
Clare	21	21	6	31	1	0	62	3	171	14	1	52	37	1	1	1	0	0	0	0	0	1	15	0	0	966
Cork	39	6	17	1280	8	3	53	7	79	13	1	152	112	4	3	9	1	2	0	0	1	5	1	1	29	3999
Kerry	33	6	6	98	7	3	33	2	70	6	0	383	30	2	3	1	4	1	1	1	0	4	33	10	0	1319
Limerick	23	0	12	67	4	2	33	3	452	4	0	91	36	0	0	4	1	0	1	3	0	6	0	0	0	1665
Tipperary	45	40	63	93	8	2	51	5	113	7	0	33	207	3	4	0	2	0	3	1	4	8	9	1	0	1360
Waterford	19	4	43	42	1	4	9	0	11	2	0	15	310	5	5	1	0	1	0	2	0	3	0	0	0	786
Galway	52	177	7	11	6	3	616	23	63	63	0	19	20	5	1	5	2	4	1	0	2	0	0	0	0	2147
Leitrim	19	18	1	1	2	0	17	15	6	61	0	1	4	1	0	1	1	0	1	0	0	2	0	0	0	252
Mayo	49	74	9	6	6	0	340	36	49	152	0	7	18	2	3	1	2	2	0	0	1	3	0	0	0	1275
Roscommon	37	81	3	2	4	2	75	10	7	75	0	4	5	0	3	2	0	1	0	0	2	0	0	0	0	542
Sligo	17	8	0	1	1	1	43	41	6	219	0	6	6	2	4	0	0	0	0	1	5	5	0	0	0	609
Cavan	60	50	7	2	45	1	29	8	2	49	3	1	14	0	1	0	0	1	0	0	1	3	0	0	0	487
Donegal	38	6	1	4	3	0	47	473	2	70	0	1	6	3	0	0	0	3	0	0	0	1	0	0	0	962
Monaghan	63	19	1	2	118	1	16	29	2	10	2	3	8	0	5	0	1	2	1	0	3	2	0	0	0	457
N.Ireland	10	0	0	0	0	0	2	2	0	2	0	0	0	2	1	0	0	3	1	1	0	0	0	0	0	255
Overseas	17	15	0	1	0	5	5	2	1	2	0	0	1	6	1	7	0	36	15	0	16	0	0	0	0	554
TOTAL	2945	1117	903	1725	1119	195	1699	761	1134	917	740	824	1604	143	249	44	55	114	105	154	137	260	62	12	31	32724

| TABLE A22 | RATES OF ADMISSION TO HIGHER EDUCATION IN DUBLIN DISTRICTS 1992 AND 1998 AND FOR SELECTED DISTRICTS IN 1978 | | |

Postal Districts	1998	1992 (Adjusted)	1978★ (Adjusted)
1 North Inner City	.09	.06	.03
3 (Clontarf - Marino)	.54	.52	.41
5 (Raheny - Harmonstown)	.38	.32	.25
7 (Cabra - Arran Quay)	.20	.14	.20
9 (Whitehall - Beaumont)	.40	.40	.48
11 (Finglas - Ballymun)	.14	.21	.18
13 (Howth - Sutton)	.40	.33	NA
15 (Castleknock - Blachardstown)	.41	.41	NA
17 (Priorswood - Darndale)	.08	.08	NA
2 South Inner City	.20	.11	.23
4 (Ballsbridge - Donnybrook)	.59	.59	.68
6 (Rathmines - Terenure)	.70	.64	.79
8 (Kilmainham - Inchicore)	.21	.18	.10
10 (Ballyfermot - Chapelizod)	.07	.07	.03
12 (Crumlin - Kimmage)	.20	.22	.15
14 (Rathfarnham - Clonskeagh)	.68	.68	NA
16 (Ballyboden - Ballinteer)	.56	.53	NA
18 (Foxrock - Glencullen)	.77	.54	NA
20 (Palmerstown)	.17	.18	NA
22 (Clondalkin - Neilstown)	.13	.19	NA
24 (Tallaght - Firhouse)	.26	.31	NA
Dublin County	.50	.58	NA
Dublin City and County	.38	.38.	38

★ Only those postal districts which did not change between 1978 and 1998 are included.

Table A23

CORRELATION MATRIX OF PREDICTOR VARIABLES USED IN MULTIVARIATE ANALYSIS OF INTER-COUNTY VARIABILITY IN RATES OF ADMISSION TO HIGHER EDUCATION

Predictor Variables	1	2	3	4	5	6	7	8	9	10	11	12	13	14
1. Distance from University	1.00	.304	.802**	.127	-.176	.120	.569**	-.661**	.409*	-.803**	-.735**	.331	.630**	-.810**
2. Distance from Institute of Technology		1.00	.143	.081	-.426*	.386	.469*	-.081	-.112	-.425*	-.566**	-.283	.232	-.473*
3. Distance from College of Education			1.00	.298	-.041	-.109	.644**	-.540**	.279	-.750**	-.732**	.240	.595**	-.570**
4. Retention Rate to Leaving Certificate				1.00	.056	-.280	.479*	.027	-.095	-.393*	-.442*	-.325	-.010-	.061
5. Proportion of Post-Primary Enrolments in Secondary Schools					1.00	-.656**	-.079	.381	-.386	.237	.298	-.177	-.506**	.318
6. Proportion of Post-Primary Enrolments in Vocational Schools						1.00	-.078	-.250	.241	-.052	.010	.240	.207	-.268
7. Proportion of Population in Farming							1.00	-.374	.008	-.767**	-.871**	-.151	.484*	-.572**
8. Proportion of Population in Higher Social Classes								1.00	-.737**	.591**	.472*	-.629**	-.833**	.782**
9. Proportion of Population in Lower Social Classes									1.00	-.442*	-.169	.663**	.503**	-.502**
10. Income per Capita										1.00	.868**	-.122	-.551**	.771**
11. Proportion of Population in Urban Areas											1.00	.063	-.638**	.674**
12. Youth Unemployment Rate												1.00	.474*	-.392*
13. Proportion of Population which left school under 15 yrs.													1.00	-.632**
14. Proportion of Population which left school at age 20 or over														1.00

TABLE A24 **DISTRIBUTION OF NEW ENTRANTS TO NATIONAL TEACHER TRAINING IN 1963, 1986 AND 1998 AND DISTRIBUTION OF ENTRANTS TO ALL COLLEGES OF EDUCATION AND ALL HIGHER EDUCATION IN 1998**

	National Teacher Training★			All Colleges of Education	All Higher Education
Province	**1963** %	**1986** %	**1998** %	**1998** %	**1998** %
Leinster	18.8	32.7	33.8	37.3	47.3
Munster	39.8	37.4	37.8	34.6	31.6
Connaught	29.8	21.8	20.8	20.9	15.1
Ulster (3 counties)	11.7	8.1	7.6	7.3	6.0
Total	**100**	**100**	**100**	**100**	**100**

★ 1998 figure includes entrants to St. Patrick's, Mary Immaculate, St. Mary's Marino, Church of Irish College and Froebal College

TABLE A25 **DISTRIBUTION OF NEW ENTRANTS TO HIGHER EDUCATION BY COUNTY AND BY SOURCE OF FINANCIAL AID**

County	Grant	Other Financial Aid	No Financial Aid
Carlow	.411	.023	.566
Dublin	.157	.025	.818
Kildare	.237	.01	.749
Kilkenny	.394	.032	.574
Laois	.446	.030	.524
Longford	.478	.023	.499
Louth	.400	.013	.587
Meath	.306	.016	.677
Offaly	.473	.033	.494
Westmeath	.419	.021	.560
Wexford	.480	.020	.500
Wicklow	.271	.012	.704
Clare	.381	.012	.607
Cork	.309	.006	.685
Kerry	.418	.008	.574
Limerick	.305	.016	.679
Tipperary	.413	.015	.571
Waterford	.356	.025	.618
Galway	.531	.010	.459
Leitrim	.552	.004	.444
Mayo	.618	.025	.357
Roscommon	.552	.006	.443
Sligo	.417	.008	.575
Cavan	.522	.008	.470
Donegal	.549	.017	.435
Monaghan	.490	.004	.505
State	.351	.017	.632

appendix b | Copy of questionnaire

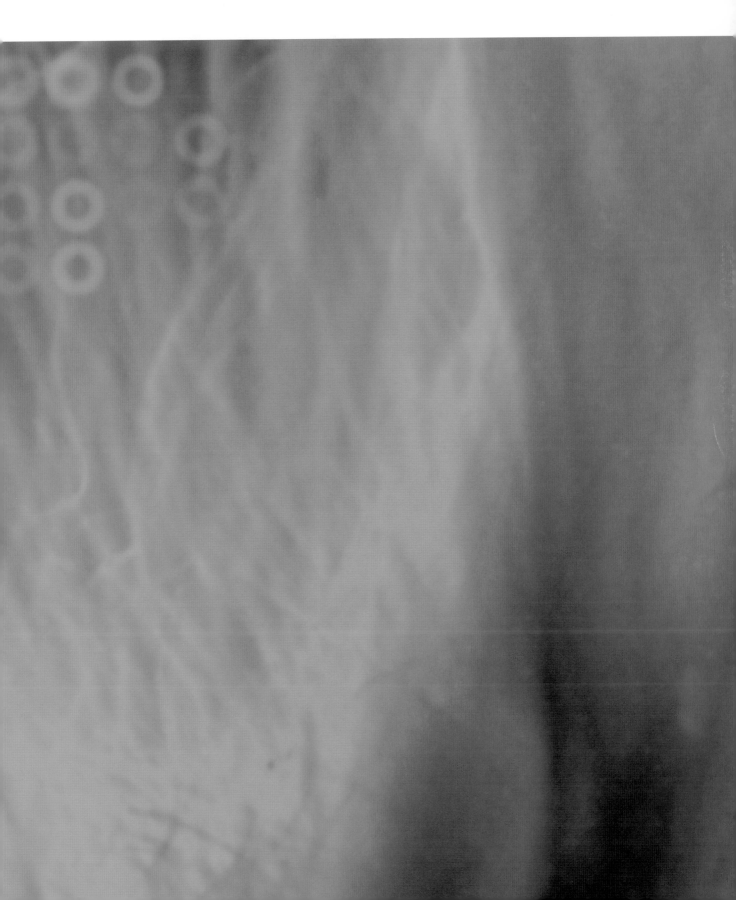

HIGHER EDUCATION AUTHORITY RESEARCH PROJECT

PLEASE COMPLETE THIS BRIEF QUESTIONNAIRE AND RETURN COMPLETED FORM IN THE PRE-PAID ENVELOPE PROVIDED.

1.   CAO No._____

2.   Please indicate the employment status of your parents/guardians (tick the appropriate box in each column).

FATHER/GUARDIAN		MOTHER/GUARDIAN	
Employed/At work	❏	Employed/At work	❏
Unemployed	❏	Unemployed	❏
Home Duties	❏	Home Duties	❏
Retired	❏	Retired	❏
Deceased	❏	Deceased	❏
Other (specify) _____		Other (specify) _____	

3.   Please state principal present occupation, giving precise job title (see explanatory note below). If not in paid employment please record LAST occupation held.

   Father/Guardian _____   Mother/Guardian_____

4.   In respect of present (or last) occupation please indicate whether:

	FATHER/GUARDIAN	MOTHER/GUARDIAN
Self-Employed with paid employees	❏	❏
Self-Employed without paid employees	❏	❏
Employee	❏	❏

   IF PARENTS/GUARDIANS ARE FARMERS:

5.   Please indicate size of farm(s) _____acres

EXPLANATORY NOTE ON OCCUPATION

In all cases please describe the occupation fully and precisely, using any special name by which the job is known, stating the type of work done and, where appropriate, the level of seniority such as supervisor or manager. The following are examples of the types of occupational descriptions which should be used:

Motor Mechanic;	Builder's Labourer;	Civil Engineer;	Gas Fitter;	Garage Manager;
Laboratory Technician;	Dock Labourer;	Electrical Engineer;	Analyst/Programmer;	Site Foreman;
Electronic Technician;	Food Process Worker;	Secretary/Receptionist;	Child Minder;	Retail Store/Shop Manager.

General terms such as "Manager", "Technician", "Labourer", "Engineer", "Fitter", "Foreman", "Mechanic", "Contractor", SHOULD NOT BE USED ALONE.

For civil service and local government employees, the grade should be stated and for Army and Garda personnel, the rank should be stated.

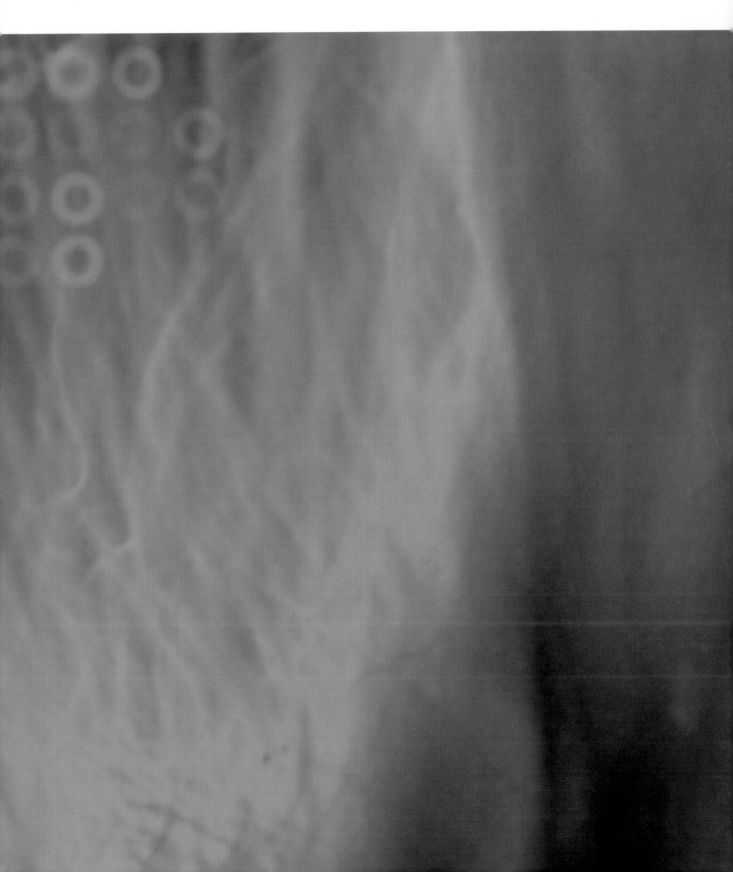

appendix c | Socio-Economic Groups
- list of constituent occupations

Socio-economic group and occupation	Employment Status*		

Employers and Managers

Socio-economic group and occupation			
Senior managers in national government	1		3,4
General Managers	1		3,4
Local Government Officers			3,4
General Administrators in national government	1		3,4
Production and works managers	1		3,4
Building Managers	1		3,4
Company financial managers	1		3,4
Marketing Managers	1		3,4
Purchasing managers	1		3,4
Personnel Managers	1		3,4
Computer Systems Managers	1		3,4
Credit Controllers	1		3,4
Bank and building society managers	1		3,4
Other financial managers n.e.s	1		3,4
Transport managers	1		3,4
Stores and warehousing managers	1		3,4
Commissioned officers in armed forces			3,4
Senior police and prison officers			3,4
Garage managers and proprietors	1		3,4
Hotel and accommodation managers	1		3,4
Restaurant and catering managers	1		3,4
Publicans, innkeepers and club managers	1		3,4
Entertainment and sports managers	1		3,4
Travel agency managers	1		3,4
Managers and proprietors of butchers	1		3,4
Managers and proprietors of shops	1		3,4
Administrators of schools and colleges	1	2	3,4
Other managers n.e.s	1		3,4
Judges	1		3,4
Librarians, archivists and curators			3,4
Draughtspersons	1		
Aircraft Officers, traffic planners and controllers	1		
Ship and hovercraft officers	1		3,4
Underwriters, claims assessors, brokers and investment analysts	1		
Matrons, houseparents, welfare, community and youth workers	1		

Socio-economic group and occupation

	Employment Status*
Authors, writers and journalists	1
Artists, commercial/industrial artists, grapic and clothing designers	1
Actors, musicians, entertainers, stage managers, producers and directors	1
Photographers, camera, sound and video equipment Operators	1
Professional athletes and sport officials	1
Vocational, industrial trainers and driving instructors	1
Accounts and wages clerks, book-keepers and other financial clerks	1
Cashiers, bank and counter clerks	1
Debt, rent and other cash collectors	1
Filing, computer, library and other clerks n.e.s	1
Stores, storekeepers, warehousemen/women, dispatch and production control clerks	1
Secretaries, medical, legal, personal assistants,typists and word processor operators	1
Computer operators, data processing operators and other office machine operators	1
Bricklayers and masons	1
Roofers, slayers, tillers, sheeters and cladders	1
Plasterers	1
Glaziers	1
Builders and building contractors	1
Floorers, floor coverers, carpet fitters and planners, floor and wall tilers	1
Painters and decorators	1
Scaffolders, riggers, steeplejacks and other construction trades n.e.s	1
Toolmakers	1
Metal working production and maintenance fitters	1
Precision instrument makers, goldsmiths, silversmiths and precious stone workers	1
Other machine tool setters and CNC setter-operators n.e.s	1
Electricians and electrical maintenance fitters	1
Telephone fitters	1
Cable Jointers and lines repairers	1
Radio, TV and video engineers	1
Computer engineers (installation and maintenance)	1
Other electrical and electronic trades	1
Smiths, forge/ metal plate workers and shipwrights	1
Plumbers, heating and ventilating engineers and related trades	1

Socio-economic group and occupation	Employment Status*
Sheet metal workers	1
Welders and steel erectors	1
Motor mechanics, auto electricians, tyre and exhaust fitters	1
Vehicle body repairers, panel beaters and spray painters	1
Weavers, knitters, warp preparers, bleachers, dyers and finishers	1
Sewing machinists, menders, darners and embroiderers	1
Coach trimmers, upholsterers and mattress makers	1
Shoe repairers and other leather makers	1
Tailors, dressmakers, clothing cutters, milliners and furriers	1
Other textiles, garments and related trades n.e.s	1
Printers, originators and compositors	1
Bookbinders, print finishers and othr printing trades n.e.s	1
Carpenters and joiners	1
Cabinet makers	1
Other woodworking trades n.e.s	1
Bakers and flour confectioners	1
Butchers and meat cutters	1
Fish mongers and poultry dressers	1
Glass product and ceramics makers, finishers and other operatives	1
Gardeners and groundsmen/groundswomen	1
Horticulture trades	1
Other craft and related occupations	1
Chefs and cooks	1
Childminders, nursery nurses and playgroup leaders	1
Educational assistants	1
Hairdressers, barbers and beauticians	1
Launderers, dry cleaners and pressers	1
Undertakers, bookmakers, and other personal service workers n.e.s	1
Importers, Exporters, commodity and shipping brokers	1
Technical and wholesale sales representatives	1
Auctioneers, estimators, valuers and other sales representatives n.e.s	1
Roundsmen/roundswomen and van salespersons	1
Market/ street traders and scrap dealers	1
Merchandisers, window dressers, floral arrangers and telephone salespersons	1
Moulders and furnace operatives (metal)	1
Electroplaters, galvanisers and colour coaters	1

Socio-economic group and occupation	Employment Status*		
Other metal making and treating process operatives n.e.s	1		
Inspectors, viewers, and laboratory testers	1		
Drivers of road goods vehicles	1		
Bus conductors and coach drivers	1		
Taxi/cab drivers, chauffeurs and couriers	1		
Seafarers (merchant navy), barge and boat operatives	1		
Mechanical plant drivers/operatives and crane drivers	1		
Fork truck drivers	1		
Other transport and machinery operatives n.e.s	1		
Pipe layers/pipe jointers and related construction workers	1		
Woodworking machine operatives	1		
Mine (excluding coal) and quarry workers	1		
Other plant, machine and process operatives n.e.s	1		
Fishing and related workers	1		
Road construction, paviors and kerb layers	1		
Other building and civil engineering labourers	1		
Stevedores and dockers	1		
Cleaners and domestics	1		
Other occupations in sales and services n.e.s	1		
All other labourers and related workers	1		

Higher Professional

	Employment Status*		
Chemists	1	2	3,4
Biological scientists	1	2	3,4
Physicists	1	2	3,4
Other natural scientists n.e.s	1	2	3,4
Civil and mining engineers	1	2	3,4
Mechanical Engineers	1	2	3,4
Electrical and electronic engineers	1	2	3,4
Software engineers	1	2	3,4
Chemical, production, planning and quality control engineers	1	2	3,4
Design and development engineers	1	2	3,4
Other engineers and technologists n.e.s	1	2	3,4
Medical practitioners	1	2	3,4
Pharmacists, pharmacologists, ophthalmic and dispensing Opticians	1	2	3,4
Dental practitioners	1	2	3,4

Socio-economic group and occupation	Employment Status*		
Veterinarians	1	2	3,4
University, IT and higher education teachers	1	2	3,4
Barristers and solicitors	1	2	3,4
Chartered and certified management accountants (including taxation experts)	1	2	3,4
Actuaries, economists, statisticians, management consultants and business analysts	1	2	3,4
Architects, town planners and surveyors	1	2	3,4
Psychologists and other social/behavioral scientists	1	2	3,4
Clergy	1	2	3,4
Social Workers and probation officers	1	2	3,4

Lower professional

Marketing Managers		2	
Civil Service executive officers			3,4
Secondary and vocational education teachers	1	2	3,4
Primary and nursery education teachers	1	2	3,4
Other teaching professionals n.e.s	1	2	3,4
Laboratory technicians	1	2	3,4
Engineering technicians	1	2	3,4
Electrical and electronic technicians	1	2	3,4
Architectural, town planning, building and			
Civil engineering technicians	1	2	3,4
Other scientific technicians n.e.s	1	2	3,4
Building inspectors and quantity surveyors	1	2	3,4
Marine, insurance and other surveyors	1	2	3,4
Computer analyst programmers	1	2	3,4
Aircraft officers, traffic planners and controllers			3,4
Nurses and midwives	1	2	3,4
Medical radiographers	1	2	3,4
Physiotherapists and chiropodists	1	2	3,4
Medical technicians, dental auxiliaries and dental nurses	1	2	3,4
Occupational and speech therapists, psychotherapists			
and other therapists n.e.s	1	2	3,4
Other health associate professionals n.e.s	1	2	3,4
Legal service and related occupations	1	2	3,4
Underwriters, claims assessors, brokers and investment analysts	1	2	3,4
Personnel, industrial relations and work study officers	1	2	3,4

Socio-economic group and occupation	Employment Status*		
Authors, writers and journalists		2	3,4
Artists, commercial/industrial artists, graphic and clothing designers		2	3,4
Actors, musicians, entertainers, stage managers, producers and directors.		2	3,4
Information officers, careers advisers and vocational guidance specialists	1	2	3,4
Vocational, industrial trainers and driving instructors			3,4
Inspectors of factories, trading standards and other statutory inspectors	1	2	3,4
Environmental health, occupational hygienists and safety officers	1	2	3,4
Other associate professional and technical occupations n.e.s	1	2	3,4
Buyers and purchasing officers	1	2	3,4

Non manual

Draughtspersons			3,4
Matrons, houseparents, welfare, community and youth workers			3,4
Nurses' aids			3,4
Photographers, camera, sound and video equipment operators			3,4
Professional athletes and sport officials			3,4
Civil service clerical officers and assistants			3,4
Local government clerical officers and assistants			3,4
Accounts and wages clerks, book-keepers and other financial clerks			3,4
Cashiers, bank and counter clerks			3,4
Debt, rent and other cash collectors			3,4
Filing, computer, library and other clerks n.e.s			3,4
Secretaries, medical, legal, personal assistants, typists and word processor operators			3,4
Receptionists and receptionist- telephonists	1	2	3,4
Telephone operators, telegraph operators and other office communication system operators	1	2	3,4
Computer operators, data processing operators and other office machine operators			3,4
Soldiers (sergeant and below)			3,4
Police officers (sergeant and below)			3,4
Fire service officers			3,4
Prison service officers			3,4
Chefs and cooks			3,4
Waiters and waitresses			3,4
Bar staff			3,4
Travel and flight attendants			3,4

Socio-economic group and occupation	Employment Status*		
Childminders, nursery nurses and playgroup leaders			3,4
Educational assistants			3,4
Hairdressers, barbers and beauticians			3,4
Housekeepers (domestic and non-domestic)	1	2	3,4
Importers, exporters, commodity and shipping brokers			3,4
Technical and wholesale sales representatives			3,4
Auctioneers, estimators, valuers and other sales representatives n.e.s			3,4
Sales assistants, check out operators and petrol pump attendants			3,4
Market/ street traders and scrap dealers			3,4
Merchandisers, window dressers, floral arrangers and telephone sales persons		3,4	
Railway station workers, supervisors and guards			3,4
Counterhands and catering assistants			3,4

Manual skilled

Bricklayers and masons			3,4
Plasterers			3,4
Builders and building contractors			3,4
Floorers, floor coverers, carpet fitters and planners, floor and wall tilers			3,4
Painters and decorators			3,4
Toolmakers			3,4
Metal working production and maintenance fitters			3,4
Telephone fitters			3,4
Cable jointers and lines repairers			3,4
Radio, TV and video engineers			3,4
Computer engineers (installation and maintenance)			3,4
Other electrical and electronic trades n.e.s			3,4
Smiths, forge/metal plate workers and shipwrights			3,4
Plumbers, heating and ventilating engineers and related trades			3,4
Sheet metal workers			3,4
Welders and steel erectors			3,4
Motor mechanics, auto electricians, tyre and exhaust fitters			3,4
Vehicle body repairs, panel beaters and spray painters			3,4
Weavers, knitters, warp preparers, bleachers, dyers and finishers			3,4
Coach trimmers, upholsterers, and mattress makers			3,4
Shoe repairers and other leather makers			3,4

Socio-economic group and occupation	Employment Status*		
Tailors, dressmakers, clothing cutters, milliners and furriers			3,4
Other textiles, garments and related trades n.e.s			3,4
Printers, originators and compositors			3,4
Bookbinders, print finishers and other printing trades			3,4
Carpenters and joiners			3,4
Cabinet makers			3,4
Other woodworking trades n.e.s			3,4
Bakers and flour confectioners			3,4
Butchers and meat confectioners			3,4
Fishmongers and poultry dressers			3,4
Glass product and ceramics makers, finishers and other operatives			3,4
Roundsmen/women and van salespersons			3,4
Bakery and confectionery process operatives			3,4
Tannery production operatives			3,4
Paper, wood and related process plant operatives			3,4
Rubber process operatives, moulding machine operatives and tyre builders			3,4
Moulders and furnace operatives (metal)			3,4
Electroplaters, galvanisers and colour coaters			3,4
Other metal making and treating process operatives n.e.s			3,4
Bus and road transport depot inspectors	1	2	3,4
Drivers of road goods vehicles			3,4
Bus conductors and coach drivers			3,4
Taxi/cab drivers, chauffeurs and couriers			3,4
Railway station workers, supervisors and guards			3,4
Rail engine drivers and other railway line operatives			3,4
Mechanical plant drivers/operatives and crane drivers			3,4
Fork truck drivers			3,4
Other transport and machinery operatives n.e.s			3,4
Woodworking machine operatives			3,4

Semi skilled

Stores, storekeepers, warehousemen/women, dispatch and production control clerks			3,4
Roofers, slaters, tilers, sheeters and cladders			3,4
Glaziers			3,4
Scaffolders, riggers, steeplejacks and other construction trades n.e.s			3,4

Socio-economic group and occupation	Employment Status*		
Sewing machinists, menders, darners and embroiderers			3,4
Gardeners and groundsmen/groundswomen			3,4
Other craft and related occupations			3,4
Security guards and related occupations	1	2	3,4
Other security and protective service occupations n.e.s	1	2	3,4
Care assistants and attendants			3,4
Caretakers		2	3,4
Launderers, dry cleaners and pressers			3,4
Undertakers, bookmakers and other personal service workers n.e.s			3,4
Tobacco process operatives			3,4
Other food and drink (incl. Brewing) process operatives			3,4
Spinners, doublers, twisters, winders and reelers			3,4
Other textiles processing operatives			3,4
Chemical, gas and petroleum process plant operatives			3,4
Plastics process operatives, moulders and extenders			3,4
Synthetic fibre and other chemical, paper, plastics and related operatives			3,4
Machine tool operatives (incl. CNC machine tool operatives)			3,4
Other automatic machine workers, metal polishers and dressing operatives			3,4
Assemblers and line workers (electrical and electronic goods)			3,4
Assemblers and line workers (metal goods and other goods)			3,4
Inspectors, viewers and laboratory testers			3,4
Packers, bottlers, canners, fillers, weighers, graders and sorters			3,4
Seafarers (merchant navy), barge and boat operatives			3,4
Electrical, energy, boiler and related plant operatives and attendants			3,4
Pipe layers/pipe jointers and related construction workers			3,4
Mine (excluding coal) and quarry workers			3,4
Other plant, machine and process operatives n.e.s			3,4
Fishing and related workers			3,4
Mates to metal , electrical and related fitters			3,4
Rail construction and maintenance workers			3,4
Postal workers and mail sorters			3,4
Hotel porters and kitchen porters			3,4
Other occupations in sales and services n.e.s			3,4

Unskilled

Water and sewerage plant attendants			3,4

Socio-economic group and occupation	Employment Status*
Labourers in engineering and other making/processing industries	3,4
Road construction, paviors and kerb layers	3,4
Other building and civil engineering labourers	3,4
Stevedores and dockers	3,4
Goods porters	3,4
Refuse and salvage collectors	3,4
Drivers' mates	3,4
Window cleaners and car park attendants	3,4
Cleaners and domestics	3,4
All other labourers and related workers	3,4

Own account workers

General managers in large companies	2
Production and works managers	2
Building managers	2
Company financial managers	2
Purchasing managers	2
Personnel managers	2
Computer systems managers	2
Credit controllers	2
Bank and building society managers	2
Other financial managers n.e.s	2
Transport managers	2
Stores and warehousing managers	2
Garage managers and proprietors	2
Hotel and accommodation managers	2
Restaurant and catering managers	2
Publicans, innkeepers and club managers	2
Entertainment and sports managers	2
Travel agency managers	2
Managers and proprietors of butchers	2
Managers and proprietors of shops	2
Other managers n.e.s	2
Draughtspersons	2
Aircraft officers, traffic planners and controllers	2
Ship and hovercraft officers	2

Socio-economic group and occupation	Employment Status*
Matrons, houseparents, welfare, community and youth workers	2
Photographers, camera, sound and video equipment operators	2
Professional athletes and sport officials	2
Vocational, industrial trainers and driving instructors	2
Accounts and wages clerks, book keepers and other financial clerks	2
Cashiers, bank and counter clerks	2
Debt, rent and other cash collectors	2
Filing, computer, library and other clerks n.e.s	2
Stores, storekeepers, warehousemen/women, dispatch and production control clerks	2
Secretaries, medical, legal, personal assistants, typists and word processor operators	2
Computer operators, data processing operators and other office machine operators	2
Bricklayers and masons	2
Roofers, slaters, tilers, sheeters and cladders	2
Plasterers	2
Glaziers	2
Builders and building contractors	2
Floorers, floor coverers, carpet fitters and planners, floor and wall tilers	2
Painters and decorators	2
Scaffolders, riggers, steeplejacks and other construction trades n.e.s	2
Toolmakers	2
Metal working production and maintenance fitters	2
Precision instrument maker, goldsmiths , silversmiths and precious stone workers	2
Other machine tool setters and CNC setter-operators n.e.s	2
Electricians and electrical maintenance fitter	2
Telephone fitters	2
Cable jointers and lines repairers	2
Radio, TV and video engineers	2
Computer engineers (installation and maintenance)	2
Other electrical and electronic trades n.e.s	2
Smiths, forge/metal plate workers and shipwrights	2
Plumbers, heating and ventilating engineers and related trades	2
Sheet steel workers	2
Welders and steel erectors	2
Motor mechanics, auto electricians, tyre and exhaust fitters	2
Vehicle body repairs, panel beaters and spray painters	2
Weavers, knitters, warp preparers, bleachers, dyers and finishers	2

Socio-economic group and occupation   Employment Status*

Sewing machinists, menders, darners and embroiderers	2
Coach trimmers, upholsterers and mattress makers	2
Shoe repairers and other leather makers	2
Tailors, dressmakers, clothing cutters, milliners and furriers	2
Other textiles, garments and related trades n.e.s	2
Printers, originators and compositors	2
Bookbinders, print finishers and other printing trades n.e.s	2
Carpenters and joiners	2
Other woodworking trades n.e.s	2
Cabinet makers	2
Bakers and flour confectioners	2
Butchers and meat cutters	2
Fishmongers and poultry dressers	2
Glass product and ceramics makers, finishers and other operatives	2
Gardeners and groundsmen/groundswomen	2
Horticulture trades	2
Other craft and related occupations	2
Chefs and cooks	2
Educational assistants	2
Hairdressers, barbers and beauticians	2
Launderers, dry cleaners and pressers	2
Undertakers, bookmakers and other personal service workers n.e.s	2
Importers, exporters, commodity and shipping brokers	2
Technical and wholesale sales representatives	2
Auctioneers, estimators, valuers and other sales representatives n.e.s	2
Roundsmen/women and van sales persons	2
Market/street traders and scrap dealers	2
Merchandisers, window dressers, floral arrangers and telephone salespersons	2
Moulders and furnace operatives (metal)	2
Electroplaters, galvanisers and colour coaters	2
Drivers of road goods vehicles	2
Bus conductors and coach drivers	2
Taxi/cab drivers, chauffeurs and couriers	2
Seafarers (merchant navy) barge and boat operatives	2
Mechanical plant drivers/ operatives and crane drivers	2
Fork truck drivers	2

Socio-economic group and occupation	Employment Status*		
Other transport and machinery operatives n.e.s		2	
Pipe layers/pipe jointers and related construction workers		2	
Woodworking machine operatives		2	
Mine (excluding coal) and quarry workers		2	
Other plant, machine and process operatives n.e.s		2	
Fishing and related workers		2	
Road construction, paviors and kerb layers		2	
Other building and civil engineering labourers		2	
Stevedores and dockers		2	
Goods porters		2	
Cleaners and domestics		2	
Other occupations in sales and services n.e.s		2	
All other labourers and related workers		2	
Farmers			
Farm owners and managers	1	2	3,4
Agricultural workers			
Horticulture trades			3,4
Farm workers			3,4
Agricultural machinery and other farming occupations			3,4
Forestry workers			3,4
All others gainfully occupied			
Gainfully occupied but occupation not stated	1	1	3,4
Librarians, archivists and curators	1	2	
Tobacco process operatives	1	2	
Refuse and salvage collectors	1	2	
Window cleaners and car park attendants	1	2	
All other gainful occupations n.e.s		2	3,4

Source: from Census 96: "*Principal Socio-economic Results, Dublin Stationery Office, 1998,*" pp. 115-24

* Employment status
   (1) Self employed with paid employees;
   (2) Self employed without paid employees;
   (3) Employees;
   (4) Assisting relative (not receiving a fixed wage or salary).

appendix d | Social Clases-
List of Constituent Occupations

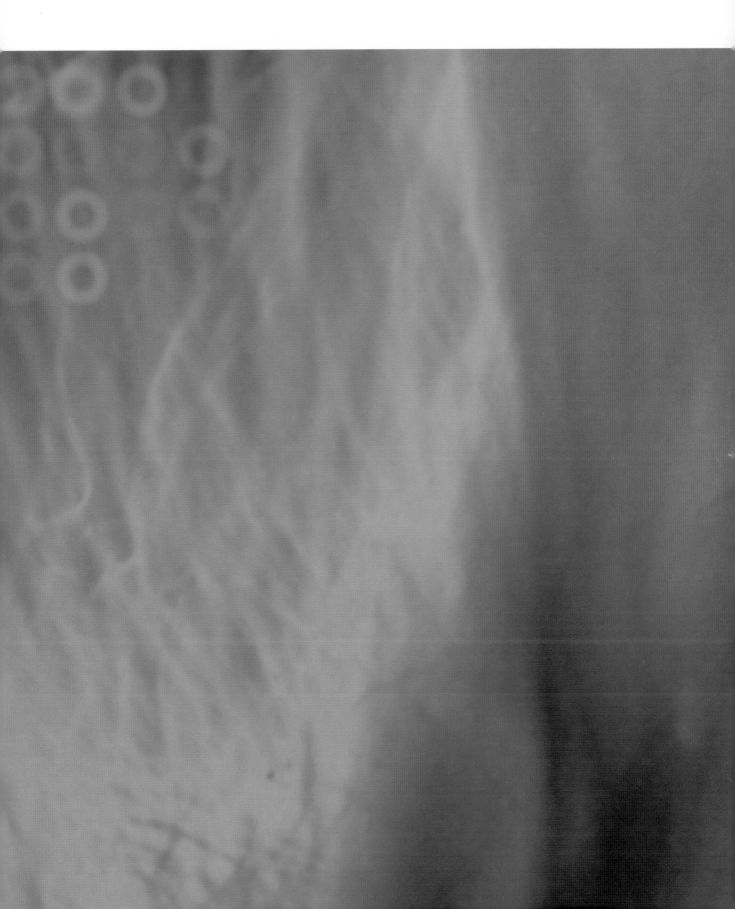

Social class and occupation

Employment Status*

1   Professional workers

Senior managers in national government	1	2	3,4
Farm owners and managers (200 or more acres)	1	2	3,4
Chemists	1	2	3,4
Biological scientists	1	2	3,4
Physicists	1	2	3,4
Other natural scientists n.e.s	1	2	3,4
Civil and mining engineers	1	2	3,4
Mechanical engineers	1	2	3,4
Electrical and electronic engineers	1	2	3,4
Software engineers	1	2	3,4
Chemical, production, planning and quality control engineers	1	2	3,4
Design and development engineers	1	2	3,4
Other engineers and technologists n.e.s.	1	2	3,4
Medical practitioners	1	2	3,4
Pharmacists, pharmacologists, ophthalmic and dispensing Opticians	1	2	3,4
Dental practitioners	1	2	3,4
Veterinarians	1	2	3,4
University, RTC and higher education teachers	1	2	3,4
Judges	1	2	3,4
Barristers and Solicitors	1	2	3,4
Chartered and certified management accountants (incl. Taxation experts	1	2	3,4
Actuaries, economists, statisticians, management			
Consultants and business analysts	1	2	3,4
Architects, town planners and surveyors	1	2	3,4
Psychologists and other social/behavioral scientists	1	2	3,4
Clergy	1	2	3,4
Social workers and probation	1	2	3,4

Social class and occupation	Employment Status*		
2 Managerial and technical			
General managers in large companies	1	2	3,4
Local government officers	1	2	3,4
General administrators in national government	1	2	3,4
Production and works managers	1	2	3,4
Building managers	1	2	3,4
Company financial managers	1	2	3,4
Marketing managers	1	2	3,4
Purchasing managers	1	2	3,4
Personnel managers	1	2	3,4
Computer systems executive officers	1	2	3,4
Credit controllers	1	2	3,4
Bank and building society managers	1	2	3,4
Civil Service executive officers	1	2	3,4
Other financial managers n.e.s	1	2	3,4
Transport managers	1	2	3,4
Stores and warehouse managers	1	2	3,4
Commissioned officers in armed forces			3,4
Senior police and prison officers			3,4
Farm owners and managers (100-199)	1	2	3,4
Garage managers and proprietor	1	2	3,4
Hotel and accommodation managers	1	2	3,4
Restaurant and catering managers			3,4
Publicans, innkeepers and club managers	1	2	3,4
Entertainment and sport managers			3,4
Travel agency managers	1	2	3,4
Managers and proprietors of butchers	1	2	3,4
Managers and proprietors of butchers	1	2	3,4
Administration of schools and colleges			3,4

Social class and occupation	Employment Status*		
2 Managerial and technical (cont.)			
Other managers n.e.s	1	2	3,4
Secondary and vocational education teachers	1	2	3,4
Primary and nursery education teachers	1	2	3,4
Other teaching professionals n.e.s	1	2	3,4
Librarians, archivists and curators			3,4
Laboratory technicians	1	2	3,4
Engineering technicians	1	2	3,4
Electrical and electronic technicians	1	2	3,4
Architectural, town planning, building and civil Engineering technicians	1	2	3,4
Other scientific technicians n.e.s	1	2	3,4
Building inspectors and other surveyors	1	2	3,4
Marine, insurance and other surveyors	1	2	3,4
Computer analyst programmers	1	2	3,4
Aircraft officers, traffic planners and controllers	1	2	3,4
Ship and hovercraft officers	1	2	3,4
Nurses and midwives	1	2	3,4
Medical radiographers	1	2	3,4
Physiotherapists and chiropodists	1	2	3,4
Medical technicians, dental auxiliaries and dental nurses	1	2	3,4
Occupational and speech therapists, psychotherapists and Other therapists n.e.s	1	2	3,4
Other health associate professionals n.e.s	1	2	3,4
Legal service and related occupations	1	2	3,4
Underwriters, claims assessors, brokers and investment Analysts	1	2	3.4
Personnel, industrial relations and work study officers	1	2	3,4
Matrons, houseparents, welfare community and youth Workers	1	2	3,4
Authors, writers and journalists		2	3,4
Artists, commercial/industrial artists, graphic and clothing Designers	1	2	3,4
Actors, musicians, entertainers, stage managers, producersAnd directors	1	2	3,4

Social class and occupation	Employment Status*		

2 Managerial and technical (cont.)

Information officers, careers advisers and vocational Guidance	1	2	3,4
Vocational, industrial trainers and driving instructors			3,4
Inspectors of factories, trading standards and other Statutory inspectors	1	2	3,4
Environmental health workers, occupational hygienists And safety officers	1	2	3,4
Other associate professional and technical occupation n.e.s	1	2	3,4
Nurses and aids and ambulance staff	1	2	3,4
Buyers and purchasing officers	1	2	3,4
Importers, exporters, commodity and shipping brokers	1	2	
Sales assistants, check-out operators and petrol pump Attendants	1	2	

3 Non-manual

Farm owners and managers (50-99 acres)	1	2	3,4
Restaurant and catering managers	1	2	
Entertainment and sport managers	1	2	
Manages and proprietors of butchers		2	
Draughtspersons	1	2	3,4
Photographers, camera, sound and video equipment Operators	1	2	3,4
Professional athletes and sports officials	1	2	3,4
Vocational, industrial trainers and driving instructors	1	2	
Civil Service clerical officers and assistants	1	2	3,4
Local government clerical officers and assistants	1	2	3,4
Accountants and wage clerks, book-keepers and other Financial clerks	1	2	3,4
Cashiers, bank and counter clerks	1	2	3,4
Debt, rent and other cash collectors	1	2	3,4
Filing, computer, library and other clerks n.e.s	1	2	3,4
Secretaries, medical, legal; personal assistants,			
Typists and word processor operators	1	2	3,4
Receptionists and receptionist-telephonists	1	2	3,4

Social class and occupation	Employment Status*		
3 Non-manual (cont.)			
Telephone operators, telegraph operator and other office			
Communication system operators	1	2	3,4
Computer operators, telegraph operators and other office Machine operators	1	2	3,4
Soldiers (sergeant and below)			3,4
Police officers (sergeant and below)			3,4
Fire service officers	1	2	3,4
Security guards and related occupations		2	
Other security and protective service occupations n.e.s	1	2	3,4
Educational assistants			3,4
Hairdressers, barbers and beauticians	1	2	
Importers, exporters, commodity and shipping brokers			3,4
Technical and wholesaler sales representatives	1	2	3,4
Auctioneers, estimators, valuers and other sales Representatives n.e.s	1	2	3,4
Sales assistants, check-out operators and petrol pump Attendants			3,4
Merchandisers, window dressers, floral arrangers and Telephone salespeople	1	2	3,4
4 Skilled Manual			
Farm owners and managers (30-49 acres)	1	2	3,4
Bricklayers and masons		2	3,4
Plasterers	1	2	3,4
Builders and building contractors	1	2	3,4
Floorers, floor coverers, carpet fitters and planner, Floor and wall tilers	1	2	3,4
Painters and decorators	1	2	3,4
Toolmakers	1	2	3,4
Metal working production and maintenance fitters	1	2	3,4
Precision instrument makers, goldsmiths, silversmiths And precious stone workers	1	2	3,4
Other machine tool setters and CNC setter-operators n.e.s	1	2	3,4
Electricians and electrical maintenance fitters	1	2	3,4

Social class and occupation	Employment Status*		
4 Skilled Manual (cont.)			
Telephone fitters	1	2	3,4
Cable jointer and lines repairers	1	2	3,4
Radio, TV and video engineers	1	2	3,4
Computer engineers (installation and maintenance)	1	2	3,4
Other electrical and electronic trades n.e.s	1	2	3,4
Smiths, forge/metal plate workers and shipwrights	1	2	3,4
Plumbers, heating and ventilating engineers and related Trades	1	2	3,4
Sheet metal workers	1	2	3,4
Motor mechanics, auto electricians, tyre and exhaust fitters	1	2	3,4
Vehicle body repairers, panel beaters and spray painters	1	2	3,4
Weavers, knitters, wrap preparers, bleachers, dyers, and Finishers	1	2	3,4
Coach trimmers, upholsterers and mattress makers	1	2	3,4
Shoe repairers and other leather makers	1	2	3,4
Tailors, dressmakers, clothing cutters, milliners and Furriers	1	2	3,4
Other textiles, garments and related trades n.e.s	1	2	3,4
Printers, originators and compositors	1	2	3,4
Bookbinders, print finishers and other print trades n.e.s	1	2	3,4
Carpenters and joiners	1	2	3,4
Cabinet makers	1	2	3,4
Other woodmaking trades	1	2	3,4
Bakers and flour confectioners	1	2	3,4
Butchers and meat cutters	1	2	3,4
Fishmongers and poultry dressers	1	2	3,4
Glass product and ceramics makers, finishers and Other operatives	1	2	3,4
Chefs and cooks	1	2	3,4
Travel and flight attendants	1	2	3,4
Childminders, nursery nurses and playgroup leaders	1	2	3,4
Educational assistants	1	2	

Social class and occupation

4   Skilled Manual (cont.)

Hairdressers, barbers and beauticians	1	2	3,4
Housekeepers (domestic and non-domestic)	1	2	3,4
Undertakers, bookmakers and other personal service Workers n.e.s	1	2	3,4
Roundsmen/women and van salesperson	1	2	
Bakery and confectionery process operatives	1	2	3,4
Paper, wood and related process plant operatives	1	2	3,4
Rubber process operatives, moulding machine operatives Tyre builders.	1	2	3,4
Moulders and furnace operatives (metal)	1	2	3,4
Electroplaters, glavanisers and colour coaters	1	2	3,4
Other metal making and treating process operatives n.e.s	1	2	3,4
Bus and road transport depot inspectors	1	2	3,4
Drivers of road goods vehicles	1	2	3,4
Bus and road goods vehicles	1	2	3,4
Taxi/cab drivers, chauffeurs and couriers	1	2	3,4
Railway station workers, supervisors and guards		2	3,4
Rail engine drivers and other railway line operatives	1	2	3,4
Mechanical plant drivers/operatives and crane drivers	1	2	3,4
Fork lift truck drivers			3,4
Other transport and machinery operatives			3,4
Woodworking machine operatives	1	2	3,4

5   Semi-skilled

Farm owners and managers (0-29 acres and area not stated)	1	2	3,4
Storekeepers, warehousemen/women, dispatch and Production control clerk	1	2	3,4
Roofers, slaters, tilers, sheeters and cladderes	1	2	3,4
Galziers	1	2	3,4
Scaffolders, riggers, steeplejacks and other construction Trades n.e.s	1	2	3,4
Sewing machinists, menders, darners and embroiderers	1	2	3,4

Social class and occupation

Employment Status★

5   Semi-skilled

Gardeners and groundsmen/women	1	2	3,4
Horticultural trades	1	2	3,4
Other craft and related occupations	1	2	3,4
Prison service officers			3,4
Security and protective service occupation n.e.s			3,4
Other security and protective service occupations n.e.s			3,4
Waiters and waitresses	1	2	3,4
Bar staff	1	2	3,4
Care assistants and attendants	1	2	3,4
Caretakers	1	2	3,4
Launderers, dry cleaners and pressers	1	2	3,4
Undertakers, bookmakers and other personal service Workers			3,4
Market/street traders and scrap dealers	1	2	3,4
Tobacco process operatives			3,4
Other food and drink (incl. Brewing) process operatives	1	2	3,4
Spinners, doublers, twisters, winders and reelers	1	2	3,4
Other textile processing operatives	1	2	3,4
Chemical, gas and petroleum process plant operatives	1	2	3,4
Plastics process operatives, moulders and extruders	1	2	3,4
Synthetic fibers and other chemical, paper, plastics And related operatives	1	2	3,4
Machine tool operatives (inc.CNC machine tool Operatives)	1	2	3,4
Other automatic machine workers, metal polishers And dressing operatives	1	2	3,4
Assemblers and lineworkers (electrical and electronic Goods)	1	2	3,4
Assemblers and lineworkers (metal goods and other Goods)	1	2	3,4
Inspectors, viewers and laboratory testers	1	2	3,4
Packers, bottlers, canners, fillers, weighers, graders and sorters.	1	2	3,4
Seafarers (merchant navy), barge and boat operatives	1	2	3,4
Electrical, energy, boiler and related plant operatives And attendants	1	2	3,4

Social class and occupation

Employment Status*

5 Semi-skilled

Occupation			
Pipe layers/pipe jointers related construction industries	1	2	3,4
Mine (excluding coal) and quarry workers	1	2	3,4
Other plant, machine and process operatives n.e.s	1	2	3,4
Fishing and related workers	1	2	3,4
Forestry workers	1	2	3,4
Mates to metal, electrical and related fitters	1	2	3,4
Labourers in engineering and other making/processing Industries	1	2	
Rail construction and maintenance workers	1	2	3,4
Road construction workers, paviors and kerb layers	1	2	
Other building and civil engineering labourers	1	2	
Stevedores and dockers	1	2	
Goods porters	1	2	
Postal workers and mail sorters	1	2	3,4
Hotel porters and kitchen porters	1	2	3,4
Counterhands and catering assistants	1	2	3,4
Cleaners and domestics	1	2	
Other occupations in sales and services n.e.s	1	2	3,4
All other labourers and related workers	1	2	

6 Unskilled

Occupation			
Water and sewerage plant attendants	1	2	3,4
Farm workers			3,4
Agricultural machinery drivers and other farming Occupations			3,4
Labourers in engineering and other making/Processing industries			3,4
Road construction workers, paviors and kerb layers			3,4
Other building and civil engineering labourers			3,4
Stevedores and dockers			3,4
Goods porters			3,4

Social class and occupation	Employment Status*		

6   Unskilled (cont.)

Social class and occupation			Employment Status*
Refuse and salvage collectors			3,4
Drivers' mates			3,4
Window cleaners and car park attendants			3,4
Cleaners and domestics			3,4
All other labourers and related workers			3,4

7   All other gainfully occupied and unknown

Social class and occupation			Employment Status*
Gainfully occupied but occupation not stated	1	2	3,4
Administrators of schools and colleges	1	2	
Librarians, archivists and curators	1	2	
Tobacco process operatives	1	2	
Fork list truck drivers	1		
Other transport and machinery operatives n.e.s	1		
Refuse and salvage collectors	1	2	
Window cleaners and car park attendants	1	2	
All other gainful occupations n.e.s	1	2	3,4

Source: Census 96: Principal Socio-economic Results, Dublin, Stationery Office, pp. 125-130

* Employment Status: (1) Self Employed with paid employees; (2) Self Employed without employees; (3) Employees; (4) Relatives Assisting relative (not receiving a fixed wage of salary.